Yeats's Daimonic Renewal

Studies in Modern Literature, No. 16

A. Walton Litz, General Series Editor

Professor of English
Princeton University

Richard J. Finneran

Consulting Editor for Titles on W.B. Yeats
Professor of English
Newcomb College, Tulane University

Other Titles in This Series

Yeats's Daimonic Renewal

by
Herbert J. Levine

UMI RESEARCH PRESS
Ann Arbor, Michigan

Produced and distributed by
UMI Research Press
an imprint of
University Microfilms International
Ann Arbor, Michigan 48106

Library of Congress Cataloging in Publication Data

Levine, Herbert J.
    Yeats's daimonic renewal.

    (Studies in modern literature ; no. 16)
    Revision of thesis (Ph.D.)–Princeton University, 1977.
    Bibliography: p.
    Includes index.
    1. Yeats, W. B. (William Butler), 1865-1939–Knowl-
edge–Occult sciences. 2. Yeats, W. B. (William Butler),
1865-1939–Criticism and interpretation. 3. Yeats, W. B.
(William Butler), 1865-1939. Per amica silentia lunae.
4. Demonology in literature. 5. Self in literature.   I. Title.
II. Series.
    PR5908.O25L4 1983   821'.8   83-6989
    ISBN 0-8357-1427-6

Contents

Preface

This work was completed at Princeton University in 1977, and entitled "'Meditation Upon a Mask': *Per Amica Silentia Lunae* and the Middle Poems and Plays of William Butler Yeats." To enhance its usefulness, I have shortened the text, but retained its most original feature, a full-scale commentary on *Per Amica Silentia Lunae*. The present work's new title, *Yeats's Daimonic Renewal*, allows me to reaffirm more directly my conviction that the daimonic argument of *Per Amica* occupies a central place in any reading of Yeats's career. My study is in many ways a polemic against *A Vision* and the overemphasis it has received in Yeats scholarship. If undertaking the study today, I would provide a firmer ground for this polemic by considering the impact of *A Vision* on the poetry of Yeats's last phase, from *The Tower* (1928) to the end of his career. Such a study would show how the strategies Yeats adopted in mid-career, correlative with the concerns elaborated in *Per Amica*, continued to shape the visionary and dramatic structure of his work in a way that *A Vision* never did.

Throughout this project, I have had generous assistance and encouragement. First among equals, A. Walton Litz nurtured the work from its inception and has continued to cheer my efforts; Lawrence Lipking helped it to develop in tandem with his own writing on *Per Amica*; Harold Bloom, at its start, and Michael Goldman, in its final stages, offered numerous suggestions that greatly enhanced the work. Numerous Yeats scholars have helped make manuscripts and unpublished information available to me: James L. Allen, Richard Ellmann, Richard Finneran, Narayan Hegde, M.M. Liberman, Edward O'Shea, and, especially, George Mills Harper, who has always been generous with his own transcriptions of Yeats's occult papers. I would also like to thank the Committee on Grants at Franklin and Marshall College for making it possible to secure the excellent services of Linda Marie Oswald for preparation of the manuscript and index. And to my colleagues in the English Department at Franklin and Marshall, a debt of gratitude for the supportive environment they foster.

Permissions have kindly been granted by Michael Yeats and Ann Yeats to quote from unpublished material; by the MacMillan Publishing Company to quote the full text of "Another Song of a Fool," from *Collected Poems of William Butler Yeats*, copyright 1919 by MacMillan Publishing Company, renewed 1947 by Bertha Georgie Yeats; and by the editors of *Colby Library Quarterly*, *ELH*, *Modern Language Quarterly*, and *Studies in the Literary Imagination* to reprint portions of articles that originally appeared in their journals.

    Finally, I record with pleasure my unpayable debt to Ellen Frankel— wife, editor, colleague—who has been my boon companion in these explorations from first to last.

Abbreviations

The following works by Yeats are regularly abbreviated within the text:

Au   *Autobiographies.* London: Macmillan, 1955.

AV(A)   *A Critical Edition of Yeats's* A Vision (1925). Ed. George Mills Harper and Walter Kelly Hood. London: Macmillan, 1978.

AV(B)   *A Vision.* London: Macmillan, 1962.

E&I   *Essays and Introductions.* London and New York: Macmillan, 1961.

Ex   *Explorations.* Sel. Mrs. W.B. Yeats. London: Macmillan, 1962; New York: Macmillan, 1963.

L   *The Letters of W.B. Yeats.* Ed. Allan Wade. London: Rupert Hart-Davis, 1954; New York: Macmillan, 1955.

Mem   *Memoirs.* Ed. Denis Donoghue. London: Macmillan, 1972; New York: Macmillan, 1973.

Myth   *Mythologies.* London and New York: Macmillan, 1959.

VP   *The Variorum Edition of the Poems of W.B. Yeats.* Ed. Peter Allt and Russell K. Alspach. New York: Macmillan, 1957.

VPl   *The Variorum Edition of the Plays of W.B. Yeats.* Ed. Russell K. Alspach. London and New York: Macmillan, 1966.

Introduction

The Centrality of *Per Amica Silentia Lunae*

Remarkably, it took more than half a lifetime for Yeats to arrive at the "freedom of speech," which established him as the foremost of twentieth-century poets.[1] Richard Ellmann has pointed to 1917 as the watershed in Yeats's poetic career: "Had Yeats died instead of marrying in 1917, he would have been remembered as a remarkable minor poet who achieved a diction more powerful than that of his contemporaries but who, except in a handful of poems, did not have much to say with it."[2] Yeats's marriage at the age of fifty-two, bringing to a close the long bachelorhood that so crucially shaped his early poetry, has naturally been seen by most critics as decisive in bringing about his poetic and emotional maturity. Marriage proved to be immensely liberating for the poet, offering the security of a settled life, normal sexuality, and, of course, the excitement of his wife's automatic writing and trance speech. We should be wary of taking an overly deterministic view of this complex of liberating experiences. The great transformation in Yeats's sense of himself as a poet was well under way in the turbulent years immediately preceding his marriage. Harold Bloom has wisely pointed our attention to the formative "two years from late 1915 to late 1917, for these were the most important in Yeats's imaginative life."[3] The present study explores the conflict and consolidation in Yeats's imaginative life during these years, particularly as they are revealed in his most moving prose work, *Per Amica Silentia Lunae* (dated February and May 1917), in order to show how Yeats transformed himself from "a remarkable minor poet" to the oracular creator of "The Second Coming" and "Sailing to Byzantium," a prophet of the doom and transcendence possible in the modern world.

Between 1909 and 1915, when Yeats was forty-four to fifty years old, he felt himself at the nadir of his poetic, dramatic, and personal development. Failure dominated his sense of life: failure to please the audience which had loved the dreamy lyrics of his youth; abortive attempts to leave that style behind and become a public spokesman for his unappreciative nation at the Abbey Theatre; inability to attain the visionary revelation that he sought for so long in hermetic studies; continued disappointment in his one-sided thirty-year love affair with Maud Gonne; and finally, failure to produce any heir for his family but his books. In October 1909, his depression was so great that he contemplated throwing himself off a cliff (*Mem*, 235-36). At the age of fifty, he faced an overwhelming imaginative impasse; after thirty years of writing poetry, there were moments when he was ready to abandon his vocation.

    Per Amica seeks to account for such adversities of the poet's fate and to articulate the possibilities of creative renewal in mid-career. Its sequential reveries are organized in two essays, "Anima Hominis" and "Anima Mundi." The first essay, more appropriately described as the soul of the poet, takes off from the invocation poem "Ego Dominus Tuus" to present a theory of poetic creation. Yeats assumes in the essay that the artist is inevitably divided between his daily self and his superior creative self. He proposes that great poets create only by imitating the image of that superior self, an antithetical mask which comprises all that the daily self lacks. The poet does not choose his antithetical image himself; instead, it is forced upon him by his personal Daimon, a figure from Greek religion and literature, who shapes the disappointments of the poet's destiny, but also grants him his visionary capacity. In "Anima Hominis" the poet enters into reverie, the prelude to all his creative activity, even reaching moments akin to trance, but his vision is inevitably broken off by reminders of his mortal limitations. The synthesis of this dialectic of reverie and disappointment is presented in "Anima Mundi," providing the means by which the poet regains his vision. With the Daimon's help the poet, through dreams and evocation, can make contact with an infinitely generative world soul, a storehouse of all images, memories, and past lives. Yeats here assumes a ghostly perspective from which he can explain the existence of the Daimon, a soul on its journey between lives. He presents a Dantesque scenario of the soul's purgatorial life, initially revisiting its earthly habitations to relive its errors, then undergoing an arduous exploration of its moral life, and reaching its apotheosis in the "condition of fire" (*Myth*, 357), the apocalyptic state dramatized in "Byzantium." Significantly, this esoteric process is analogous to the aesthetic movement in "Anima Hominis," as the artist transcends his inner divisions in the ecstasy of privileged visionary moments.

    Because of its mannered prose style, *Per Amica* has long been a step-child to *A Vision* in the history of Yeats criticism. It has been widely quoted and occasionally summarized, but most often as an *ur*-text for the later, more systematic treatise.[4] Only recently has it come to the fore in three important critical works, Harold Bloom's *Yeats* (1970), Robert Langbaum's *The Mysteries of Identity* (1977), and Lawrence Lipking's *The Life of the Poet* (1982). For Bloom, *Per Amica* is a treatise on poetic originality. His important corrective was removing *Per Amica* from the orbit of *A Vision* by showing how the former work's overt occultism is consistently subordinated to its central poetic concerns. By concentrating on the work's literary allusions, instead of its esoteric ones, Bloom shows the extent to which Yeats's imagination in middle age was dominated by a panoply of haunting poetic ghosts. While Bloom argues that the Yeatsian *Anima Mundi* is little more than the creative imagination of Romanticism (168), Langbaum sees *Per Amica* as a radical departure, especially from the expressive doctrines of Romanticism. He construes Yeats's work as a coherent theory of identity in response to "the twin problems bequeathed him by romanticism, the problem of the divided self and solipsism—the claustrophobic fear that the struggle played out within the prisonhouse of self has nothing to do with external reality."[5] Langbaum argues that in *Per Amica*'s Daimon Yeats found a means of positing an external spiritual agency through which the self defines and completes its identity; hence "the quarrel with ourselves" that Yeats posited as the key to poetic creation is also an external quarrel; "our unconscious mind lies outside us," and "our identity comes from without" (159).

Lipking sees *Per Amica*, along with Dante's *La Vita Nuova* and Blake's *Marriage of Heaven and Hell*, as a work of initiation, a genre in which the poet surveys his earlier work and learns to reread it in light of a growing conviction that he has the potential to become a master.[6] While young poets naturally expect initiation, the experience of an older poet like Yeats would seem to vitiate such hopes. In Lipking's presentation, the poignancy of *Per Amica* stems from Yeats's honesty in facing his fears, countered by the poet's equally firm adumbration of his faith in creative renewal, through the synthesis of "Anima Hominis" and "Anima Mundi."

Yeats himself recognized the central importance of *Per Amica* to his career in claiming that it was the spiritual history he needed to write before the secrets of *A Vision* could be vouchsafed to him (*AV*(B), 9). His first thought was to call it *An Alphabet*, "a kind of prose backing" to his poetry (*L*, 625). Had he kept that direct title, the history of our understanding of Yeats would certainly have been different. We would have seen *Per Amica* as the document that tells us the most about the creative struggle that stands out so dominatingly in his works. *Per Amica*, Yeats said, gave him a "new framework and new patterns" (*L*, 627). The major object of this study is to set out that framework and explicate those patterns in *Per Amica* itself and in the poems, plays, and other prose writings of Yeats's middle period (ca. 1908–21).[7] My hope is that the book will encourage a reassessment of Yeats's achievements in mid-career, so that we can learn to find in his pattern of daimonic renewal the visionary center of his art.

Studying Yeats's middle period, we confront the inadequate assumptions of much developmental psychology and literary history, which look everywhere for progressive models for understanding human behavior. Yeats did not so much develop as constantly return with new eyes to his earliest intimations of the world. "I am persuaded that our intellects at twenty," he once wrote, "contain all the truths we shall ever find."(*Au*, 189). This is a particularly useful insight into Yeats's own life cycle, for the truths about the immanence of a spiritual universe that he discovered as a young man always sustained him. At the age of fifty-one, we hear him talking metaphorically about his poetry as house-building: "There are so many rooms and corridors that I am still building upon foundations laid long ago" (*L*, 605). So too he meditates in *Per Amica* "upon certain thoughts so long habitual that I may be permitted to call them my convictions" (*Myth*, 319), the ideas and beliefs tested in a lifetime of personal application and now brought to bear in a grave crisis of the poet's imagination.

The central conviction of *Per Amica* is that a man finds and improves himself by searching for his opposite, which Yeats calls either mask, anti-self, or at its most mythological, Daimon, the Greek word for both a quasi-divine figure and an inner voice of conscience. The mask in Yeats is always assumed out of a deep-felt inner need for opposition. It is not an artificial pose, as in Wilde, nor an historical personification as in Pound, nor even a device for splitting the ego as in Eliot, but rather, a means of disciplining the ego to accept a multiplicity of selves. Through the mask of an anti-self the poet comes to terms with everything that is outside the self, with everything that has long remained hidden from daily view, with everything that puts him in touch with a collective mind greater than his own.

Yeats's self-presentation in *Per Amica* is problematic because though he is expressing his deepest convictions about the world, he is never straight-forward. Many critics, themselves writing far more rigorous analytic prose than Yeats ever did, call his style evasive, but they forget that his prose style is as much a mask as his poetic style. We are not meant to look for the real beliefs of the self beneath the plethora of opulent phrases and arcane allusions: they *are* the image of the self that is presented to us. Whether Yeats is being gnomic or effusive, the key to his mask in *Per Amica* is ceremony. A man sharing intimate experiences with a privileged audience does not want to present himself as he would in a letter to the daily paper. He chooses his images and quotations with great care to produce cameo-like sentences with immense suggestivity: "I shall find the dark grow luminous, the void fruitful when I understand I have nothing, that the ringers in the tower have appointed for the hymen of the soul a passing bell" (*Myth*, 332). Yeats is writing reveries, a word which derives not as we might expect from the French word to dream but from one similar to our word *revel*. The pleasures of the text in Yeats are an important means for restoring to him the possibilities of imaginative exuberance.

His ceremonies usher us into a realm where we can appreciate another of his most central convictions: that "the knowledge of reality is always by some means or other a secret knowledge" (*Mem*, 166). Though he often felt that poetry and occultism pulled him in opposing directions, they actually require the same mental discipline of receptivity to vision. Both the poet in reverie and the adept in ceremonial magic enter an inner world of consciousness where the divisions of time and space are shut out in a union of self and universe. Occultism only parts company with poetry when it establishes rigid categories in place of fluid visionary experience. Yeats felt that if he could only deal with the supernatural world systematically, he could be done with his researches and return to poetry, but it was never easy for him to abjure his magical books. It is extremely amusing to hear him claiming in 1915, "I am free at last from the obsession of the supernatural, having got my thoughts in order and ranged on paper "(*L*, 595). Two years later, he was reordering them by the light of the moon in *Per Amica*, and he continued to reorder them for the rest of his life.

Per Amica is very much a textbook of these visionary influences upon Yeats, both aesthetic and esoteric. The range of allusion within these general categories is vast: from Virgil to Mallarmé, from Heraclitus to the nineteenth-century magician, Stanislas de Gaeta. Yeats defines his poetic tradition with extensive quotation from Spenser and the Romantic poets, and he summarizes his spiritist researches of the previous years, which ranged from seances in modern London to study of the Eleusinian mysteries. He offers us the chance to make his reading a part of our imaginative world as he has made it an integral part of his, a gallery of poetic and magical figures who serve as models for the kind of poet-mage that he hopes to be. In "Ego Dominus Tuus," the proem of the work, he takes up Dante and Keats as contrasting figures for defining his own future poetic identity. Will he be like the Romantic Keats, singing to a nightingale of his heart's pain, or will he become a twentieth-century Dante, creating a solid visionary world as real as his own heart?

Chapter 1 takes up "Ego Dominus Tuus" and the decade of self-questionings leading up to that important enunciation of the doctrine of the anti-self. Chapters 2 and 3 attempt for the first time a full-scale reading of *Per Amica*, studying the evolution and presentation of Yeats's creative quarrels with himself, with other writers, and with the supernatural world. Wherever possible, I tie the meditations of *Per Amica* to allied concerns in Yeats's sources and in his poetry and drama, often ranging outside the middle period, since the poet in 1917 is both retrospective and projective of his own future course. Chapters 4 and 5 analyze the plays and poems of the middle period, showing the ways in which they embody the antithetical thought of *Per Amica* in new dramatic and lyric structures. The poems and plays do not need *Per Amica* for their explication, but we appreciate their complexity far better when we understand the intellectual and psychological struggles from which they grow. In the final chapter, I consolidate the polemical thrust of the whole study, namely, that *Per Amica* is a far better introduction to the visionary crux of Yeats's work than the later and far more famous *Vision*, a work ossified under the weight of its own systematic occultism.

I conclude this introduction with Yeats's own metaphor for what he gained from writing *Per Amica*: "One goes on year after year gradually getting the disorder of one's mind in order and this is the real impulse to create. Till one has expressed a thing it is like an untidy, unswept, undusted corner of a room. When it is expressed one feels cleaner, and more elegant . . ." (*L*, 627). Built in the middle of his career on old foundations, *Per Amica* is a clean and elegant new house for Yeats's poetry and drama.

1

At the Crossroads of Self and Anti-Self in "Ego Dominus Tuus"

Soon after the turn of the century, Yeats began to be dissatisfied with the shadowy image of himself that he saw in his early poetry, and sought out new rhythms, new diction to toughen his lyric persona. It was easier to repudiate that old self, and risk the displeasure of friends and critics, than to converse intimately once more with the Yeats who had seriously believed in an imminent worldwide revolution of the spirit. In 1908, two decisive events caused Yeats, aged forty-three, to begin a decade-long reevaluation of that earlier self. His publisher issued in eight deluxe volumes *The Collected Works in Prose and Verse of William Butler Yeats*, spurring Yeats to initiate a dialogue with the works of an earlier self already canonized. That same year, Ezra Pound, aged twenty-three, arrived in London to take up a place near the feet of the master; and though his critical influence on Yeats was not apparent for another five years, it would have been difficult for Yeats not to see in the exotic poses of the young aesthete images of himself at the same age, about to begin *The Wanderings of Oisin* (1889). When Yeats began keeping a journal in December 1908, his first inquiry was into his occult stories of a decade earlier and their esoteric "doctrine of the Mask" (*Mem*, 138), which he progressively made less occult and extended in "Ego Dominus Tuus" (1915) into a comprehensive theory of poetry. When in the first speech of that poem, Yeats suddenly brings back an image and character out of "Rosa Alchemica" (1896), "the open book/ That Michael Robartes left," the poet is signalling to Pound and a new generation of readers that he is now prepared to confront that nagging ghost of an earlier self and engage it in a meaningful poetic dialogue.[1]

The debate in "Ego Dominus Tuus" is central to Yeats's career because in the previous decade he had variously articulated the aesthetic positions of both of the poem's speakers, oscillating between Hic's claim that the poet has to express himself sincerely, and Ille's counterstatement that the poet must seek in his writings a visionary image of the anti-self:

> By the help of an image
> I call to my own opposite, summon all
> That I have handled least, least looked upon.

Both Hic and Ille are sides of Yeats, each wanting to denigrate the other in order to gain the upper hand in Yeats's poetic future.[2] The standard reading of the poem has always been to identify Yeats with Ille, but unfortunately this is a reading from hindsight. Yeats's career bears out Ille as the rightful spokesman for his poetic future because Yeats deliberately reshaped himself as that masked figure. He soon printed "Ego Dominus Tuus" as the proem to *Per Amica* and became a full-fledged version of Ille only in taking up Ille's arguments for the anti-self as a personal program for his poetry.

We can now see *Per Amica*, and "Ego Dominus Tuus" within it, as a major turning point, the poet's long-awaited coming of age; but when he wrote "Ego Dominus Tuus," Yeats was unsure about his own visionary pronouncements. Though he longed for an authentic revelation from a visionary anti-self, he could not be sure that one would ever come.[3] By 1919, however, when Yeats reprinted the poem in *The Wild Swans at Coole*, he could connect "the mysterious one" of Ille's apostrophe with those ghostly communicators who had brought him and Mrs. Yeats the systematic revelation of "The Phases of the Moon." As Yeats matured in the confidence of his daimonic vision, he reprinted the poem and let the context change its character as he himself had changed; but the poem has continued to seem an unswerving proclamation of the creed of antithetical revelation.[4] This chapter attempts to recover the original battle of ideas out of which the poem emerged to that we can once again see it as a meaningful debate between two opposing aesthetic positions, a quarrel that in Yeats's own mind was central to his future as a poet.

Yeats uses the term anti-self for the first time in "Ego Dominus Tuus," but the debate between the self and its opposite does not begin there, nor even with his speculations on the mask in his 1908-09 journal. It actually goes back to his needs as a timid adolescent to strike heroic poses. A second self finds its way into his earliest poetry, as in this quatrain of 1886:

> The child who chases lizards in the grass,
> The sage who deep in central nature delves,
> The preacher watching for the ill hour to pass—
> All these are souls who fly from their dread selves.

> (*VP*, 735)[5]

Though Yeats shows a profound uneasiness with the daily self, he does not suggest an escape into a mask as a precondition for writing poetry. On the contrary when he started to write he subscribed to the expressive theories of his great Romantic predecessors which his father had impressed upon him by daily readings, always from the most passionate moment of a play or poem (*Au*, 65). When he described this early aesthetic in "The Tree of Life" (1906), he explained its significance in the language of Hic, "And I would find myself and not an image":

> I had set out on life with the thought of putting my very self into poetry, and had understood this as a representation of my own visions. . . . Then one day I understood quite suddenly, as the way is, that I was seeking something unchanging and unmixed and always outside myself, a Stone or an Elixir that was always out of reach, and that I myself was the fleeting thing that held out its hand. The more I tried to make my art deliberately beautiful, the more did I follow the opposite of myself. . . . Presently I found that I entered into myself and pictured myself and not some essence when I was not seeking beauty at all, but merely to lighten the mind of some burden of love or bitterness thrown upon it by the events of life (*E&I*, 271–72).

Fifteen years after the events described, Yeats had the self-conscious distance from his earlier self to see that though he had started out with an aesthetic of self-expression, his attempts to realize it in visionary rather than dramatic terms had led him onto a quest for intellectual beauty that threatened to negate his original intentions. Whenever Yeats renewed the dramatic aesthetic of the self, he could not help but find the unchanging vision of a permanent anti-self a kind of death to the lyric poet. In 1906, as in 1891 when he first confronted the intensely personal lyrics of his Rhymers' Club friends, he was becoming conscious of the need to reunite his poetry to the energies of the whole man, through normal, active personality.

Yeats had to redirect his aesthetic toward self-expression deliberately because the lure of the anti-self, especially as he studied it in occult rituals, was so compelling to the poet awaiting a revelation from behind the veil of the temple. From Oscar Wilde he had learned about the mask as a sophisticated form of lying, the only form suitable for the alienated modern artist. In occult tradition, however, the mask had precisely the opposite function, being conceived as a way of confronting hidden truth. In the Order of the Golden Dawn, at each stage of ascension toward higher degrees of secret knowledge, Yeats received a new mystic title, in addition to his chosen occult name, "*Demon est Deus Inversus*."[6] Such multiplication of mystic selves led Yeats in his fiction to reify the anti-self as an actual mask that the self could wear, and while wearing it, share in the immemorial passions of divinity. In "Rosa Alchemica" (1896), the narrator writes of being plunged into a "dream, in which I seemed to be a mask, lying on the counter of a little Eastern ship. Many persons with eyes so bright and still that I knew them for more than human, came in and tried me on their faces, but at last flung me into a corner laughing" (*Myth*, 286–87). The image of non-human eyes becomes a crucial image to describe daimonic possession in *Per Amica* and the *Four Plays for Dancers* (1921), where once again Yeats portrays immortal anti-selves that make no allowances for the limited daily life of either poet or hero.[7]

Though total revelation of occult wisdom eluded him, Yeats was not willing to renounce the quest for secret knowledge of the self. Fully in the Romantic tradition, Yeats believed that such knowledge would be revealed through a visionary image. In "The Philosophy of Shelley's Poetry" (1900), he imagined Shelley kneeling before an altar in some remote chapel of the Morning Star:

> a single vision would have come to him again and again, a vision of a boat drifting down a broad river between high hills where there were caves and towers, and following the light of one Star; and that voices would have told him how there is for every man some one scene, some one adventure, some one picture that is the image of his secret life, for wisdom first speaks in images (*E&I*, 94–95).

Yeats elaborated on the personal myth in his essay on Shakespeare, "At Stratford-on-Avon" (1901): "The Greeks, a certain scholar has told me, considered that myths are the activities of the Daimons, and that the Daimons shape our characters and our lives. I have often had the fancy that there is some one myth for every man, which, if we but knew it, would make us understand all he did and thought" (*E&I*, 107). Though this notion is only a fancy in 1901, by 1917, in *Per Amica*, it is Yeats's central conviction: each of us has a Daimon who personally shapes for us the most difficult possible fate. I am anticipating here only because Yeats himself anticipates, in his imagined myth for Shakespeare, the crucial opposition between the myth and the man, between anti-self and self: "Shakespeare's myth, it may be, describes a wise man who was blind from very wisdom, and an empty man who thrust him from his place, and saw all that could be seen from very emptiness" (*E&I*, 107). The mind of a buried self, an inner Daimon, looking through ordinary eyes sees a broader, truer vision of reality than the daily self alone can see. Yeats looked forward to the moment when he too could gaze through another's "empty" eyes at the personal myth destiny had chosen for him.

It was not many years before Yeats was rewarded with a vision of this mysterious stranger. Yeats's 1906 description (in "A Tower on the Apennines") bears striking resemblance to the images of both Hic and Ille that he would recreate a decade later:

> I saw suddenly in the mind's eye an old man, erect and a little gaunt, standing in the door of the tower, while about him broke a windy light. He was the poet who had at last, because he had done so much for the word's sake, come to share in the dignity of the saint. He had hidden nothing of himself, but he had taken care of "that dignity . . . the perfection of form . . . this lofty and severe quality . . . this virtue." And though he had

but sought it for the word's sake, or for a woman's praise, it had come at last into his body and his mind. . . . He has in his ears well-instructed voices, and seeming-solid sights are before his eyes, and not, as we say of many a one, speaking in metaphor, but as this were Delphi or Eleusis. . . . (*E&I*, 291)[8]

The old poet has become a visionary, in the manner of Ille, ironically by his having devoted himself to self-expression, in the manner of Hic. We need no poet come out of a visionary mountain landscape to tell us that this is an idealized description of the poet Yeats himself in 1906. Yeats had moved from "the dream-burdened will" of *The Wind Among the Reeds* (1899) to a fuller articulation of the whole personality, as in "Adam's Curse" (1902), where the impassioned man speaks for the first time in common speech, hiding nothing of himself, neither his need for woman's praise, nor the difficulty of articulating this common speech into the sweet sounds of poetry.[9] Yeats had come full circle by 1906, his pursuit of the visionary anti-self having led him directly to the image of the self. The poems of *The Green Helmet* are the culmination of this phase of Yeats's development since they are based on the aesthetic assumption that Yeats needed nothing but his craft and his own passions to create a lasting personal myth.

For two years beginning in late 1908, Yeats kept an almost daily journal whose principal subject was the masks that we must constantly wear in daily life.[10] Near the start of the journal he speculated that he had "had a curious breakdown of some sort," brought on perhaps by "the fear of losing my inspiration by absorption in outer things" (*Mem*, 140). The effects of his breakdown reverberate throughout his journal; whether in the salon or in the committee room, he felt that he lacked self-possession and became crude and impersonal. "Style, personality (deliberately adopted and therefore a mask)," he wrote, "is the only escape from all the heat of the bargaining" (*Mem*, 139).

Every situation in life became a battleground, with Yeats destined to be overwhelmed unless he armed himself with the discipline of the mask. Social graciousness and poetic style, love and active virtue, and especially the deliberate Wildean pose, all were masks for the limitations of the self. The mask also became a touchstone for evaluating literary figures as well as historical epochs, anticipating Yeats's cultural speculations in "Ego Dominus Tuus," *Per Amica*, and *A Vision*. Modern culture, as exemplified in the aesthetic ideal of Pater, was weak and effeminate because it was based only on the "pursuit of self-knowledge," whereas culture in the Renaissance was "founded not on self-knowledge but on knowledge of some other self—Christ or Caesar—not on delicate sincerity but on imitative energy" (*Mem*, 159–60).

This high valuation of the mask in early 1909 suggests that Yeats had come to the end of the weary road of self-expression, yet when it came to choosing a mask for himself, it had to seem as if he wore none: "I must . . . set myself into a life of action, so as to express not the traditional poet but that forgotten thing, the normal, active man" (*Mem*, 181). We find Yeats here in a characteristic oscillation, fearing "absorption in outer things," yet denying his need to cultivate inwardness. When his theory is closest to Ille, he would make himself into Hic.

Yeats's ambivalence about the mask can be traced in his attitude to sincerity in his friends' writings. Though he knew himself to be a writer who needed to assume a mask, he could not disparage Synge, Johnson, or Dowson because they wrote directly out of personal feeling. In 1909, he viewed sincerity as a personal and cultural weakness, but in the next year, after Synge's death, he used sincerity as a term of the highest critical praise. Yeats vaunted Synge's gift of passionate self-expression and his ability to make us share in his personal vision, because Synge possessed a quality in common with all great imaginative writers, a "sincerity that makes us share his feeling" (*E&I*, 339). In the lecture "Friends of My Youth" (1910), on the Rhymers' Club poets, Yeats reidentified himself with the expressive doctrine of the group he had joined in 1891. "The poet is what he is. If a good poet, because he lives sincerely, he makes an experiment in life, good or bad, but a sincere experiment." The villains of the piece were Wordsworth and Tennyson, poets who had sacrificed personal sincerity to academic morals.[11] Yeats echoed the same thought in 1914 when he addressed a gathering of writers from the magazine *Poetry* and offered guidance they might have gotten from either Wilde or Pound: "The business of a poet. . . is merely to express himself . . . not thinking whether he is a good man or a bad man, or whether he is teaching you"[12]

Yeats's most extreme version of self-expression, appreciated by Pound as Yeats's entry into modern poetry, comes in *Responsibilities* (1914), with its dauntless final lines: "*till all my priceless things/ Are but a post the passing dogs defile*" (*VP*, 321).[13] Yeats's sincerity, or *virtù*, as Pound might have called it, enabled him to bring to English poetry the "self-portraiture" that he felt was its greatest lack, and create "a marvellous drama" of his own life. (*L*, 583).

Dramatic expression did not necessarily preclude the use of ideas in poetry. Though Yeats berated Tennyson and Swinburne for debasing their poetry with beliefs, he felt free to incorporate his own beliefs in his poems through the use of dramatic masks. In 1912-14, when he composed most of the poems in *Responsibilities*, Yeats's chief intellectual interest was investigating séances, and in 1913, he became an associate of the Society for Psychical Research. Despite the ability of the mask to let the poet identify with lives beyond his own, the beggars and fools that Yeats chose as mouthpieces did not bring him any closer to solidarity with the general middle-class Irish community. Spiritist research, Yeats felt, could establish the identity of a far more impressive community, the timeless and spaceless link between the living and the dead. In the summer of 1913, Yeats had proved to his own satisfaction the independent identity of spirits through the case of a medium who was able to write coherent sentences in ancient languages unknown either by her or by any of those present in the room, and subsequently translated by as skeptical an authority as Ezra Pound. Yeats was quick to see the literary applications of such a spirit world: "It was with this world, these temporary beings, representations in time and space of spaceless beings, that Aeneas spoke. Homer's ghosts passed into this state by drinking the blood of the sacrifice and lacking that blood had been dumb and invisible."[14] If all of ancient literature could be viewed in this way as a mediation between mortal and immortal, why could not a modern poet use his writings to make contact with a personal guardian in the spirit world?

Soon after this point in the manuscript book in which Yeats recorded his spiritist investigations, the poet began jotting down notes for poems. In May, 1914, he set down two visions which take place "in the mind's eye." One of them has been reprinted as the prose draft of "The Fisherman." I give the other one here as a possible germ for "Ego Dominus Tuus":

Subject of Poem.

Now I know what it is I have sought in the dark lanes of the wood, always thinking to find it at every new corner; what I have sought on the smooth sand of little bays of the sea, places delightful under the feet; what I have sought behind every new hillock as I climbed the shoulder of the mountain. I have sought that only I can see, if ever any can see it, the being that bears my likeness, but is without weariness or trivial desires, that looks upon far off things, bearing its burden in peace. ("Extracts," TS, 32–33).

The one with the far-off gaze no longer needs to be invoked at a hierophantic ritual attended by Michael Robartes and the immortals, but could be sought much closer to home, among the seven woods of Coole, along the shore of Sligo Bay, or climbing Ben Bulben's back, for it is, according to Yeats, a "divine image of myself."[15] The crucial querstion for Yeats to determine was the origin of this guiding image. Did it "issue forth . . . from the soul itself . . . of its own birth," as Coleridge had intuited in the midst of his dejection? More likely it descended upon one suddenly, coming from outside and from beyond the self, as in the *Vita Nuova*, where a "lord of terrible aspect" brought Dante in his sleep a vision of a woman and a flaming heart symbolic of his future love, and pronounced the words of Dante's poetic initiation "*Ego dominus tuus.*" Since we know the place that Dante came to play in the final version, furnishing both its title and its chief example of antithetical creation, it is difficult not to hear in Yeats's draft an echo of Dante's *selva oscura*, the dark wood in which the poet-hero finds himself lost at the start of the *Inferno*. Yeats too had lost his way in the middle of life, still in love with an unattainable woman, and still unable to fuse the opposing impulses of self-expression in poetry and self-transcendence in occultism.

By recognizing, as Dante had, that the image of the anti-self may be an unearthly presence that singles out the poet for its guidance, Yeats had begun to prepare himself for antithetical revelation.

Yeats's intimation of an external anti-self was severely tested in July 1915, when a spirit claiming to be the poet's personal guide asked Yeats to write a letter with all his doubts about the reality of the spirit world, and that the spirit guide would write, through Yeats, his reply. The exchange of letters with Leo Africanus, the sixteenth-century Moorish geographer and poet, came only two months before the earliest dated working drafts of "Ego Dominus Tuus," and is clearly related to that poem's structure of pitting two debaters against one another, one doubting and the other confirming the existence of an anti-self that can bring psychic wholeness to the individual. The exchange left Yeats skeptical, the poet doubting whether any of Leo's letters had come from beyond his own mind. The letters show that Yeats actually incorporated into Leo's reply much of the material on the life of the soul after death from his own recently completed essay, "Swedenborg, Mediums, and the Desolate Places" (1914), as well as a passage from a letter to his skeptical father.[16] Yeats did not need Leo to convince him of the reality of supernatural daimons intervening in the lives of men, for he attests to that conviction at the very outset of his letter to Leo. What the Leo episode gave Yeats was a means of transforming the mind's internal doubts into a debate with an external anti-self who could be conceived as supernatural. "Sometimes when you are dreaming," Yeats wrote in the name of Leo,

> "you will imagine you will dream that you witness or take part in a dispute, and afterwards, when [you] examine the opinions, discover that both disputants have made use of thoughts that are a part of your daily mind, but should that make you believe that you have not reasoned with yourself? Whose was that other that opposed you? . . . Is your own mind and your will doubled?"[17]

The turbulent Leo episode took place amidst an ongoing quarrel in Yeats's mind: Should the poet cultivate the disparate aspects of his personality as necessary antitheses or should he rather seek to unify them? We can recapitulate this argument through journal entries and through Yeats's correspondence with his father in which the two men were constantly alternating position. In May 1913, J.B. Yeats proclaimed confidently that poetry is the voice of the "whole man . . . in which is no controversy with anyone; and only when the personality is *knit* and the man at peace with himself, can poetry stream forth and there is a truce among the warring elements."[18] Yeats *fils* was unconvinced; in January 1914, he speculated that in every artist there is an antithesis "between the artistic and the daily self" (*Mem*, 270), which determines the nature of his creativity. Several months later, in August 1914, Yeats *pére* was exhorting his son with WBY's own antithetical conviction: "There is one thing never to be forgotten. *That the poet is the antithesis of the man of action.*"[19] Challenged to disagree, Yeats predictably returns to his father's earlier position in his reply the next month: "I think . . . that the poet seeks truth . . . a kind of vision of reality which satisfies the whole being" (*L*, 588). In an important letter (April 2, 1915), the core of which Yeats incorporated in "Ego Dominus Tuus," JBY classifies poets into two sorts, the one "solitary," following only the voice of his own imagination, the other "companionable," insincere and always compromising himself for others. "The solitary is the only man who retains his spiritual integrity. . . . Every thought of his mind and every feeling comes from sources beyond our utmost ken" (*Passages*, 39–43). Whenever Yeats had tried the path of the companionable, he also had found it wanting, but in 1914–15 he was not prepared to trust only in his isolated imagination.

Enter Leo in July, 1915, opposing his impulsiveness and braggart impetuosity to Yeats's timid, conscientious self and claiming that each would now complete the other. The image of the lone traveler in the desert, always acting without a thought of either deliberate pose or consequence, gave the poet a compelling opposite image, which Leo claimed was sent to bring Yeats "confidence and solitude."[20] Unfortunately, because of his doubts about Leo's veracity, what confidence Yeats had had in his imagination was severely undermined. The vision of the anti-self in the "Subject of Poem" of May 1914, was far more confident that that in "Ego Dominus Tuus," written a year and a half later. Yeats's bleak mood when he set out to write this theoretical exploration, initially entitled "The Self and the Anti-Self," can be judged by the entry on the preceding page of his manuscript book:

> No longer the moon
> Sends me dark leopards.
> Green eyed, and wavering [?] in the body . . .[21]

No wonder he turned the page and sent Ille out to walk in the moon to search for a magical resolution of his imaginative impasse. Yeats had been frustrated in his search for both the whole man and the opposite image, the two grounds of his aesthetic. Setting out amidst his uncertainty, in "Ego Dominus Tuus," Yeats attempted to create some new order out of his twenty years' quarrel with himself.

The title of the poem, signifying Dante's initiation into visionary poetry, and by extension, that of Yeats himself, did not occur to Yeats until after the entire poem had been written. Given Yeats's mood in October–December

1915, any such claims would have been extremely premature. He longed to weight the argument in favor of Ille (Pound in fact called it a debate between Hic and Willie),[22] but he nevertheless felt compelled to let us see the visionary in himself as he appeared to Pound's generation: an outmoded Romantic of the Pater-dominated 1890s, tied to the Shelleyan image of a mage in his moonlit tower, now no more than a theatrical prop:

> And, though you have passed the best of life, still trace,
> Enthralled by the unconquerable delusion,
> Magical shapes

In the final version of the poem, Ille turns back this attack with the expansive creed to which he swears allegiance:

> By the help of an image
> I call to my own opposite, summon all
> That I have handled least, least looked upon.

> *(Myth, 321)*

This bold plea for the opposite image was lost in the first draft where the second line read "I would call up my antitype," to which Yeats added a maudlin fourth line of self-denigration, "Because I am most weary of myself." Yeats could never restore himself to imaginative well-being if he continued to clothe his visionary persona with the unappealing self-loathing and world weariness of the nineties.

Though Yeats might have known the term antitype from biblical typology, where it signifies a New Testament event that fulfills the hints of an Old Testament one, it is more likely that he remembered it from Shelley's "Essay on Love," where it signifies an idealized image of a better self within us, whom we can aspire to meet in the person of our beloved. "We dimly see within our intellectual nature a miniature as it were of our entire self . . . the ideal prototype of everything excellent or lovely that we are capable of conceiving as belonging to the nature of man. The soul's "discovery of its antitype," says Shelley, is as if the chords of two exquisite lyres, strung to the accompaniment of one delightful voice, vibrate with the vibrations of our own."[23] There is something quite egotistical in Shelley's notion, both as inner, superior self and mirroring other, that Ille/Yeats rejects in favor of an antithetical self that would embody all that he lacks. Harold Bloom has noted a similar swerve from Shelleyan subjectivity in a possible source passage for Yeats's poem in *The Revolt of Islam* (201–03). Ille traces on the sand "magical shapes," just as Cythna had in the earlier poem, but Cythna had gained her knowledge through utter absorption in the depths of her own mind, where Ille hopes to have the meaning of the shapes revealed to him by an external agency who will magnify his own limited knowledge. Both the antitype and Cythna's wisdom are emblems of the nineteenth-century belief, centrally stated in Wordsworth's preface to *Lyrical Ballads*, that if the poet expresses all that is best in his own nature, he will arrive at a statement that is true for all humanity. Ille, with his intimations of occult revelation, leaves the humanistic Hic to defend this expressive theory of art.

Hic's reply is the earlier Yeatsian position of sincerity: the poet finds truth in living out and reporting his own deepest desires. Ille cannot let this pass without remarking, as Yeats had in the 1909 journal, that sincerity is the root weakness of modern culture. In the drafts, he speaks of the "subtleness and sincerity"

> That is our modern hope, and by its light
> We have lit upon the gentle, sensitive mind
> And lost the old nonchalance of the hand;
> Whether we have chosen chisel, pen or brush.
> We are but critics, or but half create,
> Timid, entangled, empty and abashed,
> Lacking the countenance of our friends.
>
> (*Myth*, 321)

Ille would restore the Renaissance ideal of *sprezzatura* and of an art created for an appreciative aristocratic coterie. Echoing Matthew Arnold's "The Function of Criticism at the Present Time," he belittles the entire modern movement in art and letters as the product of an age of criticism rather than one of genuine creativity. Bloom has noted the significant echo of Wordsworth's "Tintern Abbey" in the phrase "half create" (200). Half creation follows from empiricism, the passive commitment to reporting the moods of nature and the moods of the poet's own mind. Full creation does not depend, in Yeats's view, on imitating the world as it appears, but on portraying a visionary world that might be. Wordsworth, above all others, had abused the poetry of self-expression and given a bad name to sincerity, Yeats claimed in 1909, accepting "a discipline which he has not created" (*Mem*, 151).[24] As I have insisted, what Yeats feared more than anything else in 1915 was the drying up of his imagination. He kept before him as warning an image of "Wordsworth withering into eighty years, honoured and empty-witted" (*Myth*, 342), the end result of an expressive art that had exhausted the resources of the isolated self.

For the moment, Hic concedes the attack on modern culture, turning rather to examine specific literary figures, first Dante and then Keats, because he feels that in great literature the distinctive mark of the individual genius can always be located. As early as 1897, Yeats had attested in an essay on Blake to the personal appeal of Dante's poetry.[25] It is one's own "sorrows and angers and regrets and terrors and hopes that awaken to condemnation or repentance while Dante treads his eternal pilgrimage" (*E&I*, 141). This is why Dante has been able to make

> that hollow face of his
> More plain to the mind's eye than any face
> But that of Christ.
>
> (*Myth*, 322)

Hic has hit upon the image of the hollow face which supplies his adversary with his major argument, for behind a hollow image there must be another personality, deliberately creating emotions, Yeats wrote in 1906, as part of a "system of ordered images" ("Religious Belief Necessary to Religious Art," *E&I*, 293).

Ille goes on to paint an elaborate portrait of the man behind the hollow Dante face. His method is portraiture by opposition, finding an image that expresses all that the passionate, lecherous man Dante is not:

> I think he fashioned from his opposite
> An image that might have been a stony face
> Staring upon a Bedouin's horse-hair roof
> From doored and windowed cliff, or half upturned
> Among the coarse grass and camel-dung.
> He set his chisel to the hardest stone.
>
> (*Myth*, 322)

A recent commentator has noted the resemblance of Ille's method here to Thomas Carlyle's description of an actual portrait of Dante by Giotto, "painted as on vacancy."[26] Behind the vacant, though mournful, image, Carlyle intuits the presence of an altogether different Dante. "There is in it, as foundation of it, the softness, tenderness, gentle affection of a child; but all this is congealed into sharp contradiction, into abnegation, isolation, proud hopeless pain ... as from imprisonment of thick-ribbed ice."[27] If Yeats has indeed borrowed from Carlyle, and the likelihood is great, since Ille's comments on Keats also echo the Victorian sage, it is in the way Yeats's portrait of the stony face masks "the gentle affection" of the lover. Dante's hidden self is silent, but his stoic acceptance of a bitter fate calls out to us from the final lines, themselves a quotation from the *Paradiso*:

> Derided and deriding, driven out
> To climb that stair and eat that bitter bread,
> He found the unpersuadable justice, he found
> The most exalted lady loved by a man.
> (*Myth*, 322)[28]

It is fair to say that both Hic and Ille have oversimplified Dante's great artistic achievement for the sake of their arguments, but where Hic sees only the hollow face, Ille invests that face with a psychology of the whole man, his deepest desires as well as his need to hide them from the world in an image impenetrable as the hardest stone. In making real for us the self-denial that accompanies an artistic hunger for the unattainable, transcendent image, Ille begins to win our assent, for it is his discipline of the opposite image that grants him this broader vision of reality.

Ille's vision of Dante implies that all art is born out of a separation betwen self and mask that isolates the artist as a tragic figure. Hic refuses to accept this generalization because he has known "companionable" poets, "Impulsive men that look for happiness/ And sing when they have found it." Ille mocks Hic as a rhetorician and sentimentalist, labelling everyone who longs for the world's material rewards as a self-deceiver, though Yeats himself in 1902 had called William Morris "the one perfectly happy and fortunate poet of modern times," because he counted himself "among the worshippers of natural abundance" (*E&I*, 54). Natural abundance was a fine creed for the contented William Morris, but for the melancholy Ille, obsessed with antithesis, it could only suggest the inevitability of natural decay, the draining of the well and the withering of the tree. Yeats liked to cite the contrary example of his friends Lionel Johnson and Ernest Dowson, who, though "dissipated men," had found life out and were "awakening from the dream," to discover that "art is but a vision of reality" (*Myth*, 331). Ille arrives at this same artistic compulsion for revealing the truth about reality by way of a magnificent sentence of Keats's: "The imagination may be compared to Adam's dream—he awoke and found it truth."[29]

The discussion of Keats in "Ego Dominus Tuus" has upset more critics than almost anything else in Yeats, except perhaps his dalliance with the Blue Shirts of Irish Fascism. Hic naively proposes Keats as the supremely happy artist, ignoring the mournful resonance of the nightingale's song that echoes through Keats's major poetry. Ille also admits a happy art, but would have us penetrate the artist's mind. Unfortunately, this laudable aim is obscured by his snobbish, prudish assessment of Keats, a typical Victorian response to the poet's excess of sensuality:

> I see a schoolboy when I think of him,
> With face and nose pressed to a sweet-shop window,
> For certainly he sank into his grave
> His senses and his heart unsatisfied,
> And made—being poor, ailing and ignorant,
> Shut out from all the luxury of the world,
> The coarse-bred son of a livery-stable keeper—
> Luxuriant song.

> (*Myth*, 323)

Matthew Arnold, in his essay on Keats, went to great lengths to uphold the poet's strength of character against charges, like those of Carlyle, that "Keats is a miserable creature, hungering after sweets which he can't get." Ille's remarkably similar comments may very well derive from this and from another, even more caustic slap, "Keats wanted a world of treacle!"[30] To the Victorians, and most probably to Yeats, Keats's letters to Fanny Brawne seemed brazen in their honest expression of physical desire. Dante also had lusted after Beatrice Portinari, much as Yeats for so many years had craved a physical consummation with Maud Gonne. Yeats was beginning to understand that he could find new energy for his own art, only by renouncing the obsessive quest for Maud Gonne. "The passions," he wrote in *Per Amica*, "when we know they cannot find fulfillment, become vision" (*Myth*, 341). Yeats's/Ille's judgments of Dante and Keats, so often impugned for their literary wrongheadedness, are not really literary judgments at all, but veiled assessments of the ability of each poet to resolve the central sexual crisis of his life. Dante succeeded in transcending his passionate physical desires to create "the most exalted lady loved by a man," but Keats remained chained to his and "sank into his grave/ His senses and his heart unsatisfied." Both poets created through a kind of mask, but their achievements differ; whereas Dante's stony mask enabled him to turn away from the sorrows of his life, Keats's mask of happiness was not different enough from everything that he was in daily life to provide a strong moral discipline. Rather than finding the negative capability through which he could remake himself in his art, he was constantly reminded of his tragic separation from the happiness he desired. Ille's portrait of a pathetic Keats is an object lesson to remind Yeats that unless the artist finds some opposite image to focus the unsatisfied needs of the self, he gives himself up to "dissipation and despair." Keats himself might have answered Ille by pointing to his "Fall of Hyperion," where Moneta, a supernatural opposite, engages the poet in a chastening debate on the aims of his poetry, ironically reminiscent of "Ego Dominus Tuus" itself.

Hic's final question is overtly on the matter of style, but more importantly, he poses it as a question between two self-images of the poet:

> Why should you leave the lamp
> Burning alone beside an open book,
> And trace these characters upon the sands?
>
> (*Myth*, 323)

Hic, like Yeats's argumentative companion, Pound, would have the poet be a scholar of the poetic tradition, self-sufficient in a hermetic world of books and ideas, ensconced in "the far tower where Milton's Platonist/ Sat late, or Shelley's visionary prince" (*VP*, 373). Ille counters with the equally traditional image of the mage who, like Ahasuerus in Shelley's *Hellas*, can unveil all the wisdom of the universe. Ille is by no means stating an unequivocal case, however, when he asserts "I seek an image, not a book." Yeats had sought both and would continue to seek both, shaping the image of the anti-self into *Per Amica*, and both that and the Great Wheel into *A Vision*. He now had before him the choice of choices: either to continue collecting "the sacred books of the world" (*E&I*, 65) and making his own series of such complete, self-sufficient books, or to follow the antithetical life of a mage into an incommunicable world of lightning flashes of revelation. Yeats assumed that the choice was between poetry and occult religion, but what he could not have known at the time was that he would never have to make the choice at all. Perhaps the central paradox of Yeats's career is that his visionary aspiration constantly drew him back into the world of men where he tried to convince the skeptics of the inner workings of the universe that he had glimpsed.

In Ille's final speech, Yeats was preparing himself for a future that might very well have led him away from poetry altogether, not knowing what the meeting of self and anti-self would set in motion. Ultimately, it led him back to an image of the whole man, to what he came to call in the years following "Ego Dominus Tuus" and *Per Amica*, "unity of being."[31] The anti-self provided a new kind of unity for Yeats as soon as he learned to embody the antithetical relationship in vivid poetic images, as he does in the portrait of Dante's mask, but not in the final view of Ille's "mysterious one." There was no single image of Yeats's anti-self, not did it have to be occult as it developed in subsequent poems (although in the plays it tended to be); it merely had to be a visionary image that could be summoned to "the mind's eye," where it became the teacher, and the poet, the pupil. The more different the image from the poet, the more likely it could make its impact felt. "The Fisherman" and *Major Robert Gregory* are in every way opposite to the timid, melancholy poet who calls them to mind. The imperturbable intensity they present discloses to Yeats a conception of unity previously unknown in his own subjectivity. In Yeats's stories of the 1890s, the immortal mask had entirely overwhelmed the mortal beneath it, but after "Ego Dominus Tuus," Yeats stopped worshiping the mask and began assuming it for what he could learn from it. Even in the solitude of his marmoreal reverie, he could have confidence in the healthy diversity of his poetic resources because the concept of the anti-self had helped him locate sources of knowledge outside the self. Yeats could remain an artist within the expressive Romantic tradition because he now used the self to lay hold of everything that was opposite to the self and call it its own.

That Hic should become Ille and Ille, Hic, is a central tenet of Yeats's aesthetic, but the poet was simply not open to "unity of being" when he wrote "Ego Dominus Tuus." Instead of magnanimously extending himself to his opposites, the world's agents and doers, Ille can envision no role for the artist within the daily world. Ille's tragedy, and perhaps the central artistic failure of the poem as well, is the inability to construct a positive image of the anti-self. The entire poem has been building toward Ille's meeting with his visionary opposite, yet when the dramatic moment comes, he can only give us the theory, similarity and opposition joined in one image:

> I call to the mysterious one who yet
> Shall walk the wet sands by the edge of the stream
> And look most like me, being indeed my double,
> And prove of all imaginable things
> The most unlike, being my anti-self,
> And, standing by these characters, disclose
> All that I seek; and whisper it as though
> He were afraid the birds, who cry aloud
> Their momentary cries before it is dawn,
> Would carry it away to blasphemous men.
>
> *(Myth,* 324)

Throughout the poem, Ille has contended that the artist can actually create his anti-self by meditating on a mask. But Ille/Yeats does not have the confidence to begin. The title of the poem reminds us that neither did Dante begin that mediation on his antithetical mask until after a visionary annunciation. In the middle of his career, after having written poetry for thirty years, Yeats writes "Ego Dominus Tuus" to request an authoritative visionary initiation once and for all. He feels that he must abandon his erstwhile commitment to Hic if the communicating spirits are to believe his willingness to place himself in their hands. If Ille's anti-self whispers his secrets tentatively, it is because the poet is afraid of seeming too brash in his claims and prejudicing his visionary masters against him. Yeats was temporarily willing to renounce the ideal of the whole man if that renunciation could assure him a place in Dante's visionary company.

2

Quarrels of the Creative Self: *"Anima Hominis"*

"Per Amica Silentia Lunae" (Title and Prologue)

In his title, Yeats calls up a quiet, friendly moon to preside over this autobiography of his convictions. He deepens the link with Dante in the choice of a title phrase from Virgil, Dante's self-acknowledged master in poetry. Yeats wants to use Virgil, as Dante did, as a friendly guide to lead him from the solitude of his study into the vast and eery stillness of the *Anima Mundi*, there to receive instruction from the dead about the secret workings of both lunar and sublunar worlds. Therefore Yeats has put himself to school, he claims, "where all things are seen: *A Tenedo tacitae per amica silentia lunae*" (*Myth*, 343), referring to that shadowy realm of mediums and evocations where things are certainly not seen, as we normally understand that word. Nor were all things seen in the original Virgilian context (*Aeneid* II.255f.), since the moon, friendly enough to the Greeks, did not shine so brightly as to illuminate them for their sleeping enemy. The paradox behind the allusion points to the duality of the moon in poetic tradition. Lipking (57) comments on "Clair de Lune" by Hugo and *"Per Amica Silentia"* by Verlaine, poems that adopt the Virgilian phrase but whose scenic tranquility masks underlying violence: slave girls murdered by drowning; lesbian lovers pierced by the stigmata. G.C. Spivak finds an additional allusion to *Samson Agonistes* (lines 85-89), and construes in Yeats's title a masculinist "transaction from Homer to Virgil to Dante to Milton to Yeats," for the purposes of elaborating the transgressive figure of a woman (Helen, Dido, Beatrice, Delilah, Maud), and replacing its unspoken presence with the transumptive voice of the male poet.[1] Yeats's title and its tradition are thus both richly ironic and psychologically appropriate, while the lunar symbol itself is necessary to the definition of imaginative activity that Yeats will go on to provide.

Since Yeats is writing a theory of poetic inspiration in *Per Amica*, the moon's maddening, chastening inconstancy provides a provenance for the poet who lives for the moment of vision and must therefore "go from desire to weariness and so to desire again" (*Myth*, 340). Furthermore, the fact that the moon only reflects rather than provides its own source of light suits

Yeats's emphasis on the poet as a receptor of inflowings from the *Anima Mundi*. From Proclus, Yeats was aware of the moon as symbolizing both "the life of instinct," (a crucial connector to the dead in the *Anima Mundi*) and "'the apparition of images' in the 'imagination'" (*E&I*, 91). From the Tarot, he was aware of the moon representing both the benevolence and the dangers of the imaginative life, showing the adept glimpses of images that exist beyond the "natural mind," but unable to guide him with its merely reflected light beyond the "place of exit," to the source of those images.[2]

Per Amica is Yeats's concerted attempt to reawaken the slumbering sources of inspiration by meditating upon them. To the Ille side of Yeats, moonlight in "Ego Dominus Tuus" provided the atmosphere in which the poet could search for his imaginative vitality. In a more depressed, unmasked mood in the previous year, Yeats could only see the moon as a reminder of the inspirational energy that he had lost:

> The holy centaurs of the hills are vanished;
> I have nothing but the embittered sun;
> Banished heroic mother moon and vanished,
> And now that I have come to fifty years
> I must endure the timid sun.

(VP, 355)

At a crucial point early in his career, Yeats had found himself in the situation of "Lines Written in Dejection," divorced from his inward sources of inspiration and unable to call into action the private virtues that "earn the sun." A friend consulted a medium for him whose astrological advice Yeats followed to the letter: "'He is too much under solar influence. He is to live near water and to avoid woods, which concentrate solar power.'" A few days afterward, Yeats narrates in *Memoirs* (100–101), he began "to evoke the lunar power" known to him from his occult researches, and received a remarkable vision of a centaur and a naked woman shooting an arrow at a star, upon whose meaning he meditates in both *Per Amica* (*Myth*, 340) and *Autobiographies* (371). Yeats associated the moon not only with private vision, but also with the traditional imaginative life of the community, and when he began collecting fairy legends around Coole lake with Lady Gregory, he recognized that he was moving away from the solar isolation that had plagued him. In the years immediately preceding *Per Amica*, however, even when he tried to fuse the energy of individual discipline with images drawn from the people, as in "The Fisherman" (1914), Yeats could only write in the clear early light of dawn. He had banished, it seemed to him in "Lines Written in Dejection," what he had described as lunar in "Emotion of Multitude" (1903), "the rich, far-wandering, many-imaged life of the half-seen world" (*E&I*, 216).

The second essay of *Per Amica* begins with Yeats's protestations to the contrary; he has continually sought out the mysterious lunar influence:

I have always sought to bring my mind close to the mind of Indian and Japanese poets, old women in Connacht, mediums in Soho, lay brothers whom I imagine dreaming in some mediaeval monastery the dreams of their village, learned authors who refer all to antiquity; to immerse it in the general mind where that mind is scarce separable from what we have begun to call "the subconscious". . . . (*Myth*, 343)

Even when he is closest to the modern world, as here, in his use of the nascent Freudian terminology,[3] Yeats would "refer all to antiquity," to all ancient ideas and practices that have found their way into the book of the people. It is here, in the archaizing context of "Anima Mundi," that Yeats introduces the source of his title in Virgil's epic and its reminder of the hidden hand in human affairs.

Where the title of *Per Amica* prepares the reader for a merging of the visible and the hidden, the prologue continues expounding the inter-dependence of our intellectual and instinctive faculties. No matter how much human beings feel in control of the world through which they walk, from time to time, nature reminds them that the instinctive realm lies totally beyond their grasp.

The fable with which Yeats opens the prologue testifies in a homely way to this intimation of limits. A cat, that most cautious and reserved pet, accompanies Yeats and his pseudonymic friend on a stroll, never straying far from their supervision. Yet suddenly the flutter of a wing in a bramblebush upsets the equilibrium between the animal and the human that had seemed so unquestionably ordered. No number of endearing names could purchase that cat's attention, for he was now rapt in a concentration that only a poet in his reverie might share. This intimate anecdote is not at all casually chosen, for the black Persian cat Minnaloushe, who reappears in Yeats's poem and play, *The Cat and the Moon* (1917), represents the world of instinct lying beyond man's intellect. From the human point of view, the cat in the bushes is merely acting upon a whim, but from the cat's perspective (as seen by Yeats) his enthrallment with the flutter of a wing is determined by powers beyond the terrestrial. In Minnaloushe's behavior Yeats intimates the operation of daimonic forces in the universe. During the course of Yeats's meditation in *Per Amica*, he will attribute to such forces the motive and power for poetic, and ultimately, for all human creation.

One of the main subjects of *Per Amica*, integral to both title and prologue, is the relation between this world and another one that we do not see, which raises in turn the artistic problem of how one can write a rational treatise about matters that are not at all verifiable by reason. The narrative situation of the prologue dramatizes the problem and provides a solution. A rational conversation upon suprarational matters is interrupted by an act of animal instinct to which the conversationslist must necessarily refer if he is to validate his ideas. Minnaloushe, the concrete fact, becomes a metaphor for an abstraction, the instinctive awareness of an extraterrestrial realm.[4] The final sentence of the prologue, "Read it some day when 'Minnaloushe' is asleep," suggests one further artistic constraint. Only when the reader is at rest and his reason is playing freely over a core of instinctive experience will Yeats's "habitual thoughts" assume the authority he himself confers upon them in calling them his "convictions."[5]

The prologue not only tells us how to read *Per Amica*, but also who will read it. The book jacket of the original Macmillan edition describes *Per Amica* as "the conversation of a gifted poet, such as he only indulges in in conversing with his intimates." The intimate friend most directly concerned is "Maurice," whom we know from the allusion to Maud Gonne's home at Calvados, in Normandy, to be her illegitimate daughter Iseult, aged twenty-two. Yeats had been visiting Maud and Iseult at least once a year since 1909; Iseult took a flirting interest in her mother's old flame and had even made a lighthearted proposal of marriage in 1915. After John MacBride's execution in the Easter Rising of 1916, Yeats took one final opportunity of proposing to Maud, but after her unequivocal refusal, he began to think that he might have actually fallen in love with Iseult (witness the suite of poems to her in *The Wild Swans at Coole*; *VP*, 333-36). In the summer of 1917, after having dedicated *Per Amica* to her as the record of his most cherished convictions, he proposed to the girl. Was Yeats only acting the part of a jilted lover who lightly takes an unwanted love on the rebound; or was he seriously willing to commit the remainder of his life to a fatherly affection in the vain hope of becoming Maud's surrogate husband in their mutual commitment to Iseult?[6] Although Yeats thought of *Per Amica* as an epithalamion to Iseult, the slightness of her role in the prologue alerts the reader to look for the abiding presence of Maud Gonne as the idealized muse who disturbs Yeats's midnight repose.

The entire work, then, is a personal justification, undertaken in mid-career, of the principles by which Yeats had lived and written his poetry. Much of *Per Amica* is retrospective, harking back to his occult symbolism of the 1890s and to his theorizing about masks and the voice of poetry, circa 1910. Yet the text also demands to be read as the completion of the visionary initiation begun in "Ego Dominus Tuus," the latest elaboration of that poem's daimonic intimations. If his audience wanted to know the future direction of his career, they would have to read *Per Amica*. For its readers, Yeats invited the select few who had read everything he had written, and who he hoped would judge him most indulgently.

"A Marmorean Muse" ("Anima Hominis" I)

"Anima Hominis," Yeats's Latin title for the first essay of *Per Amica*, is misleading, for his subject is not the general soul of man, but rather the creative soul of the poet. To answer the question of what a poet is, he sets out to analyze himself, the poet he knows best, as the type of all, though in the course of the essay he alludes to over twenty other writers, both ancient and modern, to prove, as Ille had tried to do in "Ego Dominus Tuus," that every poet creates by assuming an antithetical self. The proem ends on an anticipatory note, awaiting a meeting with the anti-self. It is now up to Yeats to dramatize that meeting for us, as he describes that activity which he feels most clearly characterizes the poet as poet—meditative reverie.

Section I of "Anima Hominis" is itself a reverie with three distinct movements: the poet's extreme self-consciousness in the dinner party; the poet's retrenchment in the "marmorean" world of his muse, where he enters the state of poetic vision; and finally, a movement toward reconciliation in which the poet asks us to grant to that private, internal world the validity that we normally bestow only on our empirical perceptions. Although the section embodies the dialectical form of a debate, the combative tone of "Ego Dominus Tuus" is gone, replaced by a quiet introspection which soothes and prepares us to enter the poet's privileged world of reverie.[7]

The first movement serves as a prelude to reverie by demonstrating the inappropriateness of the social world for the artist: "My fellow diners have hardly seemed of mixed humanity, and how should I keep my head among images of good and evil, crude allegories?" Yeats's standards of judgment are those of the artist, demanding particularity and vividness. In "Edmund Spenser" (1902), he objected to his countryman's abstract moral and religious allegory because it "disappoints and interrupts our preoccupation with the beautiful and sensuous life he has called up before our eyes." Allegory could be a way of communing with God, if it maintained its "visionary strangeness and intensity," and was used, as Dante and Blake had used it, "to describe visionary things" (*E&I*, 368). Yeats's social world presented itself to him in the simplest black and white terms; divorced from everything beautiful and sensuous in life, it turned all within it, including the awkward, timid poet, into artificial caricature.

Yeats could return to life, ironically, only by eschewing it, choosing in its stead the solitude of a hermetic environment in which to re-engage his creative self. His reverie, he reports, inevitably produces a profound experience of self-discovery by calling up to his mind's eye the long-sought image of the anti-self:

> But when I shut the door and light the candle, I invite a marmorean Muse, an art where no thought or emotion has come to mind because another man has thought or felt something different, for now there must be no reaction, action only, and the world must move my heart but to the heart's discovery of itself, and I begin to dream of eyelids that do not quiver before the bayonet: all my thoughts have ease and joy, I am all virtue and confidence.

Yeats himself calls this heightened state "an heroic condition," and it is quite clear that the poet transforms himself into a poet-hero only because of the particular heroic image that comes to him in his reverie, "eyelids that do not quiver before the bayonet," a glance that sums up all the wordly courage that is so absolutely antithetical to the poet afraid of his own voice at the dinner party. This process is reminiscent of "The Fisherman" (1914), in which Yeats summons the courage to reprove the craven, the clever, the insolent, and the knave, because he has begun "To call up to the eyes/ This wise and simple man," opposed to the trivial lives surrounding the poet. In imagining the heroic anti-self, the poet relieves himself of social obligations only to incur the double responsibilitiy both to the anti-self image and to its divine source.

The most immediate reponsibility of the poet is to translate his vision into art. "It is only the shrinking from toil, perhaps, that convinces me that I have been no more myself than is the cat the medicinal grass it is eating in the garden." Only when he discovers that the experience of this reverie does not easily lend itself to self-expression, does he realize that the image of unflinching eyes in battle is not drawn from any self that he has ever known. In the final image of the medicinal grass, Yeats may be implying that the process of stumbling upon the anti-self unwittingly has been psychically medicinal for him. What Yeats has learned from this experience is that the poet does not create the images of his reverie; they come to him from "above and beyond" the self. The key words in describing such visions are "complete," "minutely organized," and "elaborate." As early as the seminal essay "Magic" of 1901, Yeats had claimed: "Our most elaborate thoughts, elaborate purposes, precise emotions, are often, as I think, not really ours, but have on a sudden come up, as it were, out of Hell or down out of Heaven" (*E&I*, 40).

Yeats is always seeking in *Per Amica* to extend the range of reference of his personal insights by alluding to other literary or religious figures who can validate them for him. Dante and Jacob Boehme serve him as models of two men for whom such visions commanded tremendous authority. Certain visions claim control over us, as the Lord of Terrible Aspect did with Dante, while others offer totally engaging worlds for us to inhabit, as does Boehme's cornucopial landscape of eternal solace. Yeats suggests that his personal intuition of "an heroic condition," beginning with the masks assumed in childhood, has made him "superstitious," but this term is not meant to suggest an evasive skepticism about visionary experience, as Richard Ellmann has characteristically suggested (*Man and Masks*, 199). Yeats's occult religion was compounded out of folk superstition and ancient magic. By acknowledging the necessity and sufficiency for his art of an authority from above and beyond, he is accepting a religious unity that binds the creative self to God.

The yoking of poet and theosophist is meant to remind us of the absolute continuity for Yeats between an aesthetic and a religious apprehension of reality. Behind the classic examples of Dante and Boehme stands the modern one of Walter Pater, clearly, the stylistic master of the work. Pater's *Marius, The Epicurean*, one of Yeats's sacred books, affirmed "the intrinsic 'blessedness' of 'vision'" for an entire poetic generation.[8] Pater's narrative of sensations and ideas moves steadily toward the revelation that the goals of art and religion, both an ecstasy of contemplation, are one. Yet for all his influence on Yeats, Pater is never quoted or cited in the work. Two years after writing *Per Amica*, Yeats was exorcising Pater through parody. "He wrote of me in that extravagant style/ He had learnt from Pater" (*VP*, 373), claims the newly resurrected Michael Robartes in "Phases of the Moon." Even before writing *Per Amica*, Yeats had begun to ascribe the tragedy of Lionel Johnson to his too literal following of the Paterian advice to cultivate exquisite impressions at the expense of all the dross in life (*Mem*, 95-96). Pater deserves a key place in Yeats's spiritual autobiography, but perhaps in 1917 Yeats is too close to thoughts of his own possible imaginative failure, and too "superstitious" to invoke one whom he blamed for the failures of his friends.[9]

"The Minds of My Friends" ("Anima Hominis" II)

Yeats, the private myth-maker, knows that he must become a public mythologist if his audience is ever to subscribe to his theory of the anti-self. Accordingly, the next three sections of "Anima Hominis" try to universalize his private insights by objectifying them in the portraits of other artists. His strategy shifts from argument between self and world to an amassing of biographical images to lend body and particularity to his myth of poetic creation.

The portraits of Lady Gregory, Florence Farr (both unnamed, because still living at the time of writing), and John Synge, are all organized around the central idea that their art stands in direct opposition to their lives, as a "compensating dream," or "an opposing virtue." Art is the anti-self of the artist's life, a necessary complement if he is to attain, as Yeats claims of Synge's art, "the fulfilment of his own life." The extent to which this was a general psychological theory for Yeats is indicated in a manuscript entry of February 1913: "All outer strengths have a corresponding inner weakness, inner strengths an outer weakness" ("Extracts," TS, 1). As shown in Yeats's portraits, life for the artist was a matter of balancing strengths against weaknesses: Lady Gregory, overly judgmental in life, celebrating indulgence in her plays; Florence Farr, living with the brashness of a buccaneer, but on stage, exquisitely representing shadowy essences; John Synge, feeble and near death, exalting a passionate adherence to all physical life. These images are familiar to any student of Yeats because he reshaped them, and others like them, again and again throughout his poetic career, from "In Memory of Major Robert Gregory" (1918) to "All Souls' Night" (1920), to "The

Municipal Gallery Revisited" (1937), without ever changing the basic pattern of the limited self finding its completion in art. His autobiographical volume, *The Trembling of the Veil* (1922), is obsessed with these and other divided personae of his friends.

Throughout his life, Yeats remained a divided being like the friends he describes, but unlike them, he continued to search for a way to unify his disparate selves. One was more or less unified, according to the insight of *Per Amica*, depending on the degree of self-consciousness with which the opposite image was pursued. Listen to Yeats's subtle hierarchy of valuation: Lady Gregory did "not know why she has created that world where no one is ever judged"; one level higher, Florence Farr, who "could not listen" had some inkling that those Burne-Jones women in her rooms, "who were always listening," were in some way necessary opposites for her; only John Synge, who hated the thought of his immanent death, was completely conscious of how he could oppose it, and in *Deirdre of the Sorrows* "accepted death and dismissed life with a gracious gesture," much as Yeats's ideally unified man, Robert Gregory, does in his triumphant exit.

"Blind Struggle" ("Anima Hominis" III)

In *Per Amica*, Yeats's scheme of self and a compensatory anti-self sometimes seems rigidly deterministic, as Ellmann notes (*Man and Masks*, 206). For Yeats, the determining forces are summed up in the word *horoscope*: "the work is the man's flight from his entire horoscope, his blind struggle in the network of the stars." Louis MacNeice correctly remarks of this passage that the "poet as poet can escape up to a point from determinism," up to a point, that is, which Yeats is not willing to specify.[10] Yeats has already hinted in the image of Dante's visionary master, of the control of the artist from beyond. Here, he interjects the sinister note that though the artist may seek to counteract that which is fated for him by adopting the mask of personality, there is no guarantee either of his probable success or of the benevolence of the supernatural forces arrayed against him. The gnostic image of the network of stars amidst which man is helplessly enmeshed serves to emphasize, rather than to dispel, the notion of a controlling horoscope. Man's ability to escape the constraints of this world is nil; in the language of Ille in "Ego Dominus Tuus," man's actions are merely "The struggle of the fly in marmalade" (*Myth*, 323).

If some men pit themselves against the outside world, still others are beset from within by their own imaginations. Yeats's description of Savage Landor is a case in point, though the beautiful modelling of the opening sentence somewhat belies the brooding intensity of Yeats's dark vision:

Savage Landor topped us all in calm nobility when the pen was in his hand, as in the daily violence of his passion when he had laid it down. He had in his *Imaginary Conversations* reminded us, as it were, that the Venus de Milo is a stone, and yet he wrote when the copies did not come from the printer as soon as he expected: "I have . . . had the resolution to tear in pieces all my sketches and projects and to forswear all future undertakings. I have tried to sleep away my time and pass two-thirds of the twenty-four hours in bed. I may speak of myself as a dead man."

To Yeats, Landor is not a figure for mockery, but a tragic instance of a man possessed, as if by a demon. To this portrait of mania, we can juxtapose the similarly obsessive melancholia of Landor's contemporary, Thomas De Quincey. In De Quincey's autobiographical reverie, *Suspiria de Profundis*, he introduced a personified Daimon, "the Dark Interpreter," who lives in the dream world of one prone to reverie and there "does his work, revealing the worlds of pain and agony and woe possible to man."[11] In *Per Amica*, Yeats casts himself as the Dark Interpreter, exposing wherever he can the pain underlying the "blind, stupefied" heart (*Myth*, 324) that creates.

"A Double War" ("Anima Hominis" IV)

"The never dying aches of the probe of pain are in every bosom; only while others resort to some kind of laudanum, the poets let these work, finding in them the root of happiness, the only sort which, though it be twin with sorrow, is without a fleck on its purity." So wrote J. B. Yeats to his son in November 1914 (*Passages*, 2). Section IV of "Anima Hominis" could almost serve as Yeats's concurring reply. The idea of a happy art, though occasionally admitted by Yeats, was antithetical to his deepest sense of life. If we think of Yeats's own early poems about supposedly happy worlds, such as "The Song of the Happy Shepherd," or "The Happy Townland," we remember that "Grey truth" (*VP*, 65) and "the world's bane" (*VP*, 214), are constant reminders there of the inadequacy of any escape into an idealized world which turns its back on the creative potential of exasperation and loss.

When Yeats returns to the arguments of "Ego Dominus Tuus," he calls happy art "'a hollow image of fulfilled desire,'" teasing us with the paradox of a hollow fulfillment. Blake wrote memorably of "the lineaments of Gratified Desire" in man and in woman,[12] but Yeats distances himself from that unattainable hope. In quoting instead from the Pre-Raphaelite Simeon Solomon, he has misremembered a passage that is not about fulfilled desire at all, but its opposite. Describing the allegorical figure of a passionate woman who sought to slay Love, Solomon writes: "her wasted beauty preyed upon itself; her face was whitened with pale fires, a hollow image of unappeased desire," and finishes by depicting her previous happy state before lust took control of her being.[13] In Solomon's fantasy, unappeased desire hollows out the body, much as Dante's "hunger for the apple on the bough/ Most out of reach," carves out that poet's "hollow face" (*Myth*, 322) in "Ego Dominus Tuus." We can assume that Yeats unconsciously reversed the long-misremembered phrase in order to validate his impulse to dismiss happy art. Happy art generates the hollowness of insincerity, whereas the antithetical hollowness of tragic art reifies a definite lack in the soul of the artist, "the poverty or the exasperation that set its maker to the work."

In taking up the issue of fulfilled or unfulfilled desires, Yeats may have been responding to a question of George Moore's in *Vale* (1914): "We had often heard him say that his poems had arisen out of one great passion, and this interesting avowal brought the no less interesting question—which produces the finer fruit, the gratified or the ungratified passion."[14] Yeats was to ask the same question rhetorically in "The Tower" (1926): "Does the imagination dwell the most/ Upon a woman won or woman lost?" (*VP*, 413). Only an unsatisfied desire could give birth to Yeats's vision of Maud's Ledaean body, with its "Hollow of cheek as though it drank the wind/ And took a mess of shadows for its meat" (*VP*, 444).

Yeats supports his position by drawing out Ille's contrast between Keats and Dante. Though each fashioned his art from disappointment, only Dante represents the tragic artist. His remaking of himself involved a dramatic confrontation with the opposite image of Beatrice, "the most pure lady poet ever sung and the Divine Justice," while Keats merely juxtaposed desire and its unattainable objects. The one is a "tragic war," the other, the plea of an unsatisfied heart.

Dante used his imaginative exasperation in a "double war"—against himself and against the moralistic world which judged him so harshly, a war that Yeats himself constantly fought against "The daily spite of this unmannerly town," Dublin (*VP*, 351). The goal for Yeats, as for Dante, was achieving a serene indifference to this public war, so that he could devote himself to tragic art. "The beauty he created," Yeats wrote of Dante in 1916, "was a victory over himself, a sign that he so ordered his thought that neither the spectacle of his time nor of his own life could break his peace."[15]

Several years earlier, in "To a Friend Whose Work Has Come to Nothing" (1914), Yeats had taken a strong stand for the artists who, in isolation, could affirm the private values that had given rise to their art:

> Bred to a harder thing
> Than Triumph, turn away
> And like a laughing string
> Whereon mad fingers play
> Amid a place of stone,
> Be secret and exult,
> Because of all things known
> That is most difficult.

(*VP*, 291)

The Quarrel With Ourselves" ("Anima Hominis" V)

Section V is extremely frustrating if we bring to it our normal analytic expectations in reading prose, since it contains some of the most clearly central statements of *Per Amica* as well as some of its most hermetic ones. The connections between them often lack the rigor of logical discourse, but are based on a highly personal system of oppositions. Yeats was drawing on ideas that he had been developing for at least a decade in some instances. His artistic problems were to select and compress this body of material from many diverse contexts into a single statement of his conviction that poetry represents a religious commitment to a total "revelation of reality." Because of the intricacies of its style, one of his most moving statements has gone largely unattended.

Yeats begins with a resonant sentence summarizing the exemplary biographies of the previous sections, and quickly extends the summary definition to establish a distinction between the poet and the crowd (familiar from *The Green Helmet* and *Responsibilities*), which he builds upon throughout *Per Amica*:

> We make out of the quarrel with others, rhetoric, but of the quarrel with ourselves, poetry. Unlike the rhetoricians who get a confident voice from remembering the crowd they have won or may win, we sing amid our uncertainty; and, smitten even in the presence of our most high beauty by the knowledge of our solitude, our rhythm shudders.

"The quarrel with ourselves," an obsession with Yeats from earliest childhood, he came to associate with Nietzsche's doctrine of self-overcoming, necessary in art and in heroism alike.[16] In 1909, Yeats asked, "Is not one's art made out of the struggle in one's soul? Is not beauty a victory over oneself?" (*Mem*, 157).

The poet's constant doubting of his knowledge of the anti-self (Is it an honest or a damned ghost urging him on?) distinguishes his genuine awareness from the untested bourgeois certainty of the rhetoricians, the sentimentalists, the conventionally religious, and the merely sensual men, castigated by Yeats in "Poetry and Tradition" (1907), because they "believe that painting and poetry exist that there may be instruction, and love that there may be children, and theatres that busy men may rest, and holidays that busy men may go on being busy" (*E&I*, 251).

To the crowd's hollow certainties, Yeats contrasts the values of his poetic and philosophic tradition: the awakening, the vision, the revelation, which he groups under the name "ecstasy." Let us listen for a moment to Pater on the same subject: "And if the life of Beatific Vision be indeed possible, if philosophy really 'concludes in an ecstasy,' affording full fruition to the entire nature of man; then, for certain elect souls, at least, a mode of life will have been discovered more desirable than to be a king" (*Marius*, II, 57-58). "Great passions may give us this quickened sense of life, ecstasy and sorrow of love. . . ."[17] Yeats developed this Paterian thought in a letter to his father in 1914: "Ecstasy includes emotions like those of Synge's Deirdre after her lover's death which are the worst of sorrows to the ego" (*L*, 587). In the defeat of the ego a joy beyond the ego could arise. J.B. Yeats, the great skeptical talker in the poet's life, exemplifies the ecstatic artist who seeks knowledge of the painful life history of a wandering woman whom he felt compelled to paint: "I would fain scourge myself spiritually, and it pained me that the image should fade" (*Letters to His Son*, 163).

Yeats's religion of ecstasy demanded a sincere avowal of man's faith in God. "We must not make a false faith by hiding from our thoughts the causes of doubt, for faith is the highest achievement of the human intellect, the only gift man can make to God, and therefore it must be offered in sincerity." Characteristic of *Per Amica*, the religious motive is tied to a mode of aesthetic apprehension. "Neither must we create, by hiding ugliness, a false beauty as our offering to the world." That is to say that there is no one in the modern world who has lived a life of unquestioning faith or of uninterrupted beauty, and the religious hypocrite or aesthete who would deny the reality of doubt or ugliness has nothing meaningful to offer either God or humanity. Yeats's goal, in art or in religion, was to excite the whole being into activity through the antagonistic conflict of the self and its opposite images: "It is the business of the intellect to call forth, to create the antagonist. The greater the intellect, the nobler the faith, the nobler the beauty" ("The Poet and the Actress," TS, 13-14).

In matters of faith, the greatest antagonists for Yeats, "the causes of doubt," were the spiritist phenomena that he had been investigating since 1911. The conflict between faith and doubt is most explicit in the "Leo Africanus" correspondence of 1915, where the Leo persona, the believer within Yeats, challenges the skeptic with evidence of the latter's intransigence in spiritual matters:

You are sympathetic, you meet many people, you discuss much; you must meet all their doubts as they arise and so cannot break away into a life of your own as did Swedenborg, Boehme, and Blake. Even the wisdom that we send you but deepens your bewilderment, for when the wisest of your troop of shades wrote you through the ignorant hand of a friend, "Why do you think faith excludes intellect? It is the highest achievement of the human intellect; it is the only gift that man can offer to God, and that is why we must leave all the winds of time to beat upon it," you but sought the more keenly to meet not your own difficulties, but the difficulties of others. Entangled in errors, you are but a public man; yet once you could put vague intuitions into verse, and that, insufficient though it was, might have led you to the path the eye of the eagle has not seen. (TS, 43)

This passage gets to the heart of what Yeats is struggling to achieve in *Per Amica*—a reinitiation into the kind of visionary poetry that he had written successfully in the 1890s. Through the persona of Leo, he reminds himself that the unadulterated visionary life of Swedenborg, Boehme, or Blake is simply not open to him because of his orientation as a "public man." In Leo's mouth the comment is certainly disparaging, but it reminds us alternatively that while Yeats affirms his mystical faith, first in reverie, and then in God, he remains a faithful observer of the human scene around him, from "old Paudeen in his shop" to the dying lady "with her Turkish trousers on" (*VP*, 291, 364). He has shown pain and ugliness as spurs to the creation of beauty in *Per Amica*. The profane has prepared him for the sacred: "Only when we have seen and foreseen what we dread shall we be rewarded by the dazzling, unforeseen, wing-footed wanderer."

From the appearance of this supernatural figure to the end of the passage, Yeats leaves the prosaic world of logical propositions. Donning his priestly vestments as the interpreter of the sacred mysteries of the anti-self, he pronounces that "the revelation of reality," which started in profane awareness of solitude and pain, seeks its consummation in the mystical marriage of self and anti-self. The "wing-footed wanderer" is Hermes, messenger of the gods, and in a later incarnation, Hermes Trismegistus, the begetter of the central principle of all occult systems of correspondence: "For things below are copies, the Great Smaragdine Tablet said" (*VP*, 556). This winged messenger bears the gods' rewards to the struggling poet in dazzling visions, but though he comes from above and beyond, he is also already part of our being, "as water with fire, a noise with silence." We recognize him as our anti-self because of the way he operates within our experience, quenching our passionate fire with his waters, or excitedly shouting us out of our calm. Yeats recognized that this supernatural control over elemental opposites (the kind of control that his cabbalistic and alchemical masters had sought to achieve in word and in deed, but most often in vain) was "of all things not impossible the most difficult," a phrase which becomes the guiding paradigm through the rest of *Per Amica*. Always eager for the widest possible application of his doctrines, Yeats summarizes the idea proverbially—"'soon got, soon gone'"—returning to his insistence on the struggle necessary to make any achievement worthwhile.

The climax of the reverie comes in the final sentence of the paragraph with the poet's paradoxical announcement of the marriage of self and anti-self: "I shall find the dark grow luminous, the void fruitful when I understand I have nothing, that the ringers in the tower have appointed for the hymen of the soul a passing bell." This Yeatsian version of Genesis is developed through two contrasting clusters of imagery; the darkness and void that greet the soul after the dirge and tolling of the death bell; the celebration of a wedding feast with light, fruit, and the conjugal bed. The one suggests that the self can join its immortal anti-self only in death, the other, that this most important of marriages can be consummated in time, following the Blakean proverb, "Eternity is in love with the productions of time" (*Complete Writings*, 151). Here I prefer the affirmative reading that would logically follow upon Yeats's renewed protestation of faith. The soul, that permanent portion of our being, must be married to the most fleeting object, the sound of "a passing bell." That loving bond between opposites begins to grow only when the self gives up all its claims to possession, even of its image-making powers, and acknowledges that it is a vessel into which the wisdom of the ages can be poured. As "Leo Africanus" explained to Yeats using a similar metaphor, "If there are marriages arranged among us, not ours the betrothal kiss" (TS, 34).

The reverie has come full circle from the marriage bell of the sentimentalist, with its momentary happiness, to the eternal wedding of the soul that is consummated in an instant. Yeats does not dare allow this transcendent union to become static, and so, shows us the beginning of a new cycle of struggle which it initiates: "The last knowledge has often come most quickly to turbulent men, and for a season brought new turbulence." Though Yeats has been rewarded by a vision of the marriage of the soul, he must still live in his turbulent body, suffering, as in his courtship of Iseult, the deceptions of "the wine cup and the sensual kiss": We can dismiss the unreality of "our Chambers of Commerce and of Commons" as Blake did,[18] but not so with love and wine, which continue to conjure with us because they have "the divine architecture of the body" (*E & I*, 62) and a "frenzy . . . ripened by the sun" (*E & I*, 262). Throughout Section V, Yeats has alternated between profane and sacred wisdom, but now he unites the two kinds of poetic fulfillment. Though not one of the saints who can "stand within the sacred house," the poet, because of his passionate life-affirming art, resides in the closest possible proximity to that sacredness, "amidst the whirlwinds that beset its threshhold." Though there are dangers in that place of sanctity, Yeats could only be grateful for the moments in which he found himself there,

> And after that arranged it in a song
> Seeing that I, ignorant for so long,
> Had been rewarded thus
> In Cormac's ruined house.

(*VP*, 384).

"That Other Flesh and Blood" ("Anima Hominis" VI)

If the vision of the anti-self, that "dazzling, unforeseen, wing-footed wanderer," comes to the poet only at rare moments of inspiration, how can he expect to create poems embodying that revelatory image at moments when he simply feels like writing verse? Can such moments of vision be reproduced through a purely poetic discipline? The question Yeats raises is central to any inspirational poetics. For an answer, Yeats turns to the example of Christian saint and hero who "make deliberate sacrifice," renouncing the ordinary frustrations and joys of life so that they might always "resemble the antithetical self." Because the poet cannot possibly give up his turbulent life, he must learn this deliberate assumption of an opposite self as an imaginative discipline, by meditating on a mask. The greater the number of masks that the poet includes within his meditation, the richer the vision of reality that he can present in his art.

Modern culture suffers, as Ille suggested in "Ego Dominus Tuus," from its total lack of discipline and its self-centered mirroring of its own sensitivity. Yeats proposes Wordsworth as his representative modern figure to be compared with "overmastering, creative" personalities like Saint Francis or Caesar Borgia. Yeats could not deny Wordsworth's greatness. Reading *The Excursion* and *The Prelude* in 1915, Yeats called Wordsworth's poetic experience "of incomparable value." Yeats distinguished, however, between the experience that shaped the poems and the subsequent "reflective power" that destroyed those precious "spots of time." "He thinks of his poetical experience not as incomparable in itself but as an engine that may be yoked to his intellect. . . . That is perhaps the reason why in later life he is continually looking back upon a lost vision, a lost happiness" (*L*, 590). Recognizing that the subjective tradition of Romanticism initiated by Wordsworth had not provided any way of insuring the permanence of the individual's fleeting experience, Yeats prefers the traditional sanction of a mask or a pose that he can copy. If the poet ever lost touch with the intensity of his vision, as Wordsworth did in his later years, there would always be the energy of the assumed role as an antagonist to spur the tired self into creativity.

Yeats himself had undergone one such period of creative exhaustion, from 1908 to 1913, when he first became obsessed with the theory of the anti-self and worked fruitlessly on draft after stilted draft of *The Player Queen*. His failure of imagination in the early versions of that play was due to his inability to get beyond his own theory of imitation. Locked into his rigid theoretical scheme, "where every character became an example of the finding or not finding of . . . the Antithetical Self" (*VPl*, 761), Yeats lost touch with his own intimation that there was an unconscious life "beyond heroic imitation."

Yeats's characters in the early versions of the play were not characters in their own right, but mouthpieces for Yeats's thoughts on the mask, making statements very similar to Yeats's in *Per Amica* on the necessary imitation of ancient models:

> Queens that have laughed to set the world at ease,
> Kings that cried "I am great Alexander
> Or Caesar come again" but stir our wonder
> That they may stir their own and grow at length
> Almost alike to that unlikely strength.
> And those that will not make deliberate choice
> Are nothing, or become some passion's voice,
> Doing its will, believing what it choose.

(*L*, 534)

This character is too conscious of the design he is supposed to be enacting ever to act on an impulse in that half-conscious, half-unconscious search for the opposite images that bring new life. The final version of the play does succeed in countering this fault, for its heroine Decima abandons herself to the masks she wears. A petty, domestic tyrant when she plays Noah's wife in the acting company, she becomes a truly magnanimous ruler when she takes over the queen's place at the end of the play. She wears the mask and no one can say that it is not her rightful role. Her transformations validate Yeats's extravagant claims for the mask in *Per Amica*:

> I think all happiness depends on the energy to assume the mask of some other life, on a re-birth as something not one's self, something created in a moment and perpetually renewed; in playing a game like that of a child where one loses the infinite pain of self-realisation in a grotesque or solemn face put on that one may hide from the terror of judgment. . . . Perhaps all the sins and energies of the world are but the world's flight from an infinite blinding beam.

From an innocent rebirth to the joy of child's play, from the solemnity of middle age to the terrors of the final judgment, man's only constant companion is the mask that allows him to say he has "lived in joy and laughed into the face of Death" (*VP*, 366).

"The Daimon Comes" ("Anima Hominis" VII)

As Yeats prepares to disclose the mysterious nature of the anti-self, he ushers us into its presence with his most mythical, allusive, and hieratic manner. He sets the scene of an ancient Greek oracle, presided over by a supernatural daimon. However, when Yeats claims originality for his contribution to the daimonic tradition ("But now I add another thought"), he is but adding to an almost continuous literary and philosophical tradition that runs from Plato to Pater.[19]

The Greek word daimon may come from one of two words: *daiomai* or *daemonas*—meaning "to divide" and "skilled,"—thus a skillful being who divides up the fates of humans (Fletcher, 42–43). To the ancients, the daimon was a subsidiary god, the tutelary genius of a place or a person. The daimon itself was morally neutral, but could be used by the higher gods malevolently or beneficently. Some daimons viciously drove people toward negative, irrational behavior (Clytemnestra, for instance, claims to be possessed by an avenging daimon, an *alastor*);[20] other daimons conducted people on their paths between lives or brought them divine messages. It is in this latter light that we see the daimon Eros in Plato's *Symposium* (203b), who attempts to draw men up toward divinity, or similarly, the soul in the *Timaeus* (90a–d), conceived as an inner daimon whose dictates we must obey in order to realize the immortal potential in each of us. In the *Symposium* passage, Plato goes still further in his claims for daimons as a sort of spiritual glue that "prevents the universe from falling into two separate halves."[21] They diminish an awesome distance and thereby make possible a personal relationship between man and his gods. For Socrates, the *daimonion* functioned as personal conscience, whose voice always prevented him from doing wrong. For Empedocles, by contrast, the daimon simply used his body, compelled, as he was "to wander thrice ten thousand years from the abodes of the blessed . . . changing one toilsome path of life for another" (Burnet, 256). Most importantly for Yeats, men as different as Socrates and Empedocles used the figure of an inner daimon in defining their identities.[22] Know thy daimon, know thyself.

The Romantic writers rediscovered the mythological daimon, lost during the intervening Christian centuries, and restored it to literature. For some of the Romantics, as for Yeats, it was an article of faith that individuals of genius (itself a Greek synonym) were driven by an inner daimon. Goethe cited Napoleon as a daimonic character (Otto, 152) and Coleridge called opium "the avenging Daemon" of his life (Beer, 112). Blake did not refer explicitly to the daimon, but the identification between man and an inner daimon is implicit in his Aristophanic myth of Spectre and Emanation. In a prelapsarian state, the two were united, but in the world of generation they are divided and endlessly pursue one another to reattain wholeness. Yeats similarly envisions the Daimon's pursuit of his chosen man, leading ultimately to their momentary creative union in a Blakean apocalypse that prefigures the ultimate beatitude of the soul at the end of its temporal journey.

Yeats also appropriates more conventional mythological uses of the daimon found in such Romantic poems as "The Rime of the Ancient Mariner," "Alastor," and "Manfred." In these works, vengeful or tutelary spirits function as allegorical aspects of the hero:[23] "Death-in-Life" wins the sinful mariner; and "Alastor," a beautiful female daimon who represents the poet-hero's own Spirit of Solitude, lures him to his death. The heroes of such poems themselves attain daimonic consciousness, as they become aware that the normal boundaries of their egos have expanded through symbolic communication with supernatural agents. As Goethe explains, "An incredible force goes forth from them and they exercise an incredible power over all creatures, nay, perhaps even over the elements. And who can say how far such an influence may not extend?" (Otto, 152). Such daimonized characters understand that their freedom is limited, yet their energy is focused and expanded, sometimes, as in the case of Manfred, even gaining them power over the daimonic realm itself. In coming to terms with their destinies, they are willing to bear a curse as a mark of their specialness. From his youth, Yeats was attracted to such characters in Romantic poems (*Au*, 42), and in his cycle of Cuchulain plays, he borrows from them both the machinery of allegorical spirits and the figure of the daimonic hero, who willingly embraces the daimonic Muse who governs his accursed destiny.

Yeats was wise not to conceive of this incredible creative force as existing solely within any individual, for just as it could miraculously appear, so too could it easily disappear. His deep love for the occult led him to see that if he projected this creative force into a supernatural realm, he could establish dramatic situations in which man would suddenly confront his hidden opposite, either in the person of a ghost or in an otherworldly image in the mind's eye. Then he could record the creative reverberations set off by such a confrontation. Behind the *Four Plays for Dancers* and "The Second Coming" lies the same experience of initiation into the unlimited imaginative power of the daimonic realm.

To describe that initial meeting between self and daimon in *Per Amica*, Yeats creates what his mentor Blake would have called "a Memorable Fancy":

> I thought the hero found hanging upon some oak of Dodona an ancient mask, where perhaps there lingered something of Egypt, and that he changed it to his fancy, touching it a little here and there, gilding the eyebrows or putting a gilt line where the cheek-bone comes; that when at last he looked out of its eyes he knew another's breath came and went within his breath upon the carven lips, and that his eyes were upon the instant fixed upon a visionary world: how else could the god have come to us in the forest?

The hero cannot simply find his mask on any sturdy oak, but has to come upon it in Dodona, the ancient sacred place where every flutter in the trees directed utterances to the oracle of Zeus. Nowhere in the passage does Yeats begin to define the nature of the daimonic force, but the stylized image of the gilded mask suggests its utter separateness from our everyday conception of the human face. All Yeats can do by way of definition is to project the aura of one internalizing the daimonic force. Theologian Rudolph Otto claims no more in his phenomenological definition of the daimonic as a "unique element of feeling, the feeling of 'uncanniness'. . . . whose positive content cannot be defined conceptually, and can only be indicated by that mental response to it which we call 'shuddering'" (119).[24]

I think we can get even closer to Yeats's image of the daimonic character by turning once more to Pater and to his most "Memorable Fancy," the brilliant evocation of the Mona Lisa from *The Renaissance.* In Pater's rendering, the Mona Lisa is a kind of daimonic mask. The visionary experience stored in it has delicately moulded its every feature. Associations from geography, history and legend become mythic in the unique presence of the image. Its individual psychic life thus blends with the storehouse of collective experience, in the kind of fusion of *Anima Hominis* and *Anima Mundi* for which Yeats hoped. When Yeats selected the Mona Lisa passage to open his *Oxford Book of Modern Verse* (1936), he wrote that she is the synthetic image of all "human experience no longer shut into brief lives." At the same time, behind her mask is a "private reality . . . always hidden" that "must be the sole source of pain, stupefaction, evil."[25] In his poems of daimonic knowledge in *The Tower* (1928), such as "Leda and the Swan," and "Meditations in Time of Civil War," Yeats learned to maintain this dual focus on the individual's pain in relation to the collective experience of Western culture.

Just as Pater extended his chosen artistic image into an emblem of modernity, so too Yeats attempts a grand synthesis through the image of the Daimon to establish a general theory of human behavior:

> the Daimon comes not as like to like but seeking its own opposite, for man and Daimon feed the hunger in one another's hearts. Because the ghost is simple, the man heterogeneous and confused, they are but knit together when the man has found a mask whose lineaments permit the expression of all the man most lacks, and it may be dreads, and of that only.

Yeats wants to claim originality for these ideas, particularly for the startling statement that the Daimon needs man as much as man needs him, but the record will not bear him out. Plutarch had already described the daimons' need to use humans to compensate for what they themselves lack, in a gory account of the "furious and imperious lusts" of these infernal creatures, who, frustrated in their own desires for consummation with the living, force men into abhorrent acts such as eating raw flesh.[26] Yeats is not prepared to say which of his Daimon's needs could be satisfied by man. As his note of 1924 suggests, he had not yet come to terms with the possible needs of permanent spiritual beings, as opposed to those of dead men making their purgatorial round and, therefore, still subject to change and human influence. One thing the poet knows for certain, however, is that the Daimon could help man achieve the single-minded intensity that makes possible the heroic quest. In personifying his spiritual opposite as a fierce, resolute being whom he could not possibly deceive and who would battle him constantly, even in his moments of creative strength, Yeats invites an anti-self to bring him new life.

"Daimon and Sweetheart" ("Anima Hominis" VIII)

How does a character who has entered into the struggle with his Daimon appear to other human beings? Probably, he would seem to us a mono-maniac, obsessed with and limited to one *idée fixe*, like the "doom-eager" heroes of "Easter, 1916." Though not obsessed with the "terrible beauty" of heroic self-sacrifice, Yeats considers himself likewise a daimonic hero, unable to shake off the curse of disappointment in love laid upon him. The Daimon brings renewal, but only as the result of a fierce lovers' quarrel: "The more close will be the bond, the more violent and definite the antipathy" (*Myth*, 335–36). From the experience of half a lifetime of violently anguished love, Yeats knows why a man continues to love a woman though she is his spiritual opposite and often hateful to him on that account. To understand the poet's love-hate relationship to his destiny, we look for the connection between the Daimon as Muse and sweetheart, and find the spectre of Yeats's beloved, the shadow of Maud Gonne.[27]

Though this daimonic liaison is, Yeats tells us, "an analogy that evades the intellect," it is worth our while to unriddle the poet's unstated reasoning. Sexual desire can force a man to remake himself as his opposite, "And live like Solomon/ That Sheba led a dance" (*VP*, 346), just as the Daimon's desire can lead man into a destiny antithetical to his own will. Both Yeats and Maud Gonne had tried to adopt the idealized images that each cherished, but neither could ever fully accept the role that had been selected by the other. The symbolist poet could not sustain the commitment to political organization, nor could the political heroine become for long a vessel of supernatural revelation. Occasionally a shared visionary life could compensate for the poet's sexual frustration, sublimated as in this remark-able vision, described in 1916:

> . . . we were sitting together when she said, "I hear a voice saying, 'You are about to receive the initiation of the spear.'" We became silent; a double vision unfolded itself, neither speaking till all was finished. She thought herself a great stone statue through which passed flame, and I felt myself becoming flame and mounting up through and looking out the eyes of a great stone Minerva. Were the beings which stand behind human life trying to unite us, or had we brought it by our own dreams? (*Mem*, 134).

Yeats does not answer his own question in the autobiographical account, but writing the next year in *Per Amica*, he replies tentatively on behalf of the supernatural powers: "I even wonder if there may not be some secret communion, some whispering in the dark between Daimon and sweetheart." Yeats felt that he had been victimized by his love for Maud, lifted up to the exhilaration of shared spiritual vision, but inevitably frustrated in an unsatisfied longing for sexual consummation and permanent commitment. Could Maud be anything else but an agent of his Daimon, forcing him to accept a solitary life, "of all things not impossible the most difficult" (*Myth*, 332).

From Empedocles onward, the heavenly curse is part of Yeats's daimonic tradition. It is strongly delineated in DeQuincey's "Levana and Our Ladies of Sorrow," an allegory inserted into DeQuincey's memoirs, in which he describes the leading images of his dreams as threatening, daimonic figures who preside over human defeat, disappointment, and madness. Like Yeats, DeQuincey felt himself cursed as a lover, yet because of that curse, blessed as a visionary. His autobiographical myth focuses on three *femmes fatales*, daimonic sisters who first plague his heart with Tears, Sighs, and Darkness, but in the end, raise him up, as the name "Levana" implies, to unfold "the capacities of his spirit." Like Yeats's daimonic partner in creation, they speak to their chosen one in the language of vision: "*They* wheeled in mazes; *I* spelled the steps. They telegraphed from afar; *I* read the signals. *They* conspired together, and on the mirrors of darkness *my* eye traced the plots. Theirs were the symbols; mine are the words."[28] DeQuincey's ladies have power over his life for good or for evil; they communicate symbolically through dream and vision; they concentrate their power over him by demanding that he worship and serve them as muses. In short, they are everything Yeats claimed of his Daimon; though the poet may be defeated in life, the Daimon comes to elicit the best of which man's imagination is capable. Yeats was trying to overcome a pervasive melancholy in writing *Per Amica*, so he naturally preferred to distance himself from a figure as morbid as DeQuincey and rely instead on more integrated personalities like Dante and Goethe, Carlylean poet-heroes who could testify with unquestioned authority to the uncanny daimonic presence at work in their creative processes.

Yeats attributes the connection between Daimon and destiny to Heraclitus, mistranslating his statement, *ethos anthropos daimon*, as "The Daimon is our destiny." A more appropriate translation would be "a man's character is his daimon, his individuality, his destiny."[29] Whereas Heraclitus hoped to combat superstition and fatalism in his demythologizing statement, Yeats subverts this intention, portraying the tragic lot of artists, heroes, and saints in terms of a daimonocentric, religious world view.

Yeats's final figure for that supernatural power involved in the events of his life is the foil in a fencing match. In "The Poet and The Actress" (1916), the Daimon is the image that battles with the poet in the depths of his soul: "One of the antagonists does not wear a shape known to the world or speak a mortal tongue." The Daimon is the central representative of a "whole phantasmagoria through which the life-long contest finds expression. There must be fables, mythology, that the dream and the reality may face one another in visible array" (TS, 6, 9–10).[30] He speaks to us in phantasmagorical images like that of the foil, as real in Yeats's mind as in a sporting bout with Ezra Pound. Are such images self-created, or are they evidence of "a hand not ours in the events of life"? "Leo Africanus" provided Yeats with the answer he adopts in *Per Amica*: "And when you lie in bed after fencing you see for certain minutes a foil darting upon you . . . what hand holds the point upon you?" (TS, 25). The warfare with the Daimon goes on "in the deep of the mind," willy nilly, whether or not we choose to take up a foil and lunge into that other Will, a figure for the Freudian subconscious, which Yeats prefers to call our antithetical destiny.

"The Saint Alone" ("Anima Hominis" IX)

Poet and hero are condemned to disappointment and defeat: the broken dreams of Yeats the lover, or the lamentable end of Cuchulain, who dies fighting the waves, are typical Yeatsian preconditions for achievements through the mask. The saint's utter exemption from this rule makes him an anomaly for Yeats. Though he lives by the mask in his imitation of Christ, the saint suffers no daily pain and loss to force him constantly to renew his commitment to the mask. He does not have to struggle to make his mask, because there is one ready-made for him to assume, a universal image of the "antithetical self of the world." "If it be true that God is a circle whose centre is everywhere, the saint goes to the centre, the poet and artist to the ring where everything comes round again," Yeats wrote in 1906 ("In the Serpent's Mouth," *E&I*, 287). The saint integrates himself, only to deny the recurrent emotional patterns of life. His severe discipline takes him outside human time in "a contemplation in a single instant perpetually renewed," but the consequence is emotional dessication: "And yet is the saint spared—despite his martyr's crown and his vigil of desire—defeat, disappointed love, and the sorrow of parting." These are the emotions at the center of Yeats's poetry, which, in the poet's tragic view, are the necessary foreground for self-transcendence.

The type of the saint illuminated for Yeats the poetic failures of his own alienated generation of the nineties, poets who had tried "to give up everything but the inmost life of thought and passion." In 1910, he judged them to be like "St. John at the Cross" [sic], who "had gone into the wilderness" and found there 'the obscure night of the soul.'"[31] Yeats's quotations in Section IX, protraying both the spiritual ecstasy and the loneliness of the saint, are drawn from that poetic generation that had renounced more of life than Yeats could ever bring himself to do.[32]

The saint deserves a place in Yeats's spiritual autobiography not only as a type that illuminates the poetic failures of Yeats's narrow contemporaries, but also as a mask that Yeats himself had assumed and would continue to assume as a perspective from which to criticize his materialist world. In the years immediately following *Per Amica*, he examines the consequences of saintly renunciation, from the easy pride of "Saint and Hunchback" (1918), to the befuddled loneliness of the Christ in *Calvary* (1920), who could not communicate with the world he had come to save. The images that ecstasy worships "But keep a marble or a bronze repose./ And yet they too break hearts" (*VP*, 445), Yeats would later explain. For all its limitations, the saint's ecstasy is powerful enough to claim this paean from the poet:

> O what a sweetness strayed
> Through barren Thebaid,
> Or by the Mareotic sea
> When that exultant Anthony
> And twice a thousand more
> Starved upon the shore
> And withered to a bag of bones!
> What had the Caesars but their thrones?
>
> (*VP*, 401)

The saint's sacrifice of the world to gain a throne greater than the world shows Yeats the kind of mask he also needed to gain mastery over his destiny. Marked out for disappointment and defeat, as he felt himself to be, the poet had to discover in poetry what the saint had realized in his antithetical life.

"To Seek Originality" ("Anima Hominis" X)

"It is not permitted to a man who takes up pen or chisel, to seek originality, for passion is his only business, and he cannot but mould or sing after a new fashion because no disaster is like another." Not seeking originality, the poet will nevertheless find it if his subject be passion and his voice, honest. T.S. Eliot, in his brief review of *Per Amica*,[33] quoted Yeats's sentence on originality approvingly, doubtless because it echoes his own ideas in "Tradition and the Original Talent" about the extinction and recreation of personality in art. Whereas in Eliot, the would-be modern master consciously aligns himself with the tradition, in Yeats's superstitious account, it is the Daimon, that illustrious dead man, who chooses the traditional mask for the aspiring artist. The most influential Daimons are therefore dead poets who choose their successors in the literary tradition among those living poets who most respect the passions that they had made great in their art.

Because Yeats sees passion as itself daimonically inspired, individuality in matters of passion, literary or otherwise, threatens the Daimon. The ideal stance for the poet was to accept passion on the Daimon's mythic terms. Yeats put the matter clearly in his preface to Lady Gregory's *Cuchulain of Muirthemne* (1902):

the Irish stories make us understand why the Greeks call the myths the activities of the daemons. The great virtues, the great joys, the great privations come in the myths, and, as it were, take mankind between their naked arms, and without putting off their divinity. Poets have taken their themes more often from stories that are all, or half, mythological, than from history or stories that give one the sensation of history, understanding, as I think, that the imagination which remembers the proportions of life is but a long wooing, and that it has to forget them before it becomes the torch and the marriage bed. (*Ex*, 10).

Through eternal passions, Daimon-sent, human beings, especially poets, come face to face with their divinity. Yet being the willful creatures that they are, poet and hero do not take their traditional passionate masks as they find them, but change their lineaments according to their own teeming imaginations. From their perspective, it is the mask, not the Daimon, which claims their total allegiance.

The artist's imagination is not dependent on the realities of the everyday world, but only on those truths seen in passion. The commonplace dream of natural renewal is easily transcended by one who claims internal vision as his "portion in the world." With such transcendence in mind, Yeats identifies with the phantom lovers in the Japanese Noh play, *Nishikigi*, who cry out: "'We neither wake nor sleep and, passing our nights in a sorrow which is in the end a vision, what are these scenes of spring to us?'"[34] Unmarried in life, they remain eternally separated in their death, and the painful fact of this separation has become the only reality in their existence. The beauty of spring, even in its yearly rebirth out of the dead of winter, is to them merely ephemeral. In his art, Yeats aspires to what the lovers have achieved unwittingly: to translate passion into vision, disappointment into destiny.

"Terrible Lightning" ("Anima Hominis" XI)

Though the poet's destiny is to "go from desire to weariness and so to desire again," Yeats reminds us that the poet continues to "live but for the moment when vision comes to our weariness like terrible lightning." Helen Vendler has taken this sentence as a summary of the main visionary impulse in the poet's work: "First, it takes place essentially in a heightened moment; second, the moment is a period in a cyclical process; third, it is a moment of illumination, when the poet is struck by an insight so clarifying that it appears as a bolt of lightning, or as a flooding of the whole being with light; and fourth, the vision comes from outside the poet, the thunderbolt from the hand of Jove" (28).

These ideas are standard ones in Yeats's Romantic tradition, but in *Per Amica*, they are all plotted on a symbolic map of human consciousness. Moments of disappointment and of illumination alike are subsumed into four geometrical forms that take on symbolic resonance from Yeats's previous speculations on character and creativity. The symbolic shapes that Yeats discusses are: the winding line of Nature or "the path of the serpent"; the straight line of the bowman's arrow, "mark of saint or sage"; the zigzag of "terrible lightning," the flash of revelation; and finally, "those heaving circles" that chart the progression of men's lives through history. The dazzling vision and the blinding beam are images for some form of divine knowledge in Sections V and VI, but these other images are new in *Per Amica*. They are not new to Yeats though, who has seen them all in the wirey, bounding lines of Blake's engravings, and has used them in previous writings. In *Per Amica*, the shapes serve as texts for meditation on conflicting modes of perceiving man's place within the cosmic scheme. They mark the start of Yeats's transition from the personal concerns of "Anima Hominis" to the cosmic explorations of "Anima Mundi."

All of his magical shapes derive, at least in part, from Yeats's deep and lasting involvement with the occult, the extent of which is only now being defined. In the Golden Dawn ritual we find a link, as in the final sentence of Section XI, between the benign serpent, having shed its Biblical skin, and the lightning flash, seen as two complementary paths, the one representing the adept's ascent toward hidden knowledge, the other, the sudden descent of divine illumination. Here is Yeats writing of these powerful symbols to his fellow occultists in 1901:

> The link that unites us to that Supreme Life, to those Adepti and teachers, is a double link. It is not merely an ascent, that has for symbols the climbing of the Serpent through the Tree of Life and of the Adepti through the degrees that we know of, but a descent that is symbolized by the lightning flash among the sacred leaves.[35]

Translated into the language of *Per Amica*, "the slow toil of our weakness" is fortuitously met; we are "smitten from the boundless and the unforeseen." The adept prepares himself for that revelation by constant study in magical texts on the assumption that they teach him the universal symbolism of the secret knowledge ultimately to be revealed. The poet, however, must find his symbols as he goes along the natural path, weary and disappointed at every turn, but occasionally perceiving that his own emotional cycle—"from desire to weariness and so to desire again"—can be projected outside the self as a pattern tracing man's history. We are reminded of the all-encompassing metaphor that Yeats rejected from *The Wanderings of Oisin*, "a breaking wave intended to prove that all life rose and fell as in my poem" ("Introduction to *The Resurrection*," *Ex*, 393). The serpentine path through life, projected three-dimensionally onto linear history, is the essence of the Yeatsian gyre, but before we can develop this fifth "magical shape," we must consider the straight line, for whose mystic meaning, in opposition to that of the wandering natural line, Yeats cites the authority of Honoré de Balzac.

The premise upon which Balzac calls the straight line the "Mark of Man" in his Swedenborgian novel, *Seraphita*, is that "the curve is the law of the material world, the straight line of the spiritual world: that one is the theory of finite creations, the other is the theory of the infinite. Man who alone on earth has knowledge of the infinite, alone can know the straight line."[36] Though all men have this potential for apprehending the infinite, only the saint can deliberately follow the straight path without wandering: but it is precisely the abstract deliberateness of his antithetical mask, out of touch with the instinctive contours of life, that Yeats holds against the saint in Section IX. The poet is committed to the serpentine realm of instinct, but the saint or adept achieves his goal by deliberate effort. The beautiful, visionary woman who shoots an arrow into the sky Yeats takes to be symbolic of the programmatic pursuit of revelation, and unable to renounce that quest himself, Yeats dwelt on her image time and again, in the poem "In the Seven Woods" (1902), here in *Per Amica*, in *The Trembling of the Veil* (1922; *Au*, 372), and finally, in "Parnell's Funeral" (1932).

Despite his longstanding commitment to visionary revelation, already in his fictions of the 1890's Yeats began to show his ambivalence toward the absolute commitment of adeptship. The Paterian narrator of "Rosa Alchemica" attempts to leave behind his private reverie for a program of mystical initiation but discovers, in the words of "Anima Hominis," that he cannot possibly "renounce experience." It has recently been argued similarly that in Yeats's novel of adeptship, *The Speckled Bird* (1896–1902), "Yeats-the-artist is . . . using the novel to lament, if not mock, the contemporaneous activity of Yeats-the-Adept."[37] When Yeats asserts in *Per Amica* that poets are "not . . . permitted to shoot beyond the tangible," he is being stringent with himself because, even after all the years of having rejected the path of magic, he yearns for its absolute consummation, though knowing full well the danger of losing a firm hold on life. The ultimate target of "the bowman who aims his arrow at the centre of the sun" is apocalypse. Harold Bloom suggests that Yeats's source is the climactic image of *Jerusalem*, where an arrow shot into the sun is an image reconciling vision and experience. Bloom infers that Yeats is likewise deciding to "renounce mere *primary* experience, even with its saving epiphanies," and "take on the state of Blake's apoca-lyptic Man." (184). Apocalyptic sainthood is an antithetical mask for Yeats, but he dons it as Ribh only toward the end of his career, when he can balance it against its opposite faces, Crazy Jane and "The Wild Old Wicked Man" (1938). Blake may have been willing to renounce the path of experience and discover in vision his private godhead, but Yeats turns his visionary eye back upon experience to discover there "those heaving circles, those winding arcs, whether in one man's life or in that of an age," which, in their magical, predictive power, embody the greatest knowledge that man can hope to gain in this life from the lightning flash of revelation.

It is by now quite clear that in this section of *Per Amica*, Yeats is very close to his mature formulation of the antithetical gyres of history in the "Dove or Swan" chapter of *A Vision*:

> I do not doubt those heaving circles, those winding arcs, whether in one man's life or that of an age, are mathematical, and that some in the world, or beyond the world, have foreknown the event and pricked upon the calendar the life-span of a Christ, a Buddha, a Napoleon: that every movement, in feeling or in thought, prepares in the dark by its own increasing clarity and confidence its own executioner.[38]

Yeats's mapping of the rise and fall of civilizations goes back to his intimation in the 1890s, expressed in such essays as "The Autumn of the Body," and "The Body of the Father Christian Rosencrux," that the movement in the arts toward greater spirituality represented a cultural vanguard that would come to dominate the new century. In "His Mistress's Eyebrows" (1906), Yeats predicts that "A careful . . . man could foretell the history of any religion if he knew its first principle, and that it would live long enough to fulfill itself" (*E&I*, 288–89). Yeats's sense of an impending, apocalypse was thus gradually integrated with a more sophisticated concept of periodicity to give him the rudiments of the philosophy of alternating and conflicting historical periods that dominated nineteenth-century historiography after Hegel.[39]

Behind Yeats's cyclical model, the antithetical reversal of every intellectual or emotional "movement,' we also hear the poet's convictions about the daimonic struggle. The more a man consciously desires to become his daimonic opposite and the closer he gets to the goal, the more likely it is that the Daimon will force him back to his emotional starting point, the limited daily self. By the same token, "Every movement, in feeling or in thought, prepares in the dark by its own increasing clarity and confidence its own executioner." A culture gradually moves toward a feeling of collective strength and self-definition, but suddenly that culture is no longer in control of its own direction: in the arts, Modernism succeeeds Victorianism; in politics, reaction and revolution both vie with the prevailing liberalism of a century. Yeats has put on his Daimon's knowledge with his power in formulating here the cyclical image of the heaving circle, the convulsive shape that explains the pattern of man's commitment to his own creativity, ever dying in the dark to be reborn in glory:

> Everything that man esteems
> Endures a moment of a day.
> Love's pleasure drives his love away,
> The painter's brush consumes his dreams;
> The herald's cry, the soldier's tread

Exhaust his glory and his might:
Whatever flames upon the night
Man's own resinous heart has fed.

(VP, 438)

"A Starved or Banished Passion" ("Anima Hominis" XII)

To do battle against the modern psychoanalytic theory that dreams result from repression, Yeats attempts a contribution to the traditional poetic *topos* on the relationship between dreams and waking life. In 1902, well before he first encountered Freud, Yeats had perceived an inverse relationship between dreams and action. "The night-knowledge-inaction, in the night dreams, from dreams the day's work afterwards perhaps." In this much-quoted annotation to Nietzsche, Yeats goes on to equate night with self-denial and day with "affirmation of self" (Thatcher, 151). Yeats's perceptive comments suggest his awareness of a strong ego center that is eclipsed at night, so we can understand his susceptibility in encountering a similar theory in Freud. In the fall of 1913, while in the thick of his spiritist research and scientific reading, he wrote, "I find an explanation of many spiritist errors in 'substitutions' similar to that which Freud discovers in our dreams" ("Extracts," TS, 24).

In what then does Yeats's disagreement with Freud lie? The poet accepts repression of "a starved or banished passion," and the distortions to which psychic repression leads in dreams. He distinguishes, however, dream from passion; the artist, we remember from "Ego Dominus Tuus," "has awakened from the common dream" (*Myth*, 323), so the same rules of dream analysis cannot apply to his passions. Whereas the normal individual is unable to tolerate the threat of starved and banished passions, and so distorts the memory of the dream just before awaking, the Yeatsian artist preserves the image, believing that his passions can release great creative energy once they have been tested in the fires of "purifying discouragement." Yeats asserts, therefore, that the artist does not use dreams, as the rest of us do, to resolve problems of identity (though an analysis of his own dreams will not support this contention).[40] Where "the doctors of medicine" find massive repression, "desires condemned by the conscience" such as incest, Yeats sees the internal psychic process moving toward the creation of visionary images.

The quality that ultimately distinguishes the visionary poet from the mystic is that the mystic would prolong the visionary moment for an eternity, while the poet knows that he must resume his critical powers and select from the images his mind has presented to him. What is the poet to do when the lightning flash of revelation suddenly breaks into the winding path he has been treading? He must for the moment become mystic or saint, allowing the contemplative ecstasy to lengthen and deepen. These are the poet's moments of bliss; to indulge in quotidian critical analysis would destroy the only true happiness the poet may ever know. Yeats yearns to give up his whole being to the vision, to become "riddled with light" (*VP*, 316), knowing that once he fixes his attention on the visionary image, it "prolongs its power by rhythm and pattern."

We are reminded of the poet's attempts in "The Symbolism of Poetry" (1900), to find the wavering rhythms that could best "prolong the moment of contemplation, the moment when we are both asleep and awake, ... in which the mind liberated from the pressure of the will is unfolded in symbols" (*E&I*, 159). In "Rosa Alchemica" (1896), Yeats had gone even further to invoke rhythm itself as a spiritual quality: "for rhythm was the wheel of Eternity, on which alone the transient and accidental could be broken, and the spirit set free." (*Myth*, 286). Yeats returns to this liberating thought twenty years later in *Per Amica*'s most gnomic utterance, "rhythm and pattern, the world where the wheel is butterfly." The butterfly was the emblem in Greek mythology for *psyche*, or soul, a fact that helps us decode Yeats's meaning: Rhythm and pattern, rhythm and pattern, turning wheel, turning world, the perpetual motion of a butterfly's wing, the perpetual incarnation of the soul.[41] The butterfly's fragility is an emblem of the vision's need for our special protection. Though every vision has a will of its own, Daimon-sent, so does the poet, who may at any moment turn his mind back to its everyday concerns and stop the wheel from turning.

Though "Anima Hominis" concludes with the poet's return to *terra firma*, Yeats wants to take one final spin on the visionary wheel. The vision

> would carry us when it comes in sleep to the moment when even sleep closes her eyes and dreams begin to dream; and we are taken up into a clear light and are forgetful even of our names and actions and yet in perfect possesion of ourselves murmur like Faust, "Stay, moment," and murmur in vain.

Self-loss and self-possession paradoxically join together when the poet renounces his ordinary identity for that of the vision, which grants him a calm nobility that he lacks in daily life. With his allusion to the penultimate scene of Goethe's *Faust*, Yeats tries to borrow some of the tragic hero's dignity for his own visionary quest. Yeats would have us believe that, like himself, Faust desired to be taken up into the "clear light" of a visionary monism. It is true that Faust cried out at a moment of illumination, but it was neither a poetic image nor a mystical secret that he wanted to make permanent, but rather a completed vision of his first altruistic project for the human race. Faust made his poignant plea knowing full well that Mephistopheles had contracted to take his life if ever he cared enough for a moment to wish to prolong it. Faust's murmur was not in vain, for it earned him heavenly intercession, and ultimately, salvation. When Yeats cries out "Stay, moment," he knows that he calls in vain, for he has long since experienced the certain fact of visionary transience. His cry is the more poignant because he has as yet no great visionary achievement, nor any definite expectation that his Daimon will lead him toward one.

"Some Bitter Crust" ("Anima Hominis" XIII)

At the start of "Anima Hominis," we might well have predicted that the work would mount toward a triumphant visionary climax. Yeats's obvious pleasure in reverie, his cogent applications of the theory of the creative anti-self in the arts, his beautiful invocation of the mysterious Daimon under the oaks of Dodona—all lead to the assumption that Yeats has gained tremendous confidence in his ability to wear the masks of hero, lover, and visionary mage that he finds imaginatively rewarding. Yet ever since he introduced the central idea that "the poet finds and makes his mask in disappointment" (*Myth*, 337), his mind has not shaken off its tragic cast. The idea of the daimonic anti-self had been worked out by the winter of 1915–16 in "Ego Dominus Tuus" and in *At the Hawk's Well*, yet the poet still had not tasted the sweet fruits of vision. It is no wonder, then, that the concluding passages of the essay show a growth in the poet's pessimism. Could the poet, Yeats soberly asks, "keep his mask and his vision without new bitterness, new disappointment?"

In one of his aphorisms, entitled "The Attraction of Imperfection," Nietzsche specifically takes up the problem of the visionary poet's identity and goes so far as to suggest that the poet's "fame benefits from the fact that he never reached his goal" of vision:

> His works never wholly express what he would like to express and what he would like to have seen: it seems as if he had had the foretaste of a vision and never the vision itself; but a tremendous lust for this vision remains in his soul, and it is from this that he derives his equally tremendous eloquence of desire and craving. By virtue of this lust he lifts his listeners above his work and all mere "works" and lends them wings to soar as high as listeners had never soared. Then, having themselves been transformed into poets and seers, they lavish admiration upon the creator of their happiness, as if he had led them immediately to the vision of what was for him the holiest and ultimate—as if he had attained his goal and had really seen and communicated his vision.[42]

Yeats would never have had the courage to describe himself either so cuttingly or so accurately. The tone of the last passages of "Anima Hominis" is completely consonant with Nietzsche's analysis of the failed visionary. In Section XII, realizing the imminent loss of vision, the poet lifts himself into an eloquent flight of imagination, but in Section XIII, he drops to the ground unsatisfied. We partly wonder at his bitterness, for has he not sampled the delicacies of vision? Sampled, yes, but not savored, for he returns full of "desire and craving," suggesting that all he can taste now is "some bitter crust," the scraps of what had been, at least for a moment, a gluttonous feast of imagination.

What does the poet's future hold in store for him as he ages? How can he survive the pain of "new bitterness, new disappointment," if he is unable to channel the new experiences into passionate vision? In one of the most poignant passages in all his works, Yeats imagines two alternate futures for himself, one boisterous, and the other so bleak that we can hardly envision the depth of the anxiety that produced it. Would he live as Savage Landor had, facing his loss of memory with songs of defiant exuberance, or would he end bitterly as William Wordsworth had, "honoured and empty-witted," nothing left him but his memory of those few glorious moments when in youth he had overcome the self's separation from the world in a willed unity with nature? Both poets far outlived the Romantic generation that had nurtured their imaginations, much as Yeats himself had outlived the "tragic generation" of the 1890s who had been his poetic peers.[43] Neither Landor's frenzy nor Wordsworth's dessication will satisfy Yeats now; his "temptation is quiet," "an acre of green grass' (*VP*, 575), like the tower at Ballylee that he had recently brought as a "setting for . . . old age," (*L*, 651), where he could attain harmony with his natural and human surroundings, "and so never awake out of vision."

With all his heart, Yeats longs to become the chosen vessel of supernatural revelation, without being cut off from home and friends. The poet can imagine nothing finer than to move from the permanent, recurring rhythms of nature to the eternity of vision. This is the note, we feel, on which "Anima Hominis" should have ended, but the comment I made about the hesitant conclusion of "Ego Dominus Tuus" applies equally here; Yeats is superstitiously afraid of prejudicing his visionary masters against him. Perhaps they have picked him out as another Wordsworth, one who has outlived his own creative force. Yeats has no intention, however, of resting with this negative verdict. When he pens the date to conclude "Anima Hominis," he already knows that he will turn the page and begin "Anima Mundi," seeking a way out of his personal dilemma through the resuscitative energy of a creative world soul.

3

The Great Memory as Anti-Self: "Anima Mundi"

"Where All Things Are Seen" ("Anima Mundi" I)

The idea of a world soul infusing itself through all of creation is as ancient as man's first religious intimation, and in written form goes back at least to Plato's *Timaeus*. Yeats leaves to other minds the task of constructing a logical argument for the *Anima Mundi* and takes upon himself the burden of putting us in touch with those minds that are most receptive to the wisdom of the ages stored in that general mind or, as he called it in earlier essays and again in *Per Amica*, "the Great Memory." Those minds are of necessity the ones that have withdrawn from the daily getting and spending of the world to seek out spiritual sustenance.

What Yeats hopes to accomplish in "Anima Mundi" depends on the sophistication of the audience, for in addition to being poetic reverie, the essay is also a doctrinal tract that refuses to speak in clear doctrinal terms. Instead of presenting an exposition of his ideas about the spirit world as he had essayed in "Swedenborg, Mediums, and the Desolate Places" (1914), in many ways a first draft of "Anima Mundi," Yeats relies on a highly wrought texture of literary and mystical symbolism and a wide range of allusions to both Western and Oriental literary and philosophical traditions. Yeats explicitly explained his intention in the Swedenborg essay: "I was comparing one form of belief with another, and, like Paracelsus who claimed to have collected his knowledge from midwife and hangman, I was discovering a philosophy" (*Ex*, 31). In the comparative spirit of Frazer's *Golden Bough*, which Yeats knew and admired,[1] he is seeking to present a universal philosophy of spirit that can be borne out by every culture in every age.

There is yet another more personal reason for Yeats's comparative approach: providing an escape from the mental isolation that he describes as his lot at the end of "Anima Hominis." From that perspective he could only see the immanence of the divine in human life in those few transient moments of reverie when he passed into a state of vision. In "Anima Mundi," the concept of the general mind allows him to accept the authority of everyone who has ever reported an experience with the supernatural, ranging from the philosophical arguments of seventeenth-century Platonists on the immortality of the soul to the ghostly encounters of Irish peasant stories. Where "Anima Hominis" grounded the theory of the Daimon in the poet's own observations of biographical patterns and psychological types, "Anima Mundi" moves beyond personal history and literature to make a home for the Daimon in the collective experience of mankind and its unceasing intimations of immortality.

The relevance to "Anima Mundi" of the Swedenborg essay, written to accompany Lady Gregory's compilation of Irish folklore, *Visions and Beliefs in the West of Ireland*, cannot be overstated. The object of the essay was to expose the underlying assumptions of Blake, Swedenborg, English and American mediums, the seventeenth-century Platonists, Noh drama, and Irish folklore; its finding is a consistent philosophy which posits the existence of a world of spirits (primarily of the dead) parallel to our world, revealed when shaped by our imagination into a visible phantasmagoria, but nevertheless, independent of our awareness of it. The essay often has the excitement of new discovery, for while its central tenet "that our imagination is king" (*Ex*, 56) appears throughout Yeats's early prose writings, especially in the Blakean volume *Ideas of Good and Evil* (1903), much of the material Yeats draws upon comes from very recent investigations into psychical phenomena and the Noh drama, the latter in the company of Ezra Pound. Though Pound scoffed at Yeats's interest in seances and Swedenborg, he nevertheless examined the literary underpinnings of his elder's researches with some care. "I don't want to be stuffy about Swedenborg's originality," he wrote to Yeats on April 30, 1914, "but I have just come on a line in the 11th book of the Odyssey . . . 'The departing soul hovers about as a dream'— it might not make a bad chapter heading or motto" (or, for that matter, the structure of a canto, as Pound would later use it in his Canto I).[2] Yeats's Virgilian title might just as easily have led him to the sixth book of the *Aeneid*, where Aeneas is instructed in the doctrine of transmigration of souls.

With confirmation from Homer, Virgil, and even the young Ezra Pound, Yeats was riding the crest of what one of his occultist-philosopher friends called "The Rising Psychic Tide." G.R.S. Mead catalogued the widespread interest in occult philosophies, ranging from ancient Gnosticism to Zen Buddhism to Henri Bergson's Intuitionism. The psychical captivated Yeats and his contemporaries, because they were susceptible to its phenomenal appeal (in the vulgar sense) and to its definition of an extraordinary epistemology: "Though invisible it is still seen, though inner it is still outer, though internal it is still external."[3] Though Yeats later found psychical research dissatisfying, he never abandoned the conviction that he had proven the reality of an independent spiritual realm from which he derived imaginative power.

The psychical is the invisible that is yet seen, a distinction we should keep in mind for appreciating the paradoxical import of Yeats's claim, "I . . . have put myself to school where all things are seen: *A Tenedo tacitae per amica silentia lunae.*" Yeats is interested in imaginative seeing under the shadowy light of a symbolic moon. In his use of the Latin quotation, he makes the symbol for his personal school of lunar knowledge seem like some "broken architrave," fallen into disuse, and now to be excavated and displayed by the poet and student of occult teachings. The image of the moon sends us back to "Ego Dominus Tuus" where Ille walks in the moonlight, "enthralled by the unconquerable delusion," tracing magical shapes. Yeats assures the readers of "Anima Mundi" that he suffers under no such delusions as Hic imputes to Ille, for he has a notebook recording "certain strange events the moment they happened." Yeats has already proven to himself the authenticity of his convictions. Now he chooses to face his readers with the blank gaze of a wise man from the desert places: "O brother, I have taken stock in the desert sand and of the sayings of antiquity."

"A Vast Luminous Sea" ("Anima Mundi" II)

The idea of a general mind as a source for supernatural revelations was by no means a new one for Yeats, as any devoted reader of his prose essays could have attested in 1917. It is one of the central formulations of *Ideas of Good and Evil*, and especially of the essay "Magic," which served in 1901 as an alphabet of Yeats's beliefs, performing the same expository function as did *Per Amica* in 1917. Yeats could very easily have quoted the following doctrinal passage from "Magic' as an introduction to the leading ideas of "Anima Mundi."

> I believe in three doctrines, which have, as I think, been handed down from early times, and been the foundations of nearly all magical practices. These doctrines are:—
> (1) That the borders of our mind are ever shifting, and that many minds can flow into one another, as it were, and create or reveal a single mind, a single energy.
> (2) That the borders of our memories are as shifting, and that our memories are a part of one great memory, the memory of Nature herself.
> (3) That this great mind and great memory can be evoked by symbols. (*E&I*, 28)

Yeats addresses all these subjects again in Section II of "Anima Mundi," beginning with the most practical applications of the theory to poetry: reverie and the evocation of symbolic forms.

It seems strange that Yeats should cite Goethe as his authority for the practice of evocation (for certainly he learned it from the Cabbalist MacGregor Mathers),[4] unless we consider evocation as a conduit to psychic unity, a quality with which Yeats associates Goethe in both *Autobiographies*

(354) and *A Vision* (B, 146). Yeats spells out Goethe's most important lesson for him in the preface to *Michael Robartes and the Dancer*: "Goethe has said that the poet needs all of philosophy, but that he must keep it out of his work" (*VP*, 853). During evocation, the controlling intellectual self must be temporarily suppressed in order to allow a buried self and its images to surface, but critical intellection is also necessary in selecting and organizing the images into traditional symbols. If the poet gives himself up wholly to criticism, he is barred from uniting these disparate selves, but if he succeeds in striking a balance between the image-making and critical faculties, then his vision can satisfy the whole being. Evocation is Yeats's most direct means of communication with a world soul that reveals itself in "sudden luminous definition of form." Poetic creativity is ultimately dependent on abjuring the will to power over this gift of the autonomous poetic image.

Yeats describes two more forms of meditation, one solitary and one communal, which comprised the "intellectual chief influence (*Mem*, 27) in his life up to the age of forty,[5] and clearly were the basis for his belief "in a Great Memory passing from generation to generation." An independent memory in nature, correlated to the individual mind by a key of symbolic forms, was the only possible explanation for the experiments that MacGregor Mathers had conducted with the young Yeats and his fellow hermetic students, in which the representation of a geometrical form inevitably called up in the minds of different people the same vision. In Yeats's own case this lifelong practice of meditation led to some of his greatest poems, and two of the most vivid of these visionary encounters, "The Valley of the Black Pig" (1896) and "The Second Coming" (1919) can be associated with visions induced by Mathers (*Au*, 336, 186). From that Cabbalist, Yeats learned to focus on a particular symbol, allow his reveries to drift according to the suggestions of that symbol, and arrive at a vivid, sensuous poetic image with definite intellectual meanings. This latter quality is what excites Yeats so greatly in "Anima Mundi" where he cites obscure alchemical symbols that Mathers' disciples all discovered in vision, while in another narrative (*Au*, 261–62), Yeats singles out Cabbalist images of the Garden of Eden that welled up from the same Great Memory. The psychologist Jung confronting the same kind of evidence for a collective unconscious of mankind proceeded to study the individual images themselves as archetypes of psychic needs. Yeats's response is characteristically different:[6] "The thought was again and again before me that this study had created a contact or mingling with minds who had followed a like study in some other age, and that these minds still saw and thought and chose." The poet-occultist wanted to make contact with those minds, the better to piece together the puzzle of the soul. If the "images showed intention and choice" in singling him and his "fellow-scholars" out for special attention, then the least he could do was devote himself to reaching them by exploring the progress of the soul after death. He could no longer be content with those narcissistic visionary unions with Maud Gonne (*Mem*, 128) that had been "the happiest and the wisest" moments of his life.

Yeats writes in "Anima Mundi" II that "our daily thought was certainly but the line of foam at the shallow edge of a vast luminous sea; Henry More's *Anima Mundi*, Wordsworth's 'immortal sea which brought us hither.'" Wordsworth had succeeded in his "Intimations" Ode, according to Yeats, in lifting his individual memory of a pre-conscious unity with the world into a universal declaration of transcendence. Though in "Anima Hominis," Wordsworth was the representative of a dessicated, isolated mind, as a stream flowing into the *Anima Mundi*, he too is numbered among the explorers of supersensual consciousness.

This new evaluation of Wordsworth is part of Yeats's general positive reassessment of the central themes and images of English Romanticism, and it leads me to take up the controversial reading of Yeats by Harold Bloom. Bloom argues that the concept of the *Anima Mundi* that Yeats claims for More and the Platonists "turns out to be the general mind of Romantic poetic tradition, as Yeats has fused it together" (186), going on to cite the numerous quotations to follow from Coleridge, Blake, Spenser (central to Bloom's view of Romanticism), and Shelley. While it is indisputable that some of the leading Romantic images for the life of the imagination—an eternal flame, a jetting fountain—are present in Yeats's version of the *Anima Mundi*, others, such as the correspondent breeze and the Aeolian harp are noticeably absent, while the ones he does draw upon can certainly be found in visionary poetry as old as the Orphic hymns. Yeats did find confirmation for his theory in the creative imagination of Romanticism, but not in its insistence on sympathy with natural forms.[7] In "Anima Mundi" he reaffirms his sense that the great Romantic poets knew how to send imagination forth to transcend the quotidian and meet the eternal reality of spirit face to face. He is not content, however, as Bloom would have him be, to have only these few poets as his fellow travelers as he sets off on his Dantesque journey into the world of shades. Indian and Japanese poets, Henry More, old women in Connacht are all necessary to establish the unassailable universality of the Yeatsian position.

Because of its inevitable pairing with "Anima Hominis," the essay and the concept of *Anima Mundi* have been seen as a completion of what the individual soul on its own lacks. Robert Langbaum sees the *Anima Mundi* as providing supernatural confirmation for identity, a way beyond "the entirely interior modern self to the completed self, which is an equivalent of God" (170), though not the same thing as God, since transcendence remains in the art work and not in the artist. Ellmann similarly sees the *Anima Mundi* concept solving the dilemmas of a radical subjectivism, so that the "image might be shared in common, instead of being limited to its creator"

(*Identity*, 219). The poet's carefully established context of reverie, evocation, and the discovery of autonomous images that *choose* among us to receive them reminds us that the *Anima Mundi*, whatever its psychological or spiritual function might be, is primarily for Yeats a means of realizing a visionary poetry at once sensuous and intellectual. Yeats now turns our attention to an occult theory of the image to explain how the images in that "vast luminous sea" become accessible to our earthbound reality.

"A Bird Born Out Of The Fire" ("Anima Mundi" III)

Perhaps the best way to understand Yeats's insistence upon fixing "the imagination upon the minds behind the personifications," is to look for a moment at the visionary poem, "The Magi." Engaged in his habitual practice of meditative reverie, Yeats begins seeing over and over again vivid images of stiff puppet-like figures:

> Now as at all times I can see in the mind's eye,
> In their stiff, painted clothes, the pale unsatisfied ones
> Appear and disappear in the blue depth of the sky.
>
> (*VP*, 318)

As the inner dome of Yeats's mind merges with the heavenly landscape of this *Anima Mundi*-sent visionary company, the figures slowly come into focus, so that Yeats knows their identity and goal. I describe the poem's mental action literally rather than symbolically because the poem itself takes pains to imitate the transformation of an image from the Great Memory into a poetic artifact with a significant, paraphrasable meaning. The poem does not question which of the illustrious dead sent this image to the poet, but Yeats might very well have speculated that it was those other questers for revelation, the Magi themselves, who were the controlling minds that sent this "living and vivid" personification to the similarly struggling poet.

In turning from the controlling minds to an occult elemental symbolism to explain the existence of images in the *Anima Mundi*, Yeats runs the risk of losing unschooled readers. Both a paraphrase and a chart will be useful here. The airy forms projected by the spirit world, lacking the solidity of our terrestrial lives, seem to us like the fluid, shimmering images that we see mirrored in water, but the spirit world itself has the constancy of Dante's purgatorial flames, "the fire that makes all simple." Arranged hierarchically, Yeats gives us:

earth—the visible images of daily life;
water—mirrored images, like the Magi, seen in the mind's eye;

air—the spiritual reality of the minds behind the images, beyond human access;

fire—an imageless condition of beatitude.

One of Yeats's great difficulties in talking about *Anima Mundi* is deciding whether to talk about the minds behind the images or the autonomous images themselves. The passage opens with the informing minds but climaxes in the most illustrious symbol of autonomous renewal, the self-resurrecting phoenix of ancient legend. Yeats creates the impression that the visionary "bird born out of the fire" is suspended in a totally independent spatial and spiritual realm, like Blake's birds of imagination that fly around the edges of his engraved plates. Yeats's unknowable, passionless bird is said to give meaning to all the other images of *Anima Mundi*, at the same time that it actively conceals an entire realm of meaning from us, and presumably from the spirits as well, "the veil hiding another four" elements. Our limited understanding is condemned to multiplicity, while this bird is the *sine qua non* of unity, the ultimate symbol of transcendence.[8] The next sections of *Per Amica* bear testimony to the fact that despite the transcendental flame with which this phoenix burns, Yeats remains fascinated with mire and blood, the personality that persists in the world of disembodied beings.

"The Family and Christian Names" ("Anima Mundi" IV-V)

The dead, Yeats is convinced, retain their personalities in the other world, yet when they appear to the living they always seem "impersonal." Yeats seems to be contradicting himself, but this duality had long been evident in Yeats's attitude to the spirit world in his work. Spirits command a reverential awe in *The Secret Rose*, while in the anecdotal reports of *The Celtic Twilight* (1893), they converse with us or terrify us out of our wits at their ease. The same division persist in such poems as "The Mountain Tomb" (1912) and "To a Shade" (1913). Eternal life both embodies mystical secrets and preserves what Yeats calls in Section V the "fragilities, infirmities, physiognomies that living stirred affection." In Sections IV and V, the transcendent and the bodily exist side by side so that we can appreciate the full range of ideal and real qualities that we share with the dead.

Yeats balances Coleridge and Saint Thomas Aquinas against Irish ghosts and the magician Stanislas de Gaeta in these two short passages, with each set of allusions drawing different readers into the orbit of his ideas. The examples also pose two different views of the life after death. Saint Thomas argues that, like Yeats's symbolic Rose, the dead have acquired "eternal possession of themselves in one single instant,"⁹ while the folk stories cited by Yeats suggest that the dead are still incomplete and revisit the living in order to gain intercession on the ghost's behalf. Later in the essay, Yeats will clarify a cycle of life after death that begins by repeating painful human emotions and moves toward the ultimate beatific completion envisioned by Saint Thomas. For the moment, the poet is content to present his divided response to life's other kingdom.¹⁰

Yeats offers Coleridge's poem of 1804, "The Phantom," to corroborate the ideal state of which Saint Thomas speaks:

> All look and likeness caught from earth,
> All accident of kin and birth,
> Had passed away. There was no trace
> Of aught on that illumined face,
> Upraised beneath the rifted stone,
> But of one spirit all her own;
> She, she herself and only she,
> Shone through her body visibly.

The central paradox of the poem is obviously the problem of the spirit's perfected identity, discernible despite the absence of physical attributes. Coleridge's poem poses the luminous image against the dark background of "rifted stone" as a way of giving visual credibility to his supernatural assertion, but this technique does not explain how one recognizes the identity of a blank-faced ghost. The answer comes in Section V, where Yeats invokes God's infinite love for the unique human soul.¹¹ The phantom, we infer, can only have "Shone through her body visibly," because her spiritual form was illuminated by the radiance of God's love.

"The Soul Has a Plastic Power" ("Anima Mundi" VI)

When Yeats pronounces his doctrine of the soul in "Anima Mundi" VI, it issues from the mouth of Henry More, the seventeenth-century theologian and Platonic philosopher. Before examining Yeats's summary of More's concept of the world soul, it is important to ask why Yeats turned to More as his authority. In his Swedenborg essay, Yeats compiled a working bibliography of his readings in Plato and neo-Platonism, and admitted to having read most of the ancient philosophers second-hand, as they are quoted in works by the seventeenth-century Platonists, More and his friends Cudworth and Glanvil. Yeats writes of them that they were "the handier for my purpose because they found in the affidavits and confessions of the witch trials, descriptions like those in our Connacht stories" (*EX*, 60). Like Yeats himself, More found confirmation for his philosophy in the facts of supernatural occurrences that he had experienced. This same point has been made in summarizing the overall thrust of More's philosophy: "with him the reality of 'spirit' was more than an intellectual conviction, it was an experience . . . The experience was the determinant, the philosophy was its rationalisation."[12]

More was especially important for Yeats because both were forging a traditional philosophy in reaction to the mainstream of modern rationalist thought in their respective ages. More's Goliath was Hobbes and his materialist, atheistical claims for the reality of body alone. Yeats, like More, also champions the reality of spirit against all purely materialist definitions, which accounts for the poet's violent antipathy to Marxism, which he saw in 1919 as "the spear-head of materialism . . . leading to inevitable murder" (*L*, 656).

Politics aside, what made More so appealing to Yeats is exactly what makes him an embarrassment to modern philosophical inquiry, the arcane terminology borrowed from ancient scientific and mediaeval scholastic writers that even in More's time was becoming obsolete. In More, Yeats had a striking example of a philosopher for whom no separation existed between science and religion, for to imply that spirit could not be scientifically analyzed would have undermined More's entire philosophical enterprise. More offered Yeats witchcraft and Hippocrates in one breath, and Yeats, ever a syncretist in his study of the *Anima Mundi*, took them both as "broken architraves" (*Myth*, 343) under which to rebuild the door opening onto the nature of the soul.

While the philosophy of More and Yeats as a whole is antimaterialistic, we are nevertheless struck by a materialistic attitude to spirit. "All souls have a vehicle or a body," writes Yeats. More resented his contemporary Descartes' definition of the soul as a *res cogitans*, a thinking thing abstracted from body, for if the soul could not be located in space, how could its obvious effects in such phenomena as witchcraft or astral projection be believed as real? More's answer to Descartes was that spirit, sovereign over matter, still partakes of matter's spatiality without its solidity, remaining itself penetrable but indivisibly there (Willey, 166-69). Yeats takes up a similar position because, unless belief in the soul is grounded in the bodily world which we all inhabit, then it loses its roots in the popular imagination and can only be propped up by the dry sticks of an artificial intellectual structure. When Yeats anticipates the conclusion of "Among School Children" (1926) in writing "beauty is indeed but bodily life in some ideal condition," he is wholeheartedly acknowledging that body must be restored to spirit, "not bruised to pleasure soul" (*VP*, 445), if the soul is once more to gain fervent believers in its immortal powers.

In a central passage from More, which Yeats fails to reproduce here, the philosopher equates the individual soul and the Daimon, clearly a major theoretical link between the two sections of *Per Amica*:

In brief therefore, if we consider things aright, we cannot abstain from strongly surmising, that there is no more difference betwixt a soul and an aereal *Genius*, then there is betwixt a sword in the scabbard and one out of it: and that a Soul is but a *Genius* in the Body, and a *Genius* a Soul out of the Body; as the Ancients also have defined, giving the same name, as well as nature, promiscuously to them both, calling them both *Daimones.* . . . (134–35).

Just as the Daimon is granted by Yeats unlimited power over the destiny of the individual life in "Anima Hominis," so here, the soul has hegemony over the human imagination. What we thought was our conscious image-making ability, Yeats now tells us is controlled by our soul, itself an agent of the *Anima Mundi*. "The soul has a plastic power, and can after death, or during life, should the vehicle leave the body for a while, mould it to any shape it will by an act of the imagination. . . ." The vehicle could even leave the body, according to Yeats, during dreams or trancelike reveries, as dramatized in such poems as "An Image from a Past Life" or "Towards Break of Day" (both 1919).

The notion of the soul's plastic power obviously has extensive ramifications for a theory of poetry and bears comparison with Coleridge's celebrated formulation of the esemplastic power of the primary imagination that moulds diverse perceptions into an imagined unity. Coleridge brought the divine into his definition of the imagination by claiming that the individual repeats "in the finite mind . . . the eternal act of creation in the infinite I AM." [13] This mortal recapitulation of the immortal provides the ultimate justification for the Romantic poet's exaltation of his own creativity, as in the central example of *The Prelude*. Yeats's theory shares the same emphasis on the joining of mortal and immortal in the creation of images, but it radically alters the balance in favor of the *Anima Mundi*. The individual is never creating anew, because "those finely articulated scenes and patterns that come out of the dark" come from the world soul that chooses to make them visible to the mind's eye. The poet should celebrate not his creativity but his receptivity, as Yeats does in the final movement of "The Double Vision of Michael Robartes."

One of Yeats's primary objectives in "Anima Mundi" is to explain in an extremely detailed way how this creative transference of images from the world soul to the individual soul takes place. [14] Yeats explains that

1. All souls have a vehicle or body;
2. This vehicle, the animal spirits, also composes the body of air and actually nourishes the body;
3. The soul has a plastic power that can mould its body to any shape;
4. Such shapes are made visible to the mind's eye by drawing particles from the medium's body, or by material offerings;

5. Once separate from the body, the vehicle can be moulded by other souls, both dead and living;
6. *Question*: How are such perfect images created by those who have no artistic facility?
7. Our animal spirits condense those of the *Anima Mundi* and embody and project its images;
8. The *Anima Mundi*, working through the mother's imagination, can even shape the unborn;
9. The images are there, whether we perceive them or not;
10. *Question*: Is this general soul the same as God?
11. "God only acts or is in existing beings or men."

The summary allows us to see that Yeats is moving constantly, if circuitously, to the final quotation from Plate XVII of Blake's *Marriage of Heaven and Hell*, which draws the connection between God and the individual and, by analogy, between *Anima Mundi* and *Anima Hominis*. The key to the aesthetic theory of *Per Amica* is here in the creative partnership between the individual and the corporate imagination. We can never know the *Anima Mundi* as a generalized abstract entity, but only as it works upon us and through us, bringing us to moments of visionary recognition of "the one life within us and abroad."

"One Sequence Begets Another" ("Anima Mundi" VII)

Most of us tend to think that thought only exists internally, and that sudden materializations of thought like hallucinations are exceptional cases. In Yeats's view such cases only exaggerate the norm, and he cites the scientific-minded, non-occultist Shelley to substantiate his claim.[15] Whereas we normally think that our thoughts pass through our minds, Yeats concludes that it is we who pass through the world's thoughts.[16]

In attributing this vast hegemony to the world of thought, Yeats seeks a concrete image to depict the *Anima Mundi* as both source and product, root and flower, of all our mental experience. He finds it by fusing his earlier image of the ocean of consciousness with the image of a garden, drawn from Spenser and Platonic tradition,[17] conducting the entire argument that follows in the organic metaphors so common to theories of imagination in the Romantic period. "I think of *Anima Mundi*," he writes, "as a great pool or garden where it moves through its allotted growth like a great water-plant or fragrantly branches in the air." We cannot conceive of a water lily giving birth to new plants outside the water that gives it life, any more than Yeats could conceive of human minds independent of the *Anima Mundi*. No more could Yeats separate our thoughts, as originating now from us, now from beyond us.[18]

The figure that Yeats repeatedly uses in *Per Amica* to suggest how individual consciousness is unified with that of the world soul is the mirror, used especially in Boehme and occult tradition: "If all our mental images no less than apparitions (and I see no reason to distinguish) are forms existing in the general vehicle of *Anima Mundi*, and mirrored in our particular vehicle, many crooked things are made straight."[19] In "Anima Hominis" VI, Yeats advised shunning the naturalistic mirror in favor of the self-imposed mask, but in recognizing a mirroring that transcends mere individuality, he has found a metaphor that comprehends individual and world soul in the same framework.

Yeats sees the relation of the *Anima Mundi* to us as infinitely generative, but at the same time he realizes that its endless sequences of images can easily overwhelm us. It is the poet's task to determine the quality of a given sequence by "the intensity of the first perception," one passionate emotion hopefully recalling another. In Section II, Yeats denigrated the self-criticism that prevented the images from forming, but now he sees a rationale for holding them "in the intellectual light where time gallops." Otherwise, "a seed is set growing and this growth may go on apart from the power, apart even from the knowledge of the soul. . . ."

When Yeats writes at the end of Section VII, "one sequence begets another," there is hardly a reader of Yeats who would not annotate the passage with the famous lines from "Byzantium" (1930), "those images that yet/ Fresh images beget" (*VP*, 498). In one of the first essays on Yeats's mythology, Cleanth Brooks connected the spirits of the poem with the theory of the soul propounded in "Anima Mundi" (*Permanence of Yeats*, 79-80), but neither he nor any other critic to my knowledge has made the obvious connection between these lines. What further light do they shed on "Byzantium"? For one thing, the negative attitude that Yeats holds toward these engulfing sequences must modify any interpretation of the poem's conclusion as an unmitigated escape for the spirits from the "bitter furies of complexity" that they have endured in human life. Who is to say that these "fresh images," originally designated as "blind," and then simply "more,"[20] do not represent another sequence of complexities beyond the spirit's control, much as they do in *Per Amica*?

The final sentence of Section VII does shed some further light on the matter. If the images in the Great Memory bear fruit for us, we are told, it is because our fertile imaginations, leading us and those images on toward some "imagined good," persuade the forms in the *Anima Mundi* that our seeds are worth nurturing. Once the dead (or, for that matter, poet and readers) enter "That dolphin-torn, that gong-tormented sea," either expanding into the sequence of fresh images or retreating into the patterns of nature and art already known, their imaginations will steer them to the destiny they will assume. To that occluded future, Yeats now turns his gaze.

"Passion Desires Its Own Recurrence" ("Anima Mundi" VIII-IX)

A useful starting point for these sections of "Anima Mundi" is the final
outburst of "The Cold Heaven":

> Ah! When the ghost begins to quicken,
> Confusion of the death-bed over, is it sent
> Out naked on the roads, as the books say, and stricken
> By the injustice of the skies for punishment?
>
> (*VP*, 316)

Yeats's vision of life after death begins in judgment and moves toward "a
measure of freedom." At first, the soul is indeed stricken, but not "by the
injustice of the skies," for the dead are imprisoned by memories, doing
penance in a purgatorial state where they relive all their passionate moments,
remembering both beneficiaries and victims. Yeats's speculations are
couched in the context of occult teachings, with allusions to Cornelius
Agrippa and Madame Blavatsky, but he lent them his full imaginative
energy. "In certain houses old murders are acted again," leads us directly to
Yeats's late masterpiece, *Purgatory* (1938), while the ghosts of the Japanese
play who cannot cease believing in their own guilt are clearly analogues for
the legendary Irish lovers of *The Dreaming of the Bones*, written the same
year as *Per Amica*. When Yeats writes that "all passionate moments recur
again and again, for passion desires its own recurrence more than any
event," we have only to think of his lifelong brooding over his passion for
Maud Gonne to see how this seemingly esoteric sentence about dead spirits
is at the very center of Yeats's emotional experience.

Yeats had worked out a model of the progress of the soul after death in
both the Swedenborg essay and in "Leo Africanus," and after *Per Amica* he
continued to develop these ideas in both editions of *A Vision*, even quoting
the same examples in the later work (222, 225, 231). Of all these expositions,
the pattern is clearest in "Anima Mundi." The persistence of individual
memory gives way to the occasional freedom of changing one's shape (an
axiom in Henry More's *Immortality of the Soul*, 150), and finally to the
greater self-loss of being absorbed into a harmonious troop of spirits,
defined by their "rhythm and pattern." Yeats is most deeply fascinated by the
initial phase where the soul is unable to free itself from its own imagination:

> For in that sleep of death what dreams may come
> When we have shuffled off this mortal coil
> Must give us pause.
>
> (*Hamlet*, III.i. 66-68)

Hamlet claims no knowledge of "the undiscover'd country from whose
bourn/ No traveller returns" (79-81), and so chooses the pains of a life that

he knows rather than those which his tormented imagination can conjure as a possible future. The Indian who is afraid of acting as Hamlet, lest he die and "be Hamlet in eternity," is no more suffering from a vain fancy than was Hamlet. For Yeats, in the *Anima Mundi*, we *are* what we *dream*.

"Death would never have been invented," Yeats wrote in the context of his spiritist research, "if we were to have the same minds and the same faculties after it as before."[21] Because the peace that tradition said was to come with age never came to Yeats, he projected that peaceful vision as the ultimate end of the dead's phantasmal journey through its remembered conscience. In "Broken Dreams" he asserts, "But in the grave all, all, shall be renewed" (*VP*, 356). Similarly, in "Shepherd and Goatherd," the pastoral elegy for Major Robert Gregory, Yeats envisions the soul journeying back through the events of its life until it reaches the bliss of prenatal harmony.

The dead spirits of "Anima Mundi" move from what Helen Vendler has called "a determined to an autonomous form" (87). She is quite right to note the aestheticism in Yeats's description of their progress. "Harmonies, symbols and patterns; refashioning by an artist; dancing in a ring; spontaneous and self-directed activity: these are all Yeats's usual words for artistic form." Vendler's ultimate claim is that "Purgatory is a symbol of the imagination at work" (198). Aesthetic pleasure is the ultimate end of the spirit's purgatorial dreaming only for those who have fulfilled a primary function of Yeatsian purgatory, the "exploration of their moral life." In "A Dialogue of Self and Soul," aesthetic pleasure comes only from accepting and then transcending the constraints of memory. Like the spirits of "Anima Mundi," Yeats passes from determined to autonomous form by contenting himself "to live it all again/ And yet again" (*VP*, 479). Similarly, when Yeats set his dance plays in a purgatorial realm, he made them exercises in the exploration of the moral life of the dead. Only when all the paths of conscience have been followed to their ends, can the spirits of these plays hope to escape their individual labyrinths. We are reminded of the dance of the spirits in "Byzantium." Though "all complexities of fury leave," the language Yeats uses to describe their dance is far from beatific:

> Dying into a dance,
> An agony of trance,
> An agony of flame that cannot singe a sleeve.
>
> (*VP*, 498).

The crooked path through the *Anima Mundi* is not so easily followed, despite Yeats's assurance that it leads eventually to "the fire that makes all simple" (*Myth*, 346).

"The Condition of Fire" ("Anima Mundi" X)

Yeats's claim for "two realities, the terrestrial and the condition of fire" makes a rigid distinction at the expense of the clarity of his argument, for all along he has been describing the independent operation of a third reality, the world of thought and images, "the condition of air." The three categories are ranged in a hierarchy borrowed from Henry More, who saw man quitting his Terrestrial Body to take on, in turn, the aereal and the Aethereal or Celestial Body, the last a sort of angelic beatitude equivalent to Yeats's condition of fire, wherein "is all music and all rest" (123). The condition of fire is problematic, because despite all of Yeats's commitment to moral explorations and a life of painful choices, he seems to elevate metaphysical stasis as the highest possible level of reality: "That condition is alone animate, all the rest is fantasy." In "Sailing to Byzantium," Yeats begs "God's holy fire" to consume his heart away, and in "Anima Mundi," the full implications of that plea are spelled out. The highest condition to which the soul attains after death is one in which no choice is possible, no Blakean contraries, no progression, no human life. The dialectic of the poem may make this seem preferable to being "fastened to a dying animal," but any reader who comes to "Anima Mundi" from its companion essay cannot help but find the tragic sense of "Anima Hominis" more useful for Yeats's poetry of unceasing oppositions.

Yeats does make poetic use of the condition of fire in *Per Amica*, because he finds ways for it to operate even in our terrestrial condition. "From thence come all the passions and, some have held, the very heat of the body." The poet fashions here a personal version of the Biblical creation myth: Divinity constantly recreates man in its own image, not merely by blowing spirit into matter, but by allowing human beings to emulate its own passionate moods. Yeats goes on the quote his own lyric "The Moods" (1895), which expresses through a rhetorical question his belief in the endurance of "the fire-born moods," archetypes of divinely inspired passion:

> What one in the rout
> Of the fire-born moods
> Has fallen away?

Yeats expects us to answer, "Not one."[22] In an essay of 1895 that shares its title with this poem, Yeats meditates on the divinity of passion: "It seems to me that these moods are the labourers and messengers of the Ruler of All, the gods of ancient days still dwelling on their secret Olympus" (*E&I*, 195). Our passions are personified daimons; the suprahuman is thus constantly being naturalized and embodied in human life. The interaction of ghosts and living beings in Yeats's poems and plays is a microcosm of the instinctive transferences between the divine and the human that represent for Yeats no less than the ordering principle of the cosmos.

"Concurrent Dreams" ("Anima Mundi" XI)

Several times in "Anima Mundi," Yeats has seen sequential experience as a roadblock to the soul's ultimate knowledge of reality. The end of sequence grants the soul its apotheosis, "an eternal possession of itself in one single moment" (*Myth*, 357). William Blake stands behind this reverie as one poet who succeeded perhaps too well in freeing himself from the constraints of narrative time in those vast panoramic prophecies, *Milton* and *Jerusalem*, which range across an historical and a mythological universe, yet transpire in a single beat of the poet's pulse, an image taken up by Yeats in Section XVI. Yeats knew that he did not share Blake's imaginative grandeur and could only break the barriers of time through occasional extrasensory experiences—simultaneous perception, prevision, and allied to these, the concurrence of dreams within dreams, all of them communications from the *Anima Mundi* calling for the poet's symbolic interpretation.

We can best understand what Yeats means by simultaneous perception if we think of it in terms of poetic structure—the juxtaposition of scenes commenting upon one another in one poem. It is in fact the characteristic mode of many of Yeats's poems of 1912-13 in *Responsibilities*, such as "The Grey Rock," "The Three Beggars," and especially "Paudeen." In the latter, the poet's rancorous view of a shopkeeper is suddenly upset by the nearly simultaneous vision of two birds whose unquestioning instinctive response to one another points up for Yeats the uncharitableness of his own human response, learned in pride, and now, chastened when he holds the two perceptions in his mind at one moment. In the language of Section XI, "intellectual power cannot but increase and alter as its perceptions grow simultaneous." The poem shows Yeats removing the proud mask assumed in other poems of the same volume in order to claim fellowship in the *Anima Mundi* where "There cannot be . . . / A single soul that lacks a sweet crystalline cry" (*VP*, 291).

Yeats's example of prevision is perhaps less psychic and more mechanical than he intended it to be. A meditative vision of a solar halo and a dream of a woman's hair burning lead Yeats to set his own hair on fire.[23] He would have done better to quote from his own recent poem, "In Memory of Alfred Pollexfen":

> At all these death-beds women heard
> A visionary white sea-bird

Lamenting that a man should die;
And with that cry I have raised my cry.

(*VP*, 361)

The onset of death and the appearance of the visionary bird may seem coincidental to the casual observer, but to the women gifted with second sight and to the poet who admires and would emulate their gift, the macabre conjunction is as necessary as death itself. Similarly, in "Towards Break of Day" (1919), Yeats and his wife dream two concurrent dreams, and though their subjects are overtly dissimilar, the very fact of concurrence demands a symbolic interpretation that will include both. Our key to the poem is in an attitude that each dreamer assumes towards his own dream. Yeats reaches out to touch and possess the waterfall, while his wife remains detached from the mythic vision of the leaping stag, allowing it the integrity demanded by an image that comes from beyond us. Yeats is denied a final interpretation of the images themselves, no doubt frustrated by his Daimon for having presumed to lay sole claim to images from the *Anima Mundi*.

Once the obscurity of concurrent dreams is penetrated, they can reward the poet with a broadened vision of himself and his art. Yeats does not analyze his dream about writing a story, but it is worth our while to do so, since it reveals Yeats's profound, unconscious understanding of himself:

I dreamed very lately that I was writing a story, and at the same time I dreamed that I was one of the characters in the story and seeking to touch the heart of some girl in defiance of the author's intention; and concurrently with all that, I was as another self trying to strike with the button of a foil a great china jar.

The dream embodies the complex relation between Yeats's life and art that he has described in "Anima Hominis." The key to the dream lies in its structure of unmasking conscious wishes. As the writer of a story in his dream, Yeats expects to direct the events of his life and art. At the same time, he understands that he is acting in defiance of his conscious intentions in "seeking to touch the heart of some girl," namely Iseult Gonne, rather than his intended bride, her mother. To touch her heart is to achieve an immediacy and intimacy beyond the decorous conventions of courtship. The fact that Yeats the author is observing Yeats the romantic actor reveals that he knows himself to be distant from this emotional involvement, something to be expected in an aging writer whose art has for so long celebrated an unrequited love.

The third concurrent image, the phallic foil with which he plays this game of passion, is significantly buttoned, emphasizing feelings of impotence that can be connected with such contemporary lyrics to Iseult as "Men Improve with the Years" (1916) and "The Living Beauty" (1917). Further interpretation turns on the key word, "foil." This manly actor with his buttoned sword is a foil for Yeats, another alter ego of the controlling writer and impulsive lover. If he strikes the china jar with this foil, breaking through the artifice of camaraderie with physical love, then he will indeed foil the relationship. The great china jar, an art object in the place of a love object—a characteristic sublimation—is an image both of Iseult's hard unreceptiveness to his advances and of her fragility. Behind this, in turn, lies the fragility of Yeats's relationship with Maud, which could hardly have stood the shock of his virtually incestuous liaison with her daughter. The china jar (perhaps associated with the Oriental *objets d'art*, great earthenware ewers, in Lady Gregory's house at Coole; *Au*, 389), stands for the whole aesthetic world of beautiful objects and poems with which Yeats has surrounded himself in lieu of Maud, and which he now puts at risk in seeking to fulfill his physical desires.

Was this dream not a warning from his Daimon? Yeats included it in *Per Amica* presumably because it dramatizes so well the central thesis of the essay, that in art, as in life, we face unconscious forces that reveal more of ourselves to us than we can consciously know. The image of the foil acting out what the conscious will had denied and what it fears is another emblem of our confrontation with the Daimon, like the foil playing before the mind's eye in "Anima Hominis" VIII. Prevision, simultaneous perception, concurrent dreams—all require the poet's interpretation, which he guards lest he mar their autonomous symbolic power. Yeats prefers to leave us with the dream within a dream sent to him from the *Anima Mundi*.

"Take the Empty Chair" ("Anima Mundi" XII-XIV)

Yeats has shown us the *Anima Mundi* working in the poet's reverie, in the dead's fantastic dreams, and in the psychic's power of prevision, but now he singles out our instinct, the one quality that applies to all natural life, both human and animal, as the most important channel of communications between us and "the dead living in their memories." Paraphrasing Henry More (200), Yeats shapes the thought into one of his liveliest sentences: "It is the dream martens that, all unknowing, are master-masons to the living martens building about church windows their elaborate nests." The animal metaphor takes us back to the prologue of *Per Amica*,[24] where Yeats introduced the cat Minnaloushe as the creature of instinct providing an object lesson for his reasoning human companions, at the same time that it looks ahead to the images of birds calmly building their nests in the midst of irrational human combat and pride (The Stare's Nest by My Window," 1923; "The Tower," 1926). Images of instinctive activity remind Yeats that despite man's destructiveness an informing mind presides over all nature.

For Yeats, the theory of instinctive sympathy that he propounds is far more than a metaphor. Meaningful contact between the living and the dead is the main subject of many of the dance plays and the frame of such major poems as "In Memory of Major Robert Gregory" and "All Souls' Night." "You are in the presence of the dead more than you can know," Yeats wrote in the Leo manuscript, "because you are never out of it" (TS, 35). That is the point of departure for the allusive climax of Yeats's reverie: "It were to reproach the power or the beneficence of God, to believe those children of Alexander, who died wretchedly, could not throw an urnful to the heap, nor Caesarion murdered in childhood, nor the brief-lived younger Pericles Aspasia bore—being so nobly born."[25] Every dead spirit, no matter how brief its life nor how wretched its end, adds to the community of spirits that comprise the *Anima Mundi*. Yeats's examples are chosen to remind his readers that no matter what the future may bring, the past as preserved in the *Anima Mundi* has ensured the permanence of nobility.

Instinct and tradition both sanction the belief in our close companionship with the dead. Yeats took upon himself the traditional poetic role of symbolically reaching out to the dead by composing elegiac tributes in verse, and it is significant that in Section XIII he describes the proximity of ghostly existence with a quotation from Stanza 44 of "Adonais," Shelley's lament for Keats.[26] Remembering their habits and their language, the objects and the places that they loved, the poet draws the dead near through fond emotional associations so that they again might "tread the corridor and take the empty chair," an occult rationale for Yeats's constant mentioning of his dead friends and heroes in his poetry. Knowing that the dead relive their passionate moments, the living poet recreates the final passionate phase before death: the heroism of "In Memory of Major Robert Gregory," the natural tranquillity of "Shepherd and Goatherd" (both 1918), the humility of "In Memory of Alfred Pollexfen" (1915), the exuberant gaiety of "Upon a Dying Lady" (1912-14). He knew that one day he would meet them all as shades. Now, it is most important that he attempt to communicate.

Yeats's prose in these sections of *Per Amica* has the best qualities of his poetry, vivid sensuous details to describe types of passion. Any attempt to annotate it leads inevitably to a catalogue of related poems. The mother who "returns from the grave" to "comfort a neglected child or set the cradle rocking" eventually finds archetypal representation in "Among School Children" (1926) and "The Mother of God" (1931). The rocks and trees that bring some moment of emotion to mind set the scene of the dance plays and of Yeats's poems of passionate heroism, from "The Grey Rock" (1913) to the testamental "Under Ben Bulben" (1939). Helen of Troy, so obviously central to Yeats's mythology of Maud Gonne in the years just prior to the writing of *Per Amica*, is for Yeats the type of the highest passion. Her intensity calls to mind Yeats's supposition in "Certain Noble Plays of Japan" (1916) "that being is only possessed completely by the dead, and that it is some knowledge of this that makes us gaze with so much emotion upon the face of Sphinx or of Buddha" (*E&I*, 226), or, we might add, on any image that Yeats had invested with the power of a passionate dream. Yeats concludes with the central paradox of his thinking about the dead. They are "so rammed with life they can but grow in life with being."[27] The insubstantial living remain behind,

> Crying amid the glittering sea,
> Naming it with ecstatic breath,
> Because it has such dignity,
> By the sweet name of Death.

(VP, 254)

"Zigzag" ("Anima Mundi" XV-XVI)

The living have only one advantage over the dead; we are free, and they are not. Our freedom lies in being able to choose whether or not we follow the lead of our Daimon, a bitter freedom at best, since it draws us most often into tragic suffering, though we can also transcend our struggles through that choice and achieve a kind of ecstatic completion. This theory of the Daimon is fully articulated in "Anima Hominis," but it remains for Yeats to show how the relationship between man and his Daimon is also determined by an "inflowing" from the *Anima Mundi*.

In "Anima Hominis" XI, Yeats sketched out three traditional symbolic approaches to life, the winding path of the natural man, the straight line of saint and sage, and the lightning flash of revelation, the way of the visionary poet. All three reappear here as mirrored aspects of the world soul. Both man and animal learn instinctive behavior from the *Anima Mundi* and put it into practice passively along with the winding path of nature. The dead who have passed through purgatory follow the straight road to the Condition of Fire (now, apotheosized in capital letters), and their aid can be invoked: "Come from the holy fire . . . / And be the singing-masters of my soul" (*VP*, 408). To his reprise of the earlier essay, Yeats adds a new thought. The lightning flash or "zigzag" is not only the way of the poet, but also that of his mentor, the Daimon, sent by the *Anima Mundi* to force upon us the major crisis of our lives.

At the moment we choose an opposite image, we move from a passive awareness of our being to an active search for a new order. The Daimon imposes "his own lucidity upon events"; without it, we cannot know exactly what action of all others is the most difficult for us, the most opposed to our natural way, and the most likely, therefore, to lead us to psychic unity. The daimonic crisis, as seen from the perspective of the *Anima Mundi*, is the way in which fate gives each of us a chance to escape from our endless cycle of disappointments. The Daimon cajoles man, suffers with him, brings him more knowledge than he can bear, but ultimately, victimizes him, because there is no escape for man into the Condition of Fire.

The lightning of total perception lasts but a moment, "a pulsation of the artery," a phrase that Yeats borrows from Blake's *Milton* (Book I, Plate 29):[28]

> For in this Period, the Poet's work is done; and all the Great
> Events of Time start forth & are conceiv'd in such a Period,
> Within a moment, a Pulsation of the Artery.

Blake's metaphor is to be taken literally. Any perception that leads to a full-blooded revelation—a poet's work or a great event—must be channelled through the whole man, body and soul, arteries and luminous vehicle. We recall Yeats's earlier quotation from Blake, "God only acts or is in existing beings or men" (*Myth*, 352). The Daimon as a messenger of God only exists as we perceive his challenge to us. He illuminates two ways of being open to us, "the passive and active properties, the tree's two sorts of fruit." Yeats does not gloss the probable Cabbalistic symbolism behind the image of the tree, but leaves us to surmise how we can best internalize the double vision of the Daimon. When he was much closer to that Cabbalism in his occult stories of the 1890s, he describes (once again echoing the passage from Blake's *Milton*) the daimonic initiation that changes our lives: "In this way all great events were accomplished; a mood, a divinity, or a demon, first descending like a faint sigh into men's mind and then changing their thoughts and their actions. . . ." (*Myth*, 285). In the more restrained mood of *Per Amica*, the daimonic zigzag only illuminates; the completion of our self-transcendence, the great event of a lifetime, is not left up to the power of the Daimon, but rather to each of us to succeed or to fail on our own paths.

"Man or Nation" ("Anima Mundi" XVII)

Not only does each Daimon single us out individually, but he can also choose us collectively, in his role as "the antithetical dream" of a nation. One of the problems in Yeats's daimonic theory is the assumption that each man has a dominant single character that naturally calls forth its opposite in the person of the Daimon. In his poetry, Yeats avoided the constraint of this singleness by constantly alternating opposite masks, allowing himself a wholesome psychological diversity. When Yeats applies the model of single character to nations and historical periods, as he does in Section XVII (and as he continued to do in both editions of *A Vision*), it leads him almost inevitably to caricature or racism. Yeats desperately wanted to believe that when a nation meets its Daimon it confronts an image that can reshape its destiny. In "The Statues" (1938), when Yeats connects Cuchulain with the heroic transformation of the Irish people during the rebellion of Easter 1916, we understand that he is dealing in myth. But when he describes the Incarnation as the necessary antithesis to the rapaciousness of ancient Jewry in the anti-semitic manner of the Gospel According to John, he pretends to be writing history, and this confusion between history and myth, especially as it shapes his political view of the modern world, is one of the most dangerous of Yeats's many pretensions.

Yeats is likely to have read about Christ as a subverter of classical Greek values in Nietzsche. Unlike Yeats, who sees Christ as being opposed to both the Jewish and Hellenistic worlds, Nietzsche saw Christ as fulfilling the Jewish prophetic promise of elevating the poor and powerless over the good, noble, and powerful. Yeats is known to have annotated a passage from Nietzsche with the anti-semitic comment that "Swedenborg thought the Jews 'chosen' because the worst—they could not corrupt the spirit having none and would obey." In *Per Amica*, Yeats adheres to the Swedenborgian thought by implying that the intransigent Jews needed Christ as their national Daimon to teach them the spiritual value of poverty and suffering. The opposition between Christ and the Jews whom he cannot save is preserved in Yeats's play *Calvary* (1920), while *The Resurrection* (1925) with its mythic "Two Songs from a Play" amplifies the Nietzschean antithesis. So does the voice of "Leo Africanus": "What was Christ himself but the interlocutor of the Pagan world, which had long murmured in his ear at moments of self-abasement and defeat, and thereby summoned?" (TS, 41). The individual calls out to his Daimon because he seeks completion outside the self, through whatever self is furthest from his will and intellect. By the same token, Yeats reasons, every nation, every culture, every age also has a "vague, unsatisfied desire," to which a national Daimon can give coherent meaning and form. Twenty centuries of Christian history, Yeats reminds us in "The Second Coming," were waiting for the Daimon of the new age that "slouches toward Bethlehem to be born" (*VP*, 402).

"Bewilder and Overmaster" ("Anima Mundi" XVIII)

A poem like "The Second Coming" may well owe a great deal to Yeats's researches into the practices of mediums and seances in the years 1911-14. Arnold Goldman has made the interesting suggestion that "the narrator's voice comes to resemble the voice of a control in a trance-vision" (*Yeats and the Occult*, 127). While it is important to assess the poet's philosophical and poetic debts to those vivid experiences of a supersensual world in contact with our own, it must also be remarked that Yeats displays considerable ambivalence to mediumistic experience as a poor substitute for the visionary experience of the poet. Yeats went to seances searching for proof, and when he found confirmation, he became extremely excited,[30] but at other times, as when he first encountered Leo, he became suspicious, convinced that he was being deceived by the medium and her control-voices. Through the theories of Henry More and Swedenborg that the suggestible spirits get their memories confused with our own, he resolved many of his doubts, and proceeded to the explanation of their phantasmagoric existence in the Swedenborg essay.[31] Nevertheless, Yeats's reluctance to value the garbled communications of the medium persisted, resulting in the distinction in "Anima Mundi" between the purity of poetic or religious meditation and the visceral stupefaction of mediumship.

Yeats's train of thought in Section XVIII is based on an axiom of Henry More's: "the purer the vehicle is, the more quick and perfect are the perceptive faculties of the soul" (149). The discipline of poetic reverie or of religious meditation aims to purify the mind of the meditator, eliminating the extraneous and the accidental. The medium, on the other hand, operates through a "coarse vehicle" that must passively await whatever spirit accidentally stumbles into its province, and cannot guide the train of association toward symbolic meaning as the poet can. Imagine a mediumistic rather than a poetic scenario for "The Second Coming." "The Second Coming! Hardly are those words out," when another voice cries out, the small, childlike voice of the control Nelly, who explains that she is in her mother's stomach and feels "'like a wet chicken.'" How long could Yeats go on expecting that such a voice, "if she could only come straight . . . could tell a lot"? (*L*, 569). If the drunken control-voices only "repeat, with brief glimpses from another state, our knowledge and our words," it was greatly preferable for Yeats to trust in his access to *Anima Mundi* through the voices and images of poetic tradition.

"Born Again" ("Anima Mundi" XIX-XX)

Eternal recurrence is one of the central doctrines of Yeats's tradition, common to philosophers from Plato to Nietzsche and to poets from Virgil to Wordsworth. Yeats takes as his *locus classicus* Spenser's Platonic description of the transmigration of souls to and from the Garden of Adonis:

> After that they agayne retourned beene,
> They in that garden planted be agayne,
> And grow afresh, as they had never seene
> Fleshy corruption, nor mortal payne.
> Some thousand years so doen they ther remayne,
> And then of him are clad with other hew,

> Or sent into the chaungeful world agayne,
> Till thither they retourne where first they grew:
> So, like a wheele, around they ronne from old to new.
>
> (*Faerie Queene*, III.6, stanza 33)

Yeats is giving body to the idea that began the essay: all our thoughts and images stem from the *Anima Mundi* and return there after we die to be drawn upon by the minds of future generations. With Spenser's image, he asserts that both our bodies and our souls grow out of that garden and return there after death to be renourished for a new incarnation of earthly life, a clear prefiguration of his later lunar wheel.

Though Yeats claims we all aspire to bypass the wheel of incarnations in favor of a direct route to the Condition of Fire, most souls are doomed to repeating lives on earth. The Sisyphean image of a friends' dream reported by Yeats, "dragons climbing up the steep side of a cliff and continually falling," creates a sombre context for the Spenserian quotation. On a cosmic scale, Yeats is reiterating his emphasis in "Anima Hominis" on the inevitable tragedy of life, as we "go from desire to weariness and so to desire again" (*Myth*, 340). The poet lives for the moment of vision, the soul for the fire that releases it from time. The first edition of *Per Amica* qualified even this belief in the ultimate end of the cycle of reincarnations: "The dead who speak to us deny metempsychosis, perhaps because they but know a little better what they knew alive; while the dead in Asia, for perhaps no better reason, affirm it, and so we are left amid plausibilities and uncertainties" (84).

Yeats calls the highest state of the soul "the rhythmic body," a term introduced in Section X and reintroduced here at the climax of his argument. The term is as abstract as any concept in *Per Amica*, yet Yeats warns us against praying "to it as a thing or a thought." Quoting Blake's "The Divine Image," Yeats asks us to follow Blake's practice and give any name to the divine image that we choose, so long as we recognize its essential humanity, since there is nothing more devastating to the imagination than a vision of abstraction. "Rhythm," Yeats writes in a letter of 1916, "implies a living body, a breast to rise and fall, or limbs that dance, while the abstract is incompatible with life" (*L*, 608). The living hero, who picks his mask from the branch of an oak tree in the sacred Dodona of his mind, is humanizing an abstract ideal. So too the dead, suffering through a prolonged exploration of their moral life, are personifications for Yeats of an ideal pursuit of apotheosis. To universalize such an ideal and to anchor it in humanity, Yeats imagines in the spirit of Blake an internal dialectical tableau, in which the essential contraries of life lead to a spiritual progression: "Within ourselves, Reason and Will, who are the man and the woman, hold out towards a hidden altar a laughing or crying child."[32] Though the wheel of rebirths represents the ultimate fate for humanity, Yeats's vision of the "laughing or crying child" reminds us that all life begins in hope confronting the unknown, a hand reaching out "towards a hidden altar." Whatever our individual fates may be, in perpetuating the life of the body or of the imagination, we perform our obeisance to God.

"Innocence" ("Anima Mundi" XXI-XXII)

"Anima Hominis" ended at a low point for Yeats, with the nagging question, Can I sustain my hard-earned mask and vision amidst the inevitable bitterness and disappointment of the world? The second essay was undertaken to allay the poet's self-doubts, attempting to bring confidence through the realization that the poet can always make contact with the *Anima Mundi* that brings life to his imagination, no matter how weary. "Anima Hominis" and "Anima Mundi" both record many triumphs for the imagination, yet despite the ability of the poet to turn from the naturalistic mirror "to meditation upon a mask" (*Myth*, 334), and despite the "pulsation of the artery" (*Myth*, 361) that brings him a daimonic revelation from the Condition of Fire, Yeats understands the disappointments of the world too well to project that ideal of self-transcendence as a norm. Though he is convinced that the individual soul mirrors the world soul and therefore has access to the final beatific state, his doubts about that mirroring persist: "When I remember that Shelley calls our minds 'mirrors of the fire for which all thirst,' I cannot but ask the question all have asked, 'What or who has cracked the mirror?'"

There is no more troubling statement in all of *Per Amica* than this conviction that something has gone desperately wrong with the human condition. Yeats's otherworldly longings seem broken by his question; the mirror that earlier seemed to make many crooked things straight (Section VII), "is broken," as in "Rosa Alchemica" (1896), "into numberless pieces" (*Myth*, 276),[33] turning Yeats back upon "the only self that I can know, myself." Yeats quotes from Shelley's "Adonais" at this point, presumably because he is bolstered by Shelley's having maintained his faith in a sustaining love in the universe; even as Shelley notes the painful disjunction of earth and heaven, he takes comfort in the vision of Adonais as a bright star illuminating his dark world (Stanzas 44-45). Yeats can take no such comfort because his practical sense of the world tells him that "the common condition of our life is hatred." How could someone like Maud Gonne, whom Yeats once respected above all other women, barter her precious soul for an "opinionated mind," "an old bellows full of angry wind"? Was there not some earthly condition of blessedness that could obviate the need for heavenly guidance, some place of truly "radical innocence"? (*VP*, 405).

No man is able consistently to shape his own world around such an ideal, but Yeats assures us that he has known privileged moments of bliss that have released him from both external and internal struggle, self and soul suddenly united in an uncommon happiness. Yeats narrates one such experience in Section XXI that he was later to put into verse in "Vacillation" (1932):

> My fiftieth year had come and gone,
> I sat, a solitary man,
> In a crowded London shop,
> An open book and an empty cup
> On the marble table-top.
>
> While on the shop and street I gazed
> My body of a sudden blazed;
> And twenty minutes more or less
> It seemed, so great my happiness,
> That I was blesséd and could bless.

(VP 501).

This blessedness does not follow from any exploration of the moral life, as it does in "A Dialogue of Self and Soul," where Yeats assesses the actions of his life and deliberately casts out remorse for his errors. Neither is the happiness described in *Per Amica* and in "Vacillation" wholly gratuitous. The self can aspire toward such wholeness but it cannot achieve it through deliberate meditation.[34] For Yeats, the best explanation for this sudden blaze of happiness is that the poet has been rewarded by the *Anima Mundi*: "It seems as if the vehicle had suddenly grown pure and far extended and so luminous that the images from *Anima Mundi*, embodied there and drunk with that sweetness, would, like a country drunkard who has thrown a wisp into his own thatch, burn up time."

What Yeats feels primarily at such moments is a kind of Shelleyan love pervading his universe, destroying the bounds between self and other. "I look at the strangers near as if I had known them all my life, . . . everything fills me with affection, I have no longer any fears or needs." The moment that Yeats dramatizes in Section XXI is initiated by neither the poet nor the *Anima Mundi*, but is rather a simultaneous inflowing and outflowing, a mutual surrender of the self to the world and of the world soul to the self.

For all the glory of such moments, it is crucial to remember that such moments are not poetic moments. Where there is no quarrel at all, but only unity, nothing is made, neither rhetoric, nor poetry. The quarrelsome poet can become a blessed saint for but a moment, for if he lingers to worship that otherworldly condition, he will never return to write poems that set "sensual music" and the soul's song in the one score. Eternity is not the poet's province, but only "What is past, or passing, or to come" (*VP*, 408).

Those who take only the world for their province, however, and forget the eternal soul, are also doomed to inconsequence. Yeats is nowhere more a rhetorician than in his condemnation of men of poetic genius, here, Carlyle and Swinburne, who sacrificed their creative spark in taking up quarrels with the world.[35] Yeats searches for an "innocence" that abjures both love and hate, separating the poet in a place apart, where he can forget about his own "irritation with public or private events or persons," forget even his literary judgments against Carlyle and Swinburne, and cultivate instead the internal quarrels of the soul that lead to poetry.

The poet cannot afford to become subsumed in the *Anima Mundi*, but neither can he cut himself off from it completely, as the rhetoricians do. The great mediating figure of *Per Amica* is of course the Daimon, without whose heavenly assistance, the poet cannot complete the work chosen for him.

"Anima Hominis" tended to see the daimonic relationship as inherently combative, but in Section XVI of "Anima Mundi," Yeats interjects a new note of tenderness. "He suffers with man as some firm-souled man suffers with the woman he but loves the better because she is extravagant and fickle" (*Myth*, 361). Having made the Daimon into his muse, Yeats has learned to become dependent on the creative intimacy they share. The mingling of those minds is so complete during the moment of creation that Yeats becomes unaware of the boundaries of his ego: "As I write the words 'I select,' I am full of uncertainty, not knowing when I am the finger, when the clay," Michelangelo's Adam turned from clay into man by the pointing finger of God.

Yeats concludes his reverie on the Daimon's role in creation with a striking account of a prior visionary initiation:

> Once, twenty years ago, I seemed to awake from sleep to find my body rigid, and to hear a strange voice speaking these words through my lips as through lips of stone: "We make an image of him who sleeps, and it is not he who sleeps, and we call it Emmanuel."[36]

A divine voice speaks through Yeats's lips to explain that his life mask has been imprinted and transferred directly to the *Anima Mundi*. Once there, the image is transformed and given the sacred name of Emmanuel, whose literal Hebrew meaning, remembered by Matthew (1:23) as a prophecy of Christ, is "God is with us." The visionary incident assured Yeats in his young manhood that he would achieve a remarkable transcendence of his own limits, but that could have come about as much through occult ritual as through poetry. The vision is far closer to the spirit of the occult initiations in Yeats's stories of the nineties than to anything else he ever wrote. It was only after many years that he came to see the vision as a foreshadowing of his theory of the mask. "Christ is but another self," Yeats wrote in his journal in December 1908, "but he is the supernatural self" (*Mem*, 138), the most exalted incarnation of the Daimon who presides over Yeats's poetry.

As a spiritual autobiography, the whole drift of *Per Amica* has been toward assessing the meaning of Yeats's past imaginative experience in order to give the poet a way of coming to terms with an uncertain future. We expect him in the final reverie of "Anima Mundi," to ask himself about his future identity as a poet, much as he did in the bitter conclusion of "Anima Hominis," but significantly, Yeats avoids this crucial question. He reserves a discussion of the totality of his poetic career for the book's epilogue, and even then, he chooses only to view it in retrospect. At the start of "Anima Mundi," Yeats introduced "old women in Connacht, mediums in Soho," as providing him with a path into "the general mind" (*Myth*, 343); now he takes one last look at magic and religion to decide if these paths still remain open to him:

> As I go up and down my stair and pass the gilded Moorish wedding-chest where I keep my "barbarous words," I wonder will I take to them once more, for I am baffled by those voices that speak to Odysseus but as the bats; or now that I shall in a little be growing old, to some kind of simple piety like that of an old woman.

Yeats had provided the key to this elliptical passage in an earlier section of "Anima Mundi," where he refers to a warning of the Zoroastrian oracle against changing "'barbarous words' of invocation" (*Myth*, 359). Even if we want to force "barbarous words" to mean poetry rather than occultism, the image from the *Odyssey* (XXIV. 5-10) of Penelope's suitors on their way to Hades, flitting and gibbering like bats in the dark, can only apply to the phantasmagoric voice of seances that Yeats described so assiduously, and doubtless preserved separately from the rest of his papers in a "gilded Moorish wedding-chest." There is considerable pathos in this image, and in light of his subsequent marriage, irony as well. By casting himself as both a barren old woman and as one who can be married only to esoteric wisdom, Yeats seems to renounce both sexuality and poetry and to rationalize a withdrawal from the world. Does Yeats mean to renounce nothing and trick us into assuming the contrary through his evasive questions? Or can we surmise that Yeats turns to rhetorical evasions because there was no other way he could possibly confront the idea of ending his poetic career?

"My Tradition" (Epilogue)

Yeats originally intended an epilogue for *Per Amica* in the manner of the contemporary dance play, *The Cat and the Moon* (1917), in which a monk, a lay brother, and a pilgrim are on their way to a holy site of ancient Ireland, St. Patrick's Purgatory, where they hoped certain theological truths would be revealed to them. They debate for a time on the possible divine creation of both good and evil, and on the prospects of redemption or reincarnation, when they are interrupted by an otherworldly communication that seems to resolve their dilemmas:

> I heard a voice talking in the hedge, and like the chirruping of a bat and it is saying that before the fall man had his head in the fire, his heart in the air, his loins in the water, and his feet on the earth, and that after Eve pulled the apple, he has had his feet on the fire, his loins in the air, his heart in the water, and his head in the earth. (Ellmann, *Identity*, 300).

The epilogue concludes with just two more lines of comment: "'What a lot the dead know,' said the pilgrim. 'I will go home in the morning. What more could I be told at the Purgatory?'"[37] This Gnostic parable of our fall into disorder is Yeats's answer to his climactic question in Section XXI, "What or who has cracked the mirror?" The supernatural voice obviates discussion of good and evil. Man's fall has assured his confusion in this life, and he can only trust in the possibilities of reincarnation to claim the ultimate knowledge that is his due.

Had Yeats actually ended *Per Amica* with this curious parable, the book would have seemed to its first readers inescapably occult, rather than poetic, despite the plethora of quotations from Spenser, Blake, Wordsworth, Coleridge, and Shelley. One of the reasons that *Per Amica* needed an epilogue was to state the poetic underpinnings of the work more directly than Yeats had yet done in his highly allusive manner. The epilogue turns on the contrast between two literary epochs, the world of European art in the 1890s that took Paris as its international capital, and the new national art of France, in the years before the Great War. Yeats contrasts his own symbolist poetic heritage with the patriotic Catholic poetry of Peguy and Claudel, to which Iseult Gonne had introduced him, the upshot being a redefinition for the poet of "my tradition . . . more universal and more ancient" than any orthodoxy or modernity.

It is important for Yeats to state at the end of *Per Amica* that fashioning a daimonic theory of creativity was his true destiny as part of a hieratic community of poets that divined a sacred purpose behind their symbolic art. "As Mallarmé had written: 'All our age is full of the trembling of the veil of the Temple.'"[38]

Yeats is interested in the revolutionary energy that the symbolist ethos imparted to a whole generation of fellow-searchers. The stories that Yeats tells in the epilogue all emphasize the rejections of materialist assumptions in favor, as he says in the *Autobiographies*, of an acceptance of "every historical belief once more."[39] Yeats's artist friends had been willing to pursue arcane secrets of alchemy and abjure the daily business of life. The artist, as in Rimbaud's "Mauvais Sang" from which Yeats quotes, felt there was bad blood between him and everything conventional.[40] "As for living," cries Villier de l'Isle-Adam's Axel, "our servants will do that for us."[41] Yeats claims for himself an artistic tradition in which all values are subservient to the spirituality of art.

Yeats does not give us a clear statement of the situation of poetry as he viewed it in 1917, although indirectly he implies a falling off from the ideals of the *fin-de-siècle*. The poets of the next French generation learned at the feet of these same masters, at Mallarmé's Tuesdays or in Verlaine's dissolute coffee-house gatherings, but they rejected the heterodox spiritual lessons of their predecessors and searched for sanction rather than sanctification, "Mother France and Mother Church," rather than "the magical soul." Because Yeats is aiming to transcend all kinds of individual distinctions by fusing the individual soul with the world soul, he cannot justly value the nationalistic work of Claudel, Jammes, and Peguy within *Per Amica*'s universalist framework.[42]

Per Amica is thus one of the few places in Yeats's work that he is willing to dispense with the primacy of nationalism (though not with his Irish ghosts). He tried to establish this universalist emphasis in yet another rejected epilogue, this time stressing his yearnings for an aesthetic and religious mythology uniting Galway, Eleusis, and Byzantium:

> I must find a tradition, that was a part of actual history, that had associations in the scenery of my own country, and so bring my speech closer to that of daily life. Prompted as I believed by certain dreams and premonitions I returned to Ireland, and with a friend's help began a study of the supernatural belief of the Galway and Aran cottages. Could I not found an Eleusinian Rite, which would bind into a common symbolism, a common meditation, a school of poets and men of letters, so that poetry and drama would find the religious weight they have lacked since the middle ages perhaps since ancient Greece. . . . In the cottages I found what seemed to me medieval Christianity, now that of Rome, now that of the Celtic church, which turned rather to Byzantium, shot through as it were with perhaps the oldest faith of man. (Ellmann, *Identity*, 305-6).

In bringing together the twin themes of poetry and religion in this draft paragraph, Yeats tries to reconcile the central aesthetic and occult ideas of *Per Amica* within the framework of his own career, seen as a return to his Irish roots. Yeats would sound this claim again and again in *Autobiographies*, but for an epilogue to *Per Amica*, he needed to see his own history as the search for a universal tradition, "the general mind" that he claims as his province at the opening of "Anima Mundi."

As a survey of Yeats's career, the epilogue provides an almost sentence-by-sentence gloss of the progression of volumes in Yeats's poetic *oeuvre*. "This new pride, that of the adept, was added to the pride of the artist." We see the mysteriously brooding poet of *The Wind Among the Reeds* (1899), who has meditated on the images from Irish folklore in his early work until they have taken on the resonance of eternal symbols. "Everywhere in Paris and in London young men boasted of the garret, and claimed to have no need of what the crowd values." The haughty poet of *The Green Helmet* (1910) appears before us, railing against the crowd in "At the Abbey Theatre" or in "At Galway Races," all the while trying desperately to protect the sanctity of his "heroic dream" (*VP*, 255). The tension between garret and crowd also animates Yeats's next volume, *Responsibilities* (1914), but by now he had discovered a theoretical reconciliation: "*In dreams begins responsibility*" (*VP*, 269). The artist can forget the criticism of the crowd and be sure of his own integrity, if he is faithful to the images and fables growing out of his *Anima Mundi*-sent dreams. "The soul, self-moving and self teaching—the magical soul": Yeats was about to compile the volume for which this phrase could best serve as epigraph. In *The Wild Swans at Coole* (1917, 1919), we hear the song of the self-moving soul in the descriptions of Robert Gregory and Mabel Beardsley; we see it embodied in the image of the swans drifting on Coole Lake. When Yeats drops the lofty tone to adopt a satiric voice, it is generally because he laments his own inability and that of his compatriots to live up to the standards he had set as a young man for "the magical soul." In the succeeding volume, the ideal of the totally unified soul is tested in love, in politics, and finally, in the family, where it receives its most noble dress: "And may her bridegroom bring her to a house/Where all's accustomed, ceremonious" (*VP*, 405).

"A Prayer for My Daughter" (1919) proposes a unity of soul that ensures its continuity by being "rooted in one dear perpetual place" (*VP*, 405). The entire doctrinal discourse of *Per Amica* displays Yeats's profound need to root his convictions in a philosophy and tradition similarly impermeable to the vicissitudes of individual thought. The epilogue places Yeats's roots in the Symbolist movement of the 1890s, though in correspondence (*L*, 592), Yeats dissociated himself from any detailed knowledge of its program. We have already observed how throughout *Per Amica* every tradition with which Yeats identifies himself subsumes an earlier one. The imagination of Romantic poetry is contained in the visions of Swedenborg and Boehme; the spiritism of Henry More can be associated both with Spenser's Renaissance Platonism and the magical practices of the medieval alchemists. Ancient Greek philosophers and the poetry of aristocratic Japanese ghost plays yield the same wisdom: The Daimon is our destiny. It was of central importance to Yeats that he offer up this truth as he himself had come to appreciate it, in bits and fragments of old writers, in the glimmerings of waking vision. For conventional teaching, Yeats's readers could turn to any pulpit, but Yeats would draw them to "our ancient Church" (*E&I*, 351), where sacrifices are offered up to the mysteries that have sustained through the ages the new births of poetic tradition.

4

The Daimonic Inner Drama of the Plays for Dancers

In *Per Amica*, Yeats writes bitterly about the sterility of his imagination during five fruitless years of work on *The Player Queen* (1907-12). In the five years after 1910, he wrote no new plays, and only took up old projects, revisions of four of his early plays.[1] When Yeats began studying with Pound the Noh drama of Japan in the winter of 1913-14, he was prepared for a new birth to come out of its wedding of natural and supernatural, man and ghost, in a concentrated expression at once aesthetic and religious. I doubt very much if he was prepared for what did happen to him. Between 1915 and 1920, he wrote five new plays in the Noh form, finished *The Player Queen*, composed in *Per Amica* his most eloquent and moving prose work, and compiled two great volumes of lyrics, *The Wild Swans at Coole* (1917, 1919) and *Michael Robartes and the Dancer* (1921), his best collections in twenty years. The social and biographical background of the period is no less astounding. In 1914, all his life seemed to him, Yeats wrote, "a preparation for something that never happens" (*Au*, 106). All the hopes of which he had long since despaired suddenly came to life. Ireland woke up in the Easter Rising of 1916, alerting Yeats to the reality of heroic action in the modern world. In that rebellion Maud Gonne's husband died, giving Yeats the chance to court her once again, and if not Maud, then at least her charming twenty-one year old daughter, Iseult. Refused on both counts, the confirmed bachelor poet married an old occultist flame, Georgie Hydes-Lee, but rather than making him succumb to pastoral temptation, marriage actually put Yeats in touch with uncanny forces dictating through the subconscious of his wife's mind. As they dreamed together of monstrous new births for the modern world, they conceived and gave birth to Anne Yeats, a daughter for whom Yeats now had to plan and dream.

This is the remarkable biographical background against which the evolution of *Four Plays for Dancers* (1921) and *The Cat and the Moon* (written 1917, published 1924) must be seen, a development which cannot be separated from the great poetry of the period. Each of the plays is associated with the central dilemmas Yeats was living through in the years of their composition and each of them helps Yeats work through private turmoil and transmute it into art.

Many critics have noted the autobiographical genesis of one or another of these plays in passing, but have seemed almost embarrassed to dwell on the wealth of biographical riches that Yeats's plays offer. Helen Vendler's uneasy noting of an autobiographical reference is typical: "there is nothing to do but admit it freely, and pass on. Nobody transformed experience more than Yeats . . . and to find the historical 'real' beneath the fiction is a task almost hopeless, it seems to me, in the plays" (207). Vendler's criticism presupposes that biographical inquiry must lose sight of the art work as it searches for hidden evidence of the life. My attempt is not to undermine the fictive in favor of the supposedly "real," but rather to show how the completed fictions reveal and become part of the pattern of the author's life. These plays are as much a part of Yeats's biography as anything else he did or said during these years, and they are perhaps a better source than most for understanding the creative life of the man because they cannot resort to the evasions of the controlling 'I'. By concentrating on the personal dilemmas in which Yeats found himself and the resolutions that writing these plays offered him, I hope to suggest how to see these plays as Yeats himself probably saw and felt them during their creation.

Curtis Bradford reminds us that "the impulse toward autobiography was always powerfully present in Yeats, perhaps most powerfully in 1914-17" (308). Bradford's work on the manuscripts of Yeats's poetry, prose, and drama shows convincingly that Yeats was an autobiographer in all his literary modes, and that in his revisions he excised only the accidental qualities of personal experience in order to emphasize what was permanent in his sense of himself and his world. Even in the dance plays, Yeats's most impersonal form, his early drafts show direct autobiographical references: in *At the Hawk's Well*, a concluding sentence lifted from his autobiography; in *Calvary*, a reference to Coole Lake in its closing song.[2] Yeats took advantage of both the freedom of the autobiographer and the restraint of the dramatist, initially projecting himself everywhere into his creations, but finally distancing himself to achieve what he described in "A General Introduction for My Work" (1937) as an embodied "idea, something intended, complete" (*E&I*, 509).

Throughout this period of intensely autobiographical writing, one of Yeats's central concerns was explaining the Daimon's role in his life history. First, in August 1915, there was the exchange of letters with Leo Africanus, the spirit voice who claimed to be Yeats's Daimon and encouraged him to take up automatic writing so that Yeats could speak with Leo's daimonic voice. Yeats undertook but was unsatisfied with this experiment, doubting whether any of Leo's words had come from beyond his own mind. Next, in "Ego Dominus Tuus," completed in December 1915, Yeats attempted another colloquy with an alter ego: Hic, the voice of the realist, debating with Ille, the voice of Yeats's otherworldly aspirations. Ille hesitantly announces the imminent revelation of his anti-self, but in the poem no such visionary being appears to him, and as the poem ends we may well question Yeats's ability to project convincingly the visionary reality in which he claims to believe.

Within a few months, however, Yeats had written the first of his dance plays, *At the Hawk's Well* (winter 1915-16), and found the form he needed to give life to the bond between man and Daimon, now envisioned dynamically as a tragic conflict.[3] Borrowing from the stylized manner of the Noh drama, he created a theatre of reverie where everything is presented by the chorus as an image in "the mind's eye" (*VPI*, 399). Any ordinary space is transformed into a "deep of the mind" (*E&I*, 225), when masked characters, speaking and moving like automatons, enact a phantasmagoric ritual that climaxes in an eery dance by the Daimon, or ghostly figure in the play. In this drama, both mortals and immortals seem equally visionary. Yeats could have found no better emblem for his conviction that the Daimon controls human life than the wordless dance of the possessed hawk-woman, which entrances the mortal Cuchulain and leads him onto his life's accursed road of heroism and inevitable defeat.

In *Per Amica*, Yeats explains his belief in the Daimon as a religious synthesis of his life and work. On the one hand, he had to believe that his negative experiences, disappointments in love, in politics, and in his quest for occult wisdom, were willed by some "hand not ours in the events of life" (*Myth*, 336), and on the other, that his very capacity for visionary experience was divinely inspired. One thus singled out by the Daimon was himself a daimonic character possessing an extraordinary inner force, and had no choice but to renounce the happiness of sentimentalists and practical men in favor of the ecstatic "revelation of reality" (*Myth*, 331). The reality revealed to Yeats's imagination by the Daimon was inevitably tragic, and in the dance plays, remarkably like his own inner reality. One of the earliest critics of these plays was most perceptive about their relation to Yeats's inner drama. In 1922, the American poet, John Peale Bishop, commented that each play was written

> out of an emotion kindled by solitary thought. They have had their beginning in the poet's convictions on the inadequacy of his life and his passionate realization of the loneliness of the half-light and have but a pale existence, they represent, as far as may be in objective presentation, the moods from which they have sprung. . . . There is no conflict except the battle of the lonely and the proud with themselves.[4]

The central characters of these plays suffer from loneliness, frustrated love, and unappreciated sacrifice. Each is thrust amidst his ignorance or bitterness into a visionary revelation where he encounters his taskmaster Daimon and is forced to test—and if possible transcend—the limits of selfhood. In the dance plays, then, Yeats continues to explore the daimonic identity articulated in *Per Amica*. He becomes a virtual daimon himself in designing the lot of mortals and immortals, vicariously living their lives and dying their deaths. Through their tragic masks and potential epiphanies, Yeats comes to know better both the suffering and the ecstasy he felt comprised his own daimonic lot.

Yeats collected *At the Hawk's Well, The Dreaming of The Bones, The Only Jealousy of Emer*, and *Calvary* as *Four Plays for Dancers* in 1921, when he was already quite far along in the development of the lunar symbolism of subjective and objective gyres for *A Vision*, and he heavily annotated all but the earliest play with that esoteric material. Helen Vendler's important study of Yeats's later plays has fully explored the thematic implications of *A Vision* for these dance plays, but does so at the peril of obscuring their literary genesis and merit. The plays for dancers never present systematic occultism and determinism as the later treatise does, but portray intense relationships between human and daimonic figures that grow out of the tragic conceptions of *Per Amica*. To readers with a biographical interest in Yeats, the plays can be seen to function as patternings, sometimes conscious, sometimes unconscious, of Yeats's sense of his own life history.

The Daimonic Initiation: *At the Hawk's Well*

The fact that Yeats patterned *At the Hawk's Well* after "the permanent sorrows" of his own life has been noted by almost every commentator to write on the play.[5] A recent critic has summed up the extent of Yeats's biographical projection into his characters: "Cuchulain in his temerity . . . images what the artist, the man of contemplation most lacks and the Old Man in his timidity and atrophy what he most dreads."[6] Through these personae, Yeats is not merely protesting against impotent old age, nor nostalgically longing for an unattainable exuberant youth. Cuchulain and the Old Man, a reimagined pairing of Hic and Ille, are centrally opposed to one another because of the way each pursues his quest for the waters of immortality. Immortality cannot be attained simply by waiting patiently for fifty years beside a magical well. The Daimon who grants that gift is a hard taskmaster, who demands that the quester recast the lineaments of his own image through some transforming mask. Both characters are masked in the play, but whereas the Old Man's mask simply embodies his natural self, Cuchulain's mask can transform him from a plucky youngster to a dedicated hero. Terrified of the aura of the place where he waits, the Old Man will simply wheedle and whine till the end of his days. Cuchulain, however, shows that he is destined for the immortality of the hero by his willingness to encounter mysterious forces beyond his own control. He abandons the water that plashes in the well to pursue instead the sexually alluring image of the hawk-woman. He is drawn magnetically into the orbit of the being that has possessed her, the *genius loci* who is his Daimon. Gazing into her eyes invokes a curse, but he willingly takes it on to pursue his destiny as a hero, whatever the bitter cost.

Yeats understood that the choice of a mask in life or in literature was made in partnership with the Daimon. He needed to believe that his Daimon had not destined him for the passive mask of the Old Man, but that like Cuchulain, he could choose and be chosen as a hero in his own imaginative world if he was willing to undertake the risks and suffering of the heroic lot. One thing his Daimon demanded was subjecting the imagination to pain before it could be rewarded by a vision of beauty (*Myth*, 332). Yeats needed to imagine himself in his play as an utterly dessicated scarecrow of a man, in order to set off the antithetical splendor of Cuchulain and the frenzy of the hawk-woman, an important aesthetic choice he repeated in such later poems as "The Double Vision of Michael Robartes" (1919), "Among School Children," and "Sailing to Byzantium" (both 1927). Yeats's chief aesthetic goal in this middle period of his life was to transcend the frustrations of middle age and recreate himself as a hero. To do so, he had to subject himself to the muse of adversity, embodied in the unfriendly female Daimon of *At the Hawk's Well*.

The main focus of the action is the irrational lure of the daimonic, as it manifests itself in the dance of the Guardian of the Well, and in Cuchulain's undaunted exit to face the terrors of that supernatural hawk that suddenly possesses the dancer, "a horrible deathless body/ Sliding through the veins of a sudden" (*VP*, 410). One of the central ironies of the play is that just such a spontaneously overwhelming force once possessed the now withered Old Man. At setting out, he was hardly to be distinguished from this plucky youngster:

> I came like you
> When young in body, and in mind, and blown
> By what had seemed to me a lucky sail.
> The well was dry, I sat upon its edge,
> I waited the miraculous flood, I waited
> While the years passed and withered me away.
>
> (*VPl*, 405-6)

The consequences for the audience of this *déjà-vu* are horrifying. Whatever force lured the Old Man to the well also turned it into the source of his utter dessication. The pivotal moment of daimonic initiation for the Old Man stopped his life fifty years before, but for Cuchulain that shaping moment still remains to be acted out at the hawk's well. Cheated time and again by the dancers, deluded by the shadows who curse his quest, the Old Man is an unheeded object lesson on the destructive power of the daimonic force that has already begun to entangle the hero. It is the bitter fate of Chuchulain that persuades Yeats of our "blind struggle in the network of the stars" (*Myth*, 328).

The most important moment of the play is Cuchulain's ecstatic awakening to the presence of the possessed dancer. Twice during the play he hears the cry of the hawk, but sees no wing. Even when he learns from the Old Man that the voice comes through the Guardian of the Well, who has been possessed by the Woman of the Sidhe in her changed form as a hawk, he remains unmoved by being in the presence of something so unnatural. Resolute in his desire to drink of the water, he challenges the silent staring figure with his own penetrating gaze. When she unconsciously rises, we watch an hypnotic ritual: she is the medium whose passive vehicle is stupefied by the presence of another, far stronger being within her, and Cuchulain in turn is magnetically drawn into the orbit of her movements. He rises to take the place she has vacated by the well, their bond growing deeper during her hawk-like dance.

The focus of the Old Man's fear and of Cuchulain's attraction are the dancer's eyes. Her otherworldly gaze is so blank that each sees himself mirrored there. "Nor moist, nor faltering, . . . those eyes of a hawk" (*VPl*, 409) extinguish the faculties of any viewer who persists in seeking transcendence. They are the same transfixed, daimonic eyes that drank up the soul of the decadent narrator in "Rosa Alchemica" (1896), when he took his place in the dance of initiation for Michael Robartes's mystical order (*Myth*, 290), and the same as those "eyelids that do not quiver before the bayonet" (*Myth*, 325), which carry Yeats off into reverie in the ceremonial opening of *Per Amica*. Possession by the Daimon is a form of madness, and though it can be but a momentary fixation, Yeats knows that the hero can never truly accept his calling until his eyes have been "fixed upon a visionary world" (*Myth*, 335).

Though Cuchulain marches off in glory, Yeats's audience knew the bitter continuation of his history from Irish legend and Yeats's own play, *On Baile's Strand* (1904). Yeats wisely chooses not to vaunt the heroic destiny, but on the contrary, to reassert the balanced human perspective of the chorus. The most problematic issue in criticism of this play is defining the role of the distinctly non-daimonic chorus, and the relation it bears to Yeats's own views. John Rees Moore has warned against identifying Yeats with the Chorus, advising us to look ironically at their innocent affirmative vision of natural sexuality and plenitude:[7]

> "The man that I praise",
> Cries out the leafless tree,
> "Has married and stays

> By an old hearth, and he
> On naught has set store
> But children and dogs on the floor.
> Who but an idiot would praise
> A withered tree?"

(VPI, 413-14)

The fact that Yeats printed these lines as part of a lyric in *Responsibilities and Other Poems* (1916) alerts us to his willingness to appropriate the praise of normality as one of his lyric personae. We hear in these final stanzas of the play the poignant cry of Yeats, the yearning bachelor, atypically calling out for a life of natural abundance, because he is painfully aware of what can happen to one's life when it becomes daimonized.

Bradford prints the original ending to the first prose version of *At the Hawk's Well*, then called "The Well of Immortality," and changed no doubt because that immortality is so unattainable in the play. It stresses the quality of autobiographical lament underlying the play: "Accursed the life of man— between passion and emptiness what he longs for never comes. All his days are a preparation for what never comes" (181). The gravity of this statement is not easily discounted, since Yeats wrote it out in three different versions in his journal,[8] and also used it as the climactic thought of *Reveries over Childhood and Youth* (1914), another attempt to plot beginnings before the play.

The parable of *At the Hawk's Well* was deeply threatening to Yeats for it reminded him of the inevitable frustration of the heroic and visionary callings: "Wisdom must live a bitter life" (*VPI,* 413), sings the chorus, but how to escape the horrifying possibility of ending life as "a withered tree?" Yeats's only hope lay in self-knowledge. He needed to recognize that the chorus's temptation was as real for him as Cuchulain's pursuit of a visionary image. Why else would he echo the same temptation among the confessions of *Per Amica* and again, late in life, in "An Acre of Grass?" Having acknowledged his temptation to abjure the daimonic struggle, he could see himself as one even more firmly committed to a heroic life in pursuit of antithetical images, whatever the personal cost.

The Daimonic Crisis of Conscience: *The Dreaming of the Bones*

Yeats was soon reminded of how great the cost of commitment to a heroic image could be by the martyrdom of the sixteen dead men in the Easter Rising. The crisis that gave rise to Yeat's next play, *The Dreaming of the Bones* (spring-summer 1917) was Yeats's guilt in the aftermath of the Easter Rising. "I keep going over the past in my mind and wondering if I could have done anything to turn those young men in some other direction" (*L*, 614).

Yeats had spent the previous years far from the causes of Irish nationalism, and instead had delved heavily into spiritism and ghost lore, another aspect of the Irish experience to be sure, but one that the sixteen dead men could hardly associate with Ireland's future. The play sets the political and ghostly worlds in conflict, and past critics, depending upon their biases, have emphasized one at the expense of the other. But when we put the play in a biographical context and realize that Maud Gonne is both the ghost that Yeats is trying to exorcise, and the political force he hopes to assuage (she had not approved of "Easter 1916"),[9] we no longer have to decide between Yeats as ghost-lover or Irish patriot.[10] Although the ghosts have "mummy truths" to tell, the young rebel has historical facts about the consequences of their legendary betrayal, which led to seven hundred years of English subjugation of Ireland. Yeats does not ask us to accept the truth of the one and deny that of the other. Both ghosts and man leave the lonely scene with the bitter knowledge that the sorrows of ghostly love are eternal and that the tragic past of Ireland can never be undone.

The ghostly pair are Diarmuid and Dervorgilla, two lovers damned for all time by Irish legend because in their fight against Dervorgilla's cuckolded husband, they are said to have called in the Norman princes of England to fight on their side. In reward, Diarmuid ceded his part of the Irish kingdom to the Normans, thus marking the beginning of Ireland's seven centuries of English subjugation. The Young Man whom the lovers meet on a dark, lonely hillside near the ruins of a deserted Abbey is their complete antithesis, because he has just fought that same English oppressor, and now is headed back to the Aran Islands to save himself from hanging. Yeats has loaded the opposition between the lovers, who were willing to give up their country for their love, and the fighter, who risks his life for his country, with an immense burden of historical judgment; those who sold their country into slavery are seeking absolution from one who, with his own blood, sought to have bought it back once and for all. How could such a man, under such historical conditions, possibly forgive the infamous traitors? Twice his answer rings out, "O, never, never/ Shall Diarmuid and Dervorgilla be forgiven" (*VPl*, 773).

Behind the irreconcilability of the play's protagonists lies Yeats's sense that his own world view, as embodied in a hieratic art like that of the dance plays, was utterly irreconcilable with the revolutionary energies of Ireland in the aftermath of the Easter Rising. The loneliness that pervades *The Dreaming of the Bones* is Yeats's own loneliness as he contemplates the world of possibilities swept away by the murder of the rebels-become-martyrs. Cuchulain gave himself up to an heroic destiny because for him there was no other choice. But for those shot after the Rising, there might well have been some other political choice. Like the Young Man of this play, they might have left the scene of fighting to go into hiding, contributing to

Ireland's future with their lives rather than with their deaths. Though Yeats gave them credit for having been "transformed utterly," he sincerely wished that their form of "terrible beauty" had never been born.

Yeats's sympathies are more fully engaged by the pair of ghostly lovers, as we might expect from one who had so recently described the sad plight of the spirit world in "Anima Mundi." These dead lovers, who appear to the Young Man as spirits, are trapped in the deterministic prison of their guilty, passionate memories. But the living are free, at least in theory, to help the sufferers escape the endless recurrence of their earthly passion by forgiving them their trespasses. This is what happens in the Noh play, *Nishikigi* (referred to in "Anima Hominis" X and "Anima Mundi" X), which Yeats used as his source.[11] Yeats turned this essentially religious scenario into a daimonic crisis of conscience in the life of a young Irish patriot by offering him the option of defying his nationalist faith in sympathizing with the ghosts. Instead, he chooses to be bound by the conscience of history. Though "the terrestrial condition" theoretically offers the "full freedom" lacking in the daimonic realm (*Myth*, 356), the Irish memory is as long and unforgiving as that of ghosts.

As in the earlier dance play, Yeats's presentation is motivated by personal concerns. The sufferings of the ghostly lovers are partly modeled on his own. In the woman's agonized recitation of a burning desire that cannot be consummated throughout eternity, we are at the deepest point of feeling in the play, where Yeats's own painful experience with Maud Gonne in a long, unfulfilled love merges most fully with his occult subject matter:

> These have no thought but love; nor any joy
> But that upon the instant when their penance
> Draws to its height, and when two hearts are wrung
> Nearest to breaking, if hearts of shadows break,
> His eyes can mix with hers; nor any pang
> That is so bitter as that double glance,
> Being accursed.
> . . . .
> Though eyes can meet, their lips can never meet.
>
> (*VPl*, 771)

As Yeats confessed in *Per Amica*, when the lineaments of the artist's mask "express also the poverty or the exasperation that sets its maker to the work, we call it tragic art" (*Myth*, 329).

There were many exasperated double glances, no doubt, during the summer of 1917 when Yeats was courting Iseult Gonne and finishing his play at Colleville-sur-Mer, with mother and daughter looking on approvingly. "Here they say it is my best play," wrote Yeats (*L*, 629), probably because the Gonnes applauded the Young Man's strong rejection of the traitorous pair.

Still the tireless revolutionary even in middle age, "joyless and self forgetting" in her political hatred (*L*, 631), Maud Gonne must have approved especially of the Young Man's politicizing rhetoric (lines 56-58, 247-58), so full of ideological disdain.

Though the Young Man is clearly not Yeats's spokesman in the play, he is far more than just a rhetorical stalking horse to set off the sufferings of the ghosts. Susceptible to the supernatural from the start, he becomes increasingly fascinated as the strangers undertake to educate him about ghosts, and when the woman begins obliquely to describe her own awful sufferings, he sympathetically tries to envision a crime so monstrous that it could demand such enduring penance. Only when finally recognizing that the lovers are Diarmuid and Dervorgilla, and that their guilt is not personal but political, does he pull back. At this point the ghosts, realizing that they have exhausted verbal persuasion, dance the sweet but strange dance of frustrated longing that virtually ensnares their amazed observer:

> Why do you dance?
> Why do you gaze, and with so passionate eyes,
> One on the other; and then turn away,
> Cover your eyes, and weave it in a dance?
> . . . .
> So strangely and so sweetly. All the ruin,
> All, all their handiwork is blown away
> As though the mountain air had blown it away
> Because their eyes have met.
>
> (*VPl*, 774-75)

Faced with their passion itself and not mere folkloric description of ghostly suffering, he hesitates: "I had almost yielded and forgiven it all—/Terrible the temptation and the place! " (*VPl*, 775).

I think we can see in the ghosts' visionary strategy to lure the Young Man something of the entire history of Yeats's relationship with Maud Gonne. Yeats always tried to fascinate Maud with the supernatural world, while she urged the exigencies of politics upon him, but neither could ever fully accept the role that had been selected by the other. Despite this incompatibility, similar to that of the ghosts and rebel in the play, Yeats continually tried to manipulate Maud Gonne spiritually. In an extremely revealing passage of autobiography, virtually contemporary with the play, Yeats writes: "I, who could not influence her actions, could dominate her inner being. I could therefore use her clairvoyance to produce forms that would arise from both minds, though mainly seen by one . . . There would be, as it were, a spiritual birth from the soul of a man and a woman" (*Mem*, 124-25). A shared visionary life, then, could compensate for the poet's immense sexual frustration. We find something akin to this shared visionary life in the sexually sublimated dance of the ghostly lovers, who can neither end their penance nor reconsummate their love unless they can attract the potent Young Man as a surrogate partner. He participates in the vision they create up to a point, but withdraws at the crucial moment when he might have assured the lovers a new spiritual burth. Yeats knew the temper of Maud and of Ireland too well in the summer of 1917 to allow his fantasy of forgiveness and union to complete itself. Ireland could not throw off its burden of guilt and hatred, nor Yeats, his lonely remorse:

> Dry bones that dream are bitter,
> They dream and darken our sun.

(VPI, 776)

The Daimonic Bargain: *The Only Jealousy of Emer*

Yeats had the remarkable opportunity to cast out remorse and virtually begin life again when he married in October 1917. After so many years of obsessive love for another woman, it was only natural that he wonder whether he could start and maintain a marriage at the age of fifty-four that would not be overwhelmed by the dark shadows of the past. *The Only Jealousy of Emer*, conceived in 1916 but mostly written in 1918, is exactly contemporary with the poems that helped Yeats cope with the crises of his new marriage, almost all of which he collected in *Michael Robartes and the Dancer*. Like Solomon and Sheba in the poems, Cuchulain and Emer are legendary masks for the newly married pair, embodying in their own drama some of the conflicts of Yeats's marriage.

Where *The Dreaming of the Bones* dramatizes the suffering of the ghostly world, *The Only Jealousy of Emer* presents its frightening malevolence together with its consummate beauty, in the persons of the two Daimons, Bricriu and Fand. Each Daimon has a personal agenda: Bricriu wants to thwart Fand, who seeks through the capture of the mortal, Cuchulain, to transcend the cycles of time. Though these desires orginate in an exclusively daimonic realm, they help the human heroes to learn to know what they value most highly in human life. To affirm the values of love and fidelity, Emer and Cuchulain must perform heroic renunciations, the best actions of which they are capable.

Yeats gives Emer the possibility of being jealous over two women resembling Iseult and Maud, the lovely young mistress Eithne Inguba, introduced in the play with imagery of "white shell, white wing" (*VPI*,533) and Fand, the glittering moon goddess, "more an idol than a human being" (*VPI*,551), who comes to tempt Cuchulain with the unremembering pleasures of immortality. Though she hates the very name of the supernatural Sidhe, she accepts the terms of Bricriu's malicious bargain: renounce

Cuchulain's love forever so as to prevent him from being seduced away from earthly life by his brazen female Daimon. Unsuspected by his wife, Cuchulain meanwhile values the memories of his love for Emer so highly that he willingly rejects the proffered charms of gorgeous Fand, the erstwhile hawk-woman of his first heroic quest. As he explains to Fand,

> How could you know
> That man is held to those whom he has loved
> By pain they gave, or pain that he has given,
> Intricacies of pain.

(VPl,559)

These lines were excised from the final version of the play, perhaps because they revealed too clearly how deeply *The Only Jealousy* is concerned with the pain of Yeats's relationships with the women he has loved, both the "pain they gave" and the "pain that he has given." Through Emer's and Cuchulain's sacrifice of both earthly and otherworldly fulfillment, Yeats acted out his own need to put Maud Gonne and the paradisal visions of his dreamy youth behind him and accept together with his wife the mature pains of memory.

According to the play's title, Emer is jealous of only one woman, the supernatural moon goddess, Fand. Yeats's dramatic means for making that jealousy vivid to us are the most interesting in the play. He shifts his focus from two-person encounters (Emer-Eithne Inguba, Emer-Bricriu) to a presentation of two scenes at once, as Bricriu suddenly makes visible to Emer the dance with which her inhuman rival tempts her husband. "The Daimon . . . brings man again and again to the place of choice, heightening temptation that the choice may be as final as possible" (*Myth*, 361).[12] The temptation is heightened by what Yeats calls in *Per Amica*, simultaneous perception. Emer must compare herself with the immense attractiveness of the goddess, and powerless to plunge her knife into the other's breast, she is made to realize that unless she performs the Daimon's bidding, she will lose her husband to this metallic creature.

Fand is a problematic figure, not so easily rejected as the deformed, malicious Bricriu, because she represents to Yeats and to Cuchulain a kind of visionary ideal, akin to the lunar dancer of "The Double Vision." Cuchulain and the audience see the external vision of perfection that she presents, but the goddess herself knows that her image is subject, like all other bodily images, to the wheel of reincarnation. There is no doubt that Fand suffers when Cuchulain chooses his painful memories rather than releasing her from the wheel of time. Neither Emer's aspirations for emotional security, nor Fand's for apotheosis, can survive against Bricriu's daimonic opposition. In the final song, the chorus of musicians sympathetically recommends that Fand return to her lunar world to await her own form of completion in the cycle of full moons to come.

Many previous commentators have noted that the play presents a farewell to Maud,[13] but new biographical information sheds light on the difficulty Yeats had, even after marriage, in taking that stand once and for all. It should be remembered that in a poem written just three days after his marriage, Yeats felt the need to apologize to his wife for the determined drift of his mind to the past: "O but her heart would break to learn my thoughts are far away" (*VP*, 450). Two months later while *The Only Jealousy* was gestating, Yeats was preoccupied with his wife's automatic script, in which the supposedly daimonic communicators informed him that his "own sin exactly correspond[s] to those of C[uchulain]," presumably meaning the hero's continued attraction to Fand. The automatic script goes on to record that Yeats asked the Control, "'Who will C love?' The Control replied, 'I cannot tell you till you know yourself and you do know I think but perhaps unconsciously.' When he asked if it were Emer, the Control did not reply" (Notes to *AV*(A), 78). Though Mrs. Yeats's unconscious must have been serving her own best interests in helping with the play, she could hardly take the liberty of resolving her husband's wavering marital commitment for him. The poet would have to make up his own mind.

This biographical imperative helps explain why in the first version of the play Yeats gave Cuchulain such a large role in determining his own future. By the time that Yeats printed the revised version in *The Collected Plays* (1934), his decision to fully commit himself to his wife was far behind him and he could afford to mute both Cuchulain's and Fand's role considerably in favor of the greater renunciation of Emer, whose choice alone now determines what happens to her husband. In the earlier version printed in *Four Plays for Dancers*, husband and wife each has to choose his or her own pain. Ironically, as Emer renounces her love, Cuchulain affirms his:

> What a wise silence has fallen in this dark!
> I know you now in all your ignorance
> Of all whereby a lover's quiet is rent.
> What dread so great as that he should forget
> The least chance sight or sound, or scratch or mark
> On an old door, or frail bird heard and seen
> In the incredible clear light love cast
> All round about her some forlorn lost day?
> That face, though fine enough, is a fool's face
> And there's a folly in the deathless Sidhe
> Beyond man's reach.

(*VPl*,559)

Cuchulain is literally bent over on stage under the weight of his memories, yet he will not put them off to attain the easy transcendence that Fand offers him in a kiss. He claims to love only what passes away, not out of sentimentality, but out of the remembered knowledge that human love is nurtured by remorse for things it has lost or might soon lose. Although most of the ironies in the final version of the play are directed against Emer, Cuchulain also comes in for his share after speaking these loving words. He does not realize that the greatest remorse of all is yet to come when he awakens from his temporary death. There has been "some whispering in the dark between Daimon and sweetheart" (*Myth*, 336), and by a trick of fate he is deprived of the woman for whom he bargained away immortality. He awakes to the pain of mortality, diminished in strength, in courage, and most tragically, in love.

Cuchulain and Emer, as I said earlier, are masks for the married Yeatses, but not proxies. They have their own pasts, their own futures, and clearly, the final turn of the plot with Cuchulain falling into the arms of Eithne Inguba does not offer a parallel to Yeats's biography. Yet I contend that buried in *The Only Jealousy of Emer*, as the seed from which the drama has grown, is a hidden image of Yeats's marriage, its strengths and its compromises. Yeats doubtless gave Emer her prominent tragic role because he felt that he had asked his wife to sacrifice some of her potential for love in marrying a man burdened by an obsessive romance in his past. Yeats may also have felt that her part in the automatic writing behind *A Vision* constituted more of a sacrifice than she had bargained for, when she designed a project to captivate his wandering attention. To compensate for these sacrifices, Yeats stresses in the early version Cuchulain's intense loyalty to Emer and to their shared memories of pain. Cuchulain's role is an emblem of his own marital devotion, a large enough commitment, he hoped, to mitigate the sway of his other past. The speeches Cuchulain delivered after Emer's renunciation were perhaps too private in their tenderness and insistence on inner pain to remain in the public domain, for they seem almost like love letters to Yeats's wife. In excising them, along with other private references to *A Vision*, Yeats freed the play for its proper heroic impact, and it is proud Emer, not Yeats, who lingers longest in our memory.

The Rejected Daimon: *Calvary*

The first three *Plays for Dancers* are all deeply autobiographical in the way that Yeats uses their fictional settings and characters to work through problems in his own life. *Calvary* (1920) is not autobiographical in the same way, and in fact, has not elicited any comments placing it in the context of Yeats's biography. Critics have preferred to explain the play as an illustration of the historical concepts Yeats was developing in the drafts of *A Vision*. While the play bears out this position, such a reading begs the question of why Yeats felt the need of dramatizing the story of Christ's loneliness and why he presented it along with these other biographically-oriented plays. Probably because he had received such startling daimonic communications through his wife's unconscious, Yeats increasingly saw himself as a prophet to his civilization, who had to alert his world to the imminent death of subjectivity. He felt compelled to present nightmare images of the present to make his audience believe in the horrifying visionary images sent by his own Daimon, that "rough beast" slouching "towards Bethlehem to be born" (*VP*, 402). Christ had been the Daimon of his people (*Myth*, 362), but they had chosen to ignore him. Would the modern audience pay any more attention to the prophetic message of Yeats's Daimon? In *Calvary*, Yeats reaches out to Christ as a fellow martyr to the widening gyre of civilization.

The central tragedy of *Calvary* is that Christ is powerless to change his historical circumstances. He offers the people of his time something better than self-interest, but they are just coming into their own right as individuals, and prefer to reject Christ's teachings rather than to deny themselves. Yeats felt himself in an analogous situation as a privileged critic of society, whose just criticisms would inevitably be ignored because the drift of his civilization was counter to the subjectivity that he constantly affirmed. The most important difference between the two figures is that when Yeats feels rejected, he can still wear his aloof mask, whether as legendary Irish hero, suffering ghost, or hierophant in a moonlit tower. When Christ is rejected by those whom he has come to save, there is no other mask for him to wear; his very divinity is called into question. Like the Magi of Yeats's poem, who are "by Calvary's turbulence unsatisfied" (*VP*,318), Christ returns in his mind to assess the meaning of these fated events and to reenact the painful moment of his rejection.

Christ came to offer eternal salvation in order to save people from themselves. Yeats's play dramatizes how people simply cannot give up being themselves. Lazarus is miserable in being the one singled out to be raised from the dead. He wanted to die as normal people do, and now, cannot accept the notion that Christ has conquered death for all time. Judas cannot bear the thought that even his betrayal of Christ was preordained, for he needs to believe in his unique effect on history:

> It was decreed that somebody betray you—
> I'd thought of that—but not that I should do it,
> I the man Judas, born on such a day,
> In such a village, such and such his parents;
> Nor that I'd go with my old coat upon me
> To the High Priest. . . .
>
> (*VPl*, 785)

Judas's illusory belief in his own power is typical of the characters in a play where no one unites with an opposite image and everyone believes that reality is the way that he understands the world. Even the dancing Roman gamblers, who are not interested in individuality, cannot allow themselves to be absorbed in Christ, who is not "the God of dice," but a God of determinism. At the end of the play, Christ stands at center-stage, his cross supported by his betrayer, his circle formed by the pagan dancers who ironically try to comfort him with the notion that he has nothing that they need. "Things fall apart; the centre cannot hold" (*VP*, 402).

The final tableau of the play quite literally realizes the dramatic possibilities of the situation described in the first stanza of "The Second Coming." Christ can be considered a type of the falconer, while the self-sufficient Romans are like those ominous falcons whirling away out of his control. Similarly, the solitary birds that dominate the opening and closing songs are crucial to the play as emblems of an autonomy that Christ fears, for they deny any need for the salvation he brings:

> The ger-eagle has chosen his part
> In blue deep of the upper air
> Where one-eyed day can meet his stare;
> He is content with his savage heart.
>
> (*VPl*, 787)

Imagine for a moment this savage bird's perspective on the play. What does he need with a man-god? Let things fall apart. Let the anarchic Roman soldiers gamble all values away. Let the cowardly Judas and the selfish Lazarus puff themselves up with passionate intensity. Let Christ lacerate his breast over his failures. After all, "what can a swan need but a swan?" (*VPl*, 788).

The proud birds of the closing song offer a critique of the whole pitiful world of *Calvary*. Not subject to human criticism, their aloof poses call to mind the eagle's-eye position Yeats occupies in "The Second Coming" in his dual role as social critic of the present and vatic prophet of the new dispensation. Yeats did not always speak to his civilization from such a towering height. Like Christ, he often felt victimized by those in Ireland whom he and his friends had come to save. It was one thing to rail at the ruffians from the proscenium of the Abbey Stage, another thing entirely to have them beating down one's door during the long nightmare of "the Troubles". In *Calvary*, the only comfort that Christ can take from his troubles is to live for a moment in the love of "Martha, and those three Marys" (*VPl*, 783), women whose identity depends on living in God's love. Yeats has to forge a similar comfort in the poem that responds to the bleak vision of "The Second Coming", his "Prayer for My Daughter". He proposes a set of values by which his civilization can live if only the soul

> ... learns at last that it is self-delighting,
> Self-appeasing, self-affrighting,
> And that its own sweet will is Heaven's will.
>
> (*VP*, 405)

In the best of all possible worlds, the soul might learn this lesson. In the fallen world of *Calvary* and "The Second Coming", such lessons are not easily learned. If they were, Yeats might long since have thrown away his quarrelsome poetry and drama, and been content to live.

A Daimonic Parable: *The Cat and the Moon*

Written shortly before Yeats's marriage and in a mood of expansive comic release, *The Cat and the Moon* expresses a light-hearted side of Yeats familiar from his lyrics, but excluded from the more troubled concerns of his contemporary dance plays. Like the others, this too is a parable about daimonic transformations, but one that has no obsessive personal agenda. It revels in the joyous energy of a character who unites with his daimonic opposite, and by contrast, deplores the limitations of a character who fails to do so. The only other participant is the saint, to the challenges of whose unseen presence the other two respond.

The dramatic purpose of *The Cat and the Moon* is to enlighten and entertain through programatically recreating the Yeatsian doctrine of the Mask. It is the kind of play that Yeats might have written more often, had he been able to escape the wearying cycle of disappointments, bargains, and compromises that he took to be the artist's normal lot. In this parable of the untrammeled imagination, we sense Yeats fully in control of the joy and power he felt in assuming an antithetical mask.

The legend is quickly told. Steeped in the superstitions of the local peasantry, two roguish beggars seek out the well of a saint because they have heard that he can restore to the one his eyesight and to the other the use of his limbs. When they arrive at the well and tree (parodically reminiscent of *At the Hawk's Well*),[14] the saint does not reveal himself, but proposes in an oracular voice that each man make a final choice, either to be cured or to be blessed. The blind man only wants his eyes back so that he can beat the other for having stolen his sheep. Though a sinner like his fellow, the flighty and foolish lame man cannot help but feel that it is a grander thing to be blessed and have one's name inscribed in the book of the blessed. The blind pragmatist is granted vision so that he can pursue his selfish goals, but the lame beggar, though not choosing the cure, is granted the far greater gift of internal, spiritual vision. He alone sees the saint, believes in him, comes to believe in his own blessedness, and miraculously, completes his transformation by dancing and curing his own lameness.

The blind beggar is one of those whom Yeats calls in *Per Amica* rhetoricians, always quarreling with others, and never suspecting the possibility of an internal quarrel. Saint and sinner are yoked together, he surmises, so that they can argue endlessly. The Lame Beggar, far less adept at argument, understands intuitively that saint and sinner meet because of the bond of a possible conversion. When he first mentions the saint, he imagines that the sight of him "will be a grander thing than having my two legs" (*VPl*, 796), for the lame man can imagine "a re-birth as something not one's self" (*Myth*, 334). His imagination for the mask is so strong, in fact, that he believes his own playful lies to his blind companion about the color of his sheepskin. The play begins by illustrating in the cantankerous blind man and deceitful lame man Yeats's contention that "the common condition of our life is hatred," but once the lame man strikes a blessed bargain with his daimonic opposite, he can forget the quarrel and say with Yeats in his moments of aesthetic joy, "everything fills me with affection" (*Myth*, 365).

The play's underlying spiritual meanings are brought to the fore, perhaps more than in any of Yeats's more serious dance plays, by the framing daimonic lyric, from which the play derives its title. Before the beggars even enter, the first stanza is sung to establish the mood of potential correspondences between the instinctive natural world (cat), and an abstract heavenly counterpart (moon):

> The cat went here and there
> And the moon spun around like a top,
> And the nearest kin of the moon,
> The creeping cat, looked up.
> Black Minnaloushe stared at the moon,
> For, wander and wail as he would,
> The pure cold light in the sky
> Troubled his animal blood.
>
> (*VPl*, 792-93)

The opening stanza correlates natural instinct, especially animal sexuality, and the moon's course, through the mirrored movements of cat and moon. The second stanza relates the symbolic action of the lyric to the movement on stage. While the beggers make a circuit of the stage to the beat of drum taps, their instinctive counterpart, Minnaloushe, steps out of his initially cautious movements into the deliberate patterning of a dance. The moon's movements no longer trouble Minnaloushe, as the burden of the song shifts from the supernatural to the natural: "Do you dance, Minnaloushe, do you dance?," and soon enough the cat is teaching the distant moon "a new dance turn." Just as the stanza concludes, the partners arrive at the saint's well, and though neither character yet realizes it, Minnaloushe's dance with his opposite image in the sky predicts that one of the beggars will soon call his own dance tune.

The final stanza of the song, celebrating the moon's (predetermined?) entrance to a new phase, is postponed until the action of the play is completed, and the lame beggar has likewise entered a new phase of his selfhood. As the coda to the action of the play, this stanza extends its meaning considerably. Minnaloushe has progressed, stanza by stanza, from staring at the moon, to dancing with it, and finally to a "wise" understanding of its cyclic changes, which earlier "troubled his animal blood":

> Does Minnaloushe know that his pupils
> Will pass from change to change,
> And that from round to crescent,
> From crescent to round they range?
> Minnaloushe creeps through the grass
> Alone, important and wise,
> And lifts to the changing moon
> His changing eyes.

(VPI, 804)

The lame beggar has likewise longed for the saint from afar and danced in front of him. The erstwhile simpleton has become whole, physically and spiritually. He has received the reward sought by poet and hero from the "mysterious one" of "Ego Dominus Tuus," who disclosed far more than the beggar in a comedy ever dreamed of seeking. "Aren't you a miracle?" "I am, Holy Man" (*VPI*, 804). It does not matter, finally, whether he understands the daimonic creed that wrought this miracle, or those in the rest of Yeats's dance plays. It only matters that we do.

There is no telling what would have happened to Yeats's dramatic career had he not discovered the model of the Japanese Noh when he did. He might well have stopped writing plays out of disgust with the growing objectivity and mechanistic portrayal of life in the popular theatre. That aversion was productive, however, for in reaction to the realistic stage that he had come to abhor, Yeats succeeded in creating what he called for in "A People's Theatre" (1919), namely, "the theatre's anti-self" (*Ex*, 257). He eventually wrote half a dozen more plays that adopted some or all of the Noh conventions already used because he could not easily abandon the clean outline of a ritual that freed the imagination to disregard verisimilitude. As Yeats's imagination grew progressively more violent in old age, he needed a stage where he could easily imagine murders reenacted and severed heads dancing on the floor.

    The dance plays also allowed Yeats to experiment with lyrics that were far less discursive than any he had written since the dense symbolic mode of *The Wind Among the Reeds*. In his new theatre, he indulged himself in the role of hierophant, which he assumed in his verse collections only for such momentous poems as "The Magi" or "The Second Coming." Of all of the dance plays' lyrics, only "The Cat and the Moon" was colloquial enough to remain as part of Yeats's *Collected Poems*.[15] As poet, Yeats could not abandon the public voices he had learned to shape to his will. Instead, he put new matter into the mouths of old masks.

5

Poetic Renewal Through Lyric Debate: 1910–21

Just as Yeats's plays for dancers are an arena in which he struggles with the major biographical and intellectual perplexities of his life, so too his poems of the same period become dialectical vehicles for working through his creative quarrels with himself. In the poetry of *Responsibilities*, *The Wild Swans at Coole*, and *Michael Robartes and the Dancer*, *Per Amica*'s aesthetic of self and anti-self operates everywhere as an intellectual structure for largely autobiographical verse. When poems dramatize a quarrel between two speakers, or between two opposing images, they do so because Yeats needs to find a temporary resolution of conflicting impulses within the self.

The poems of this period reflect his gradual success in making an integrated personality that can confront the pains and losses of aging without resorting either to sentimental self-pity or to rhetorical abuse hurled against an unfeeling world. His stated objective for his poetry is to try for more self-portraiture, yet when we survey the output of these years, we find him more and more speaking through some traditional mask: Solomon as lover, Robert Gregory as hero, Tom O'Roughley as fool, or Michael Robartes as mage. In a note to himself headed "First Principles" (December 1912), he explains the central tension that would underlie the next three volumes of his verse: "One must be both dramatist and actor and yet be in great earnest" ("Extracts," TS, 1).

The story of Yeats's middle period is one of belated emotional maturity. In theory, Yeats was seeking "a vision of reality which satisfies the whole being" (*L*, 588), but between 1908 and 1915, his poetic vision is primarily divisive, characterized by a vitriolic hatred of the ascendant Catholic middle class in Ireland. If Yeats had continued in the bitter vein of many of the political poems of *Responsibilities* (1914), he would have turned himself into the dreaded rhetorician of *Per Amica*, constantly quarreling with others and never realizing his inner potential for transcending the rancor and hatred that isolate and warp the self. His movement toward a more capricious vision of reality is the subject of this chapter.

William Pritchard has marked out two distinct phases of Yeats's poetic and emotional development beginning with the poems of *The Green Helmet* (1910). In the first phase, characterized by such poems as "No Second Troy," or "To a Wealthy Man . . . ," "the poet creates tightened structures of rhetoric which protect and exalt him . . . even as they frequently say that he has been vanquished, is harassed and worn out." This movement of self-protection gives way to "subjective exploration," beginning with "Ego Dominus Tuus" in 1915, a process more fully articulated after the writing of *Per Amica* in the spring of 1917. Pritchard characterizes this second phase as "a felt necessity to ask harder and less rhetorical questions about the self which spins out the dream. How is responsibility incurred? What does it have to do with the kind of poem most worth writing, most subjectively . . . passionate, most sincere?"[1] Such poems turn out to be inclusive structures with room for the opposing visions of self and anti-self, doing justice to the actual, while proposing some method of transcendence. They express the poet's uncertainties without falling into hesitant, passionless rhythms, and likewise, his certainties without becoming rigid or dogmatic. The flowering of this poetry comes in *The Wild Swans at Coole* (1917, 1919), a volume characterized by intensely palpable images, dynamic actions, cogent voices, and a direct, yet symbolic mode of speech. In this volume, Yeats reaches a sturdy poetic and human balance,[2] attained again only in the equally searching poems of *The Winding Stair* (1933).

In this period, Yeats wrote more poems in dialogue form than at any other time in his career. The genre of debate characterizes even those poems that are not explicitly dialogues between different voices. Within a poem each image is tested against its opposite, or against a whole series of opposites, before any particular resolution satisfies the quarrelsome poet. And no answer is final. The conflict between wisdom and beauty, for instance, is debated in poem after poem with entirely different voices. These poems test and prove the validity of Yeats's poetic in *Per Amica*, for Yeats asks us to stand with him amidst the uncertainty of his quarrel in order to appreciate the full force of his song.

Within a single volume, Yeats groups poems by theme and tone, and often he excludes poems chronologically associated with one another, waiting to compile them in a new book with other similar poems. In this way, each new book seems to answer questions raised by an earlier one.[3] In returning to problems previously confronted, Yeats consciously shapes a record of evolving attitudes toward the central issues of his *oeuvre*—time and aging, beauty and wisdom, limitation and transcendence. What had seemed a decisive stance in *Responsibilities* is often undermined by a more exploratory poem in *The Wild Swans at Coole*, while in *Michael Robartes and the Dancer* (where most of the poems are contemporary with those in the previous volume), the poet strikes a very different balance and once again strives for strong affirmations of his opinions. Where the personae of

Responsibilities are generally aloof, those of *The Wild Swans at Coole* are committed to searching for new values to sustain them. With "Ego Dominus Tuus" as its theoretical centerpiece, the primary emphasis of *The Wild Swans at Coole* is on the subjective search for antithetical images to enlighten the struggling self. The succeeding volume offers the fruits of enlightenment. Yeats's martyrologies and apocalyptic visions point toward definite morals—terrible beauty and passionate intensity destroying themselves for lack of the poet's wisdom. In *Michael Robartes and the Dancer*, then, Yeats tries to consolidate the gains from this eleven-year exploratory phase.

Prior to his marriage in 1917, Yeats's poetry was dominated by a pattern of private loss. Increasingly from 1918 on it becomes dominated by the luminous images created in the mind's eye through the partnership of poet and Daimon. The central texts for considering Yeats's liberation of his antithetical images are the two versions of "The Wild Swans at Coole." As first published in 1917, this lament for the onset of a premature and passionless old age reads quite differently than the familiar version in Yeats's *Collected Poems* (the order of the stanzas being 1–2–5–3–4). We can best come to terms with the original poem if we think of it as Yeats's last epithalamium to a bride that would never be his, written just a few months after Maud refused his final proposal. At Coole, Yeats first conceived the image of Maud as an enchanted lover inhabiting the body of a swan.[4] Counting the nine-and-fifty swans, he doubtless imagined them all paired in love, all but the solitary one who was destined to be his bride.[5] Now, in 1916, "All's changed" (*VP*, 322). For the first time in Yeats's myth-making imagination, the swans were merely swans on the lake, and nothing more. As he wrote in an early draft: "They're but an image on a lake/ Why should my heart be wrung" (Bradford, 50). Yeats obviously knew the answer to that question as no one else could. Out of the profound disjunction between past and present meanings of that image on the lake, "The Wild Swans at Coole" was born.

In the poem written in 1916, the poet is stuck in static despondency. He opens and closes in the present, and whenever he moves backward or forward in time, he is brought up short. For the rejected suitor who has built the myth of his life around one woman for over twenty-five years, there are no sustained flights, either of imagination or memory. In the more familiar later version of the poem, the climactic final stanza speculates on the departure of the swans to an open future. But in 1916, with that stanza effectively buried in the center of the poem, that departure cannot take place. The perception, "When I awake some day/ To find they have flown away," is broken off by Yeats's lament for his broken heart: "I have looked upon those brilliant creatures and how my heart is sore." Yeats prefers to keep the swans floating on the lake, where he can continue to possess what is left for him of their special meaning. The climax of 1916 is an anti-climax; rather than dramatic departure and new life, he offers the stasis of landscape painting:

> Unwearied still, lover by lover,
> They paddle in the cold
> Companionable streams or climb the air;
> Their hearts have not grown old;
> Passion or conquest, wander where they will,
> Attend upon them still.

> > (*VP*, 323)

It makes no difference whether the swans paddle or climb. What matters is the contrast between their "companionable" hearts, which have not grown old, and the solitary poet's, which has.[6] While "passion or conquest . . ./ Attend upon them still," the only attendant the poet has is the nagging memory of an ideal past out of reach and of a present filled with self-pity.

The version of the poem that Yeats printed in 1919 is no longer an ode to private memory, but rather to the poet's symbolic vision. Instead of concluding with the image of the swans as his private possession, Yeats projects a concluding vision that acknowledges their autonomy as "mysterious, beautiful" beings that the poet can never truly know, despite his earlier attempts to count and personify them:

> But now they drift on the still water,
> Mysterious, beautiful:
> Among what rushes will they build,
> By what lake's edge or pool
> Delight men's eyes when I awake some day
> To find they have flown away?

> > (*VP*, 323)

The final stanza opens *after* the invidious comparisons between Yeats's heart and the swans' have been drawn. The swans' flight is no longer aborted either by Yeats's present heartache or by his retreat to the past when he "trod with a lighter tread." Instead, our attention is focused on two possibilities that are hinted at, but virtually denied in the first version: that the poet can awake to a future without the swans and that the swans can "delight men's eyes" other than Yeats's. With this deliberate and important revision, Yeats began to liberate himself from the obsessive burden of the past, and what's more, to include us in that symbolic act of liberation.

The revision Yeats made in "The Wild Swans at Coole" (sometime between November 1917 and March 1919) seems natural enough in light of his marriage, his purchase of a permanent home at Thoor Ballylee, and the onset of automatic communication that led to the symbolic system of *A Vision*. These biographical changes are naturally reflected in *The Wild*

Swans at Coole of 1919, a very different volume than its predecessor of two years earlier (See Appendix).[7] The first printing, including *At the Hawk's Well*, is dominated by Yeats's intense disappointments in love and his sense that all life is a preparation for what never happens. The irresolution of "Ego Dominus Tuus" is a touchstone, reminding Yeats's readers that the daimonic revelation of the anti-self that he longed for had still not come. Though all of the previous poems remain in the 1919 volume, seventeen new poems have been added, and a far more cheerful mood prevails. Underlying all of the new poems is Yeats's greatly extended ability to assume the mask of an anti-self. Ten of the seventeen new poems are spoken by personae distinctly unlike Yeats, and four of these are dialogues which encourage debate between voices of self and anti-self. We see Yeats actively putting to work the lessons of *Per Amica*, engaging in creative quarrel with himself in poems ranging in form and mood from the serious sustained meditation of "In Memory of Major Robert Gregory" to the curious intuitive dialectic of "Another Song of a Fool."

The masks Yeats assumes in this second collection of *The Wild Swans at Coole*—lover, hero, fool, and mage—are by no means new to his *oeuvre*. In a passage of *Autobiographies*, he describes his important discovery as a young man that the lyric poet had to be "shaped by nature and art to some one out of half a dozen traditional poses, and be lover or saint, sage or sensualist, or mere mocker of all life" (84). In his early poetry, Yeats obviously emphasized the ideal lover at the expense of the sensualist, and when he turns to mocking the life around him in *The Green Helmet* (1910), there is no trace in his work of the secret knowledge or discipline of the saint. *Responsibilities* (1914) marks a new beginning for Yeats in his managing of all his characteristic poses without sacrificing to the artifice of the mask the personal voice of the man who both suffers and creates. After *The Wild Swans* and *Michael Robartes and the Dancer*, no later volume contains as many fine examples of all Yeats's poetic voices, private and public, colloquial and hieratic. Different volumes bring different masks to the fore: *The Tower*, the old man; *The Winding Stair*, the last Romantic; *Words for Music Perhaps* and *Last Poems*, the wild old sensualist. In the volumes published between 1914 and 1921, we have them all in embryo, and by studying the development of each persona across several volumes, we can trace Yeats's renewal in mid-career.

"The Narrow Theme of Love" (*VP*, 333)

Yeats's love poetry is the most private mode in which he wrote. We hear in poems like "The Cold Heaven" (1912), "On Woman" (1914), or "The Living Beauty" (1917), a speaking voice that we identify with Yeats's own, particularly because he so often exposes his heart's anguish directly. He probably made more poetic capital out of the intensely personal "rag-and-bone shop of the heart" (*VP*, 630), than any English poet since the Petrarchan sonneteers of the Renaissance. His poetic strategy is to hold up an image for contemplation—Maud as classical heroine, Iseult as dancer, Maud and Mrs. Yeats as versions of Sheba—and attempt to come to terms with its positive or negative impact on his image of himself as lover. Personal emotion is distanced by a doubly ironic contemplation of self and beloved. Yeats's poetry thus gives him a chance to control his various loves, who in life never bent to his will.

The program piece for Yeats's love poetry in this period is "The Mask" (1910), a duet for antagonistic lovers written for *The Player Queen*. The poem proposes elevating the ideal image of lover and beloved as a means of fanning the sparks of their sexual attraction into an all-consuming, passionate flame. What is not often noted about the poem is the simultaneous ironic impulse to question and reject that ideal image. The woman views the mask as a discipline for creating beauty, but the man finds its disguise a threat to passionate sincerity.

Does Yeats stand by his own doctrine of the mask, and praise the woman's cold marble façade, unbroken by the slightest ripple of emotion, or does he identify with the turbulent emotions of the man, who may be doctrinally naive, but is emotionally alive? Yeats gives the woman the last word:

> 'O no, my dear, let all that be;
> What matter, so there is but fire
> In you, in me?'
>
> (*VP*, 263)

The insecure lover in Yeats hangs back, and the artist chooses the powerful talisman of a romantic image, as a way of bearing his disappointments without constant surrender to self-pity.

In "Fallen Majesty" (1912), we have a striking example of the way in which Yeats elevates his disappointed passion into a subject fit for tragic treatment.[8] Hymning Maud's praises ensures the immortality of his own role as Homer to her Helen of Troy:

> The lineaments, a heart that laughter has made sweet,
> These, these remain, but I record what's gone. A crowd
> Will gather, and not know it walks the very street
> Whereon a thing once walked that seemed a burning cloud.
>
> (*VP*, 315)

The heroic image of the "burning cloud," the dignity of the repeated insistence on the historical record, the validation of the poet's subjective feeling by the crowd, all combine to invest Yeats's diminished feeling with the kind of grandeur normally associated only with consummation. Yeats even manages to lend a touch of wild exhilaration to his appreciation by associating himself with a "gypsy camping-place," as the mask of the noble survivor reconciles him temporarily to his loss.

We respond to a more powerful Yeatsian voice in "The Cold Heaven," a greater poem of the same year, greater perhaps in the degree to which the agonizing tension between past and present is seen as irreconcilable. The poet's paradoxical vision of burning ice that will not burn gains the quality of a waking nightmare when it reawakens the memory of his lost love, even while the common sense acquired with age reminds him that the flame of that love has long since died down. The very idea of its being fanned anew drives the poet wild:

> And I took all the blame out of all sense and reason,
> Until I cried and trembled and rocked to and fro,
> Riddled with light.
>
>   (*VP*, 316)

Yeats's sudden overpowering sorrow is triggered by a literal application of the symbolic vision to his own condition. "Ice burned and was but the more ice"; so too, the aging poet burns once more "With the hot blood of youth," yet for all that, is to all other eyes a cold, passionless middle-aged man.

The concluding appeal of the poem to a possible justice on the other side of the grave is one to which Yeats resorted increasingly in his love poetry. In "On Woman" (1914), he prays that his rebirth will allow him "To find what once I had/ And know what once I have known" (*VP*, 346). Similarly, "Broken Dreams" (1915) shares the certainty that "in the grave all, all, shall be renewed" (*VP*, 356). Yeats places the emphasis differently in "The Cold Heaven." Shaking his fist at "the injustice of the skies," demanding whether the dead are also forced to endure the dizzying cycle of passionate life over again. Yeats directs our attention away from his present confusion to consider the possibility of some otherworldly fate—punishment or renewal. In the Swedenborg essay and in *Per Amica*, Yeats assures us that the soul is indeed stricken after death because it cannot escape from its own painful memories, just as Yeats himself cannot in the poem. The image of wild, icy love continues to burn because the poet cannot escape from the hypersensitivity of his own imagination.

Yeats wrote over a dozen love poems in the years 1915–16, and his central obsession with "that monstrous thing/ Returned and yet unrequited love" (*VP*, 358) is almost never out of sight. Several of the more self-pitying poems ("A Song," "To a Young Girl") are embarrassing in the hyperbolic way in which they bare the heart's pain. When the bitterness is translated into a less confessional idiom, as in "The Collar-Bone of a Hare," Yeats achieves a clearer self-definition: the persona of a romantic hero who prefers his solitary dreams of innocent dancing to the reality of "the old bitter world where they marry in churches" (*VP*, 330). The best of these love poems are of two kinds: balanced appreciations, in which youthful memories sustain the poet without obscuring their generative pain ("Her Praise," "Broken Dreams"); and chilling visionary encounters where images of the beloved have an almost magical power ("A Thought from Propertius," "Presences," "A Deep-Sworn Vow," and "Lines Written in Dejection"). These latter poems share *Per Amica*'s excitement in reverie's images that grant Yeats the opposite selves to broaden his existence, if only for the moment of creation.

The solitary setting and marmoreal mood of *Per Amica* are echoed in almost every line of "The Living Beauty" (1917), a love poem written to Iseult Gonne:

> I bade, because the wick and oil are spent
> And frozen are the channels of the blood,
> My discontented heart to draw content
> From beauty that is cast out of a mould
> In bronze, or that in dazzling marble appears,
> Appears, but when we have gone is gone again,
> Being more indifferent to our solitude
> Than 'twere an apparition. O heart, we are old;
> The living beauty is for younger men:
> We cannot pay its tribute of wild tears.

> (*VP*, 333–34)

Yeats's fear of the marble façade in "The Mask" is carried one step further in this poem, where even the self-created beauty of mental images allures only to deceive the already discontented heart. Knowing that "the wick and oil" of the body are spent, Yeats must light his own aesthetic candle in search for some imperturbable content. But instead of controlling the image, he discovers that he is manipulated by it. We remember that Yeats associates the malevolence of Daimon and sweetheart. And so, "the living beauty" becomes an agent of the daimonic force that has cursed the poet's life, forcing him to turn away from both statue and beating heart.

Bereft of both living and imagined beauties to love, Yeats describes in another poem the resulting mental breakdown:

> A strange thing surely that my Heart . . .
> Should find no burden but itself and yet should be worn out.
> It could not bear that burden and therefore it went mad.

> (*VP*, 449)

He goes on in "Owen Aherne and His Dancers" to describe how longing, despair, pity, and fear have all conspired against his solitary heart. Written three days after his marriage, this poem provides a new consolation, for he can now turn away from the indifferent aesthetic image to the loving wife at his side.[9]

The love poems that Yeats writes to his wife in 1918–19, all but one collected in *Michael Robartes and the Dancer*, revel in a new affectionate freedom. The poet studies himself and his wife talking about love ("Solomon and Sheba"), making love ("Solomon and the Witch"), dreaming the completion of each other's dream ("Towards Break of Day"), and confronting unknown images that rise up from the subconscious ("An Image from a Past Life"). He neither idolizes nor debases the love object, but allows himself a mature, deferential irony toward both self and beloved. The main change in poetic strategy is a shift in focus toward a point of view that incorporates both lovers without constantly subordinating the image to the observer, as Yeats had done in so many self-gratifying poems where he alone of all old men was privileged to cherish the memory of Maud Gonne. I suspect that the revision of "The Wild Swans at Coole," with its new knowledge that the beautiful swans are not his to possess, came early in the poet's marriage when he must have learned to appreciate his wife's freedom to shape her own destiny. In 1909, Yeats thought that the great wisdom of Solomon was his successful manipulation of the ideal image of the beloved (*Mem*, 144–45), but by 1918–19, when he directly assumes the role of Solomon in his verse, Yeats has learned that all images relayed to the self from the *Anima Mundi* have an uncanny will of their own.

The terms of *Per Amica* are appropriate here, because in several of these marriage poems Yeats includes esoteric material. The most bizarre, "An Image from a Past Life" (1919), dramatizes a manifestation of the supernatural in the interpenetrating minds of two lovers. A woman that the man loved in a previous existence appears to expose an unacknowledged rift between husband and wife, and to flout the conscious mind's smug self-assurance that it understands all its own secrets. Though Yeats overloads the poem with a three-page note based on his wife's automatic writing (*VP*, 821–23), the drama turns mainly on one assertion from *Per Amica*: Images that come to us from the *Anima Mundi* show "intention and choice" (*Myth*, 345). The dead spirit appears to the woman and not to the man because it senses that being more vulnerable emotionally, she will not wish the vision away, as her husband does with an easy rationalization. The poem contains no dramatic resolution of the conflict between husband and wife, but instead, concludes by reaffirming the mysterious power that the visionary image of the anti-self, "the hovering thing" (*VP*, 390), exercises over human consciousness.

The meeting with the daimonic image takes a very different turn in the love duet "Solomon and the Witch" (1918), which raises similar esoteric concerns but subordinates them more fully to the human drama. The poem contemplates the eschatological possibility that the passionate union of two lovers might initiate a divine apocalypse, a subject considered with similar ironic detachment in the contemporary, final version of *The Player Queen* (1919). The key to the poem is the ironic interplay of two voices, the passionate Sheba and the coolly rational Solomon, distant even during the heat of her passion when, daimonically possessed, she "suddenly cried out in a strange tongue/ Not his, not mine." Solomon, purported to have the wisdom of the ages, claims to understand these strange crowings as signals of the imminent apocalypse set into motion by their love. Sheba's naive response, "Yet the world stays," debunks her husband's philosophic pretensions. If they are to attain any form of unity, it cannot be through witty pretense or occult speculation about the power of the cockerel's crow. They have to begin where all lovers find their resuscitative energy:

> "And the moon is wilder every minute.
> O! Solomon! let us try again."
>
> (*VP*, 389)

Solomon's esoteric explanation of apocalypse, the union of Choice and Chance, has been tied by many of Yeats's critics to the newly developed lunar system,[10] but Yeats gives us other interpretive clues:

> Aye, though all passion's in the glance—
> For every nerve, and tests a lover
> With cruelties of Choice and Chance;
> And when at last that murder's over
> Maybe the bride-bed beings despair,
> For each an imagined image brings
> And finds a real image there.
>
> (*VP*, 388)

Solomon has been deceived by fate, for he had hoped that the lover whom chance might bring him would harmonize with his own chosen image of what a lover should be. He no doubt expresses what Yeats has discovered in marrying—that the ideal never synchronizes with the real. Eight years earlier in "The Mask," Yeats believed that unity in love could only be achieved by both partners' idealizing one another. Now, neither partner wears a mask that effaces individuality. Solomon, the occultist side of Yeats, enjoys the hypothetical creation of doctrine, yet always grounds it in his tragic sense of life's inescapable divisions. And Sheba is not so much Mrs. Yeats as a passionate side of the poet, impatient with his own need for abstract statement. Her daimonic cock-crow therefore needs to be evaluated by the meditative persona. "Maybe an image is too strong/ Or maybe is not strong enough," Solomon wonders. Yeats's answer is that no image or mask can be strong enough without being tested by the experience of meeting with its opposite in a poem. Speculation about the poetic image yields the field to concrete experience, and finally, the "oil and wick are burned in one."

"Men and Women Made Like These" (*VP*, 272)

In such poems as "To a Wealthy Man . . . ," or "To a Shade," and the other *Poems Written in Discouragement* (1913), Yeats exalts heroic anti-selves as a way of disparaging all that he dislikes in bourgeois Ireland, while aggrandizing his own persona that is able to conceive of such opposites. In several groups of elegiac tributes—to Mabel Beardsley, to the martyrs of the Easter Rising, to Major Robert Gregory—Yeats assumes heroic masks without creating such easy triumphs of self over world. The greater his own desire to strain against personal disappointment by marvelling at heroic grandeur, the more likely he is to satisfy that insatiable desire of becoming a legitimate hero in his poetic world.

More than any other poem in *Responsibilities*, the multiple maskings of "The Grey Rock" most clearly predict the development of Yeats's middle period. Its themes of sacrifice in love, in heroism, and in art ally it to such later poems as "On Woman" (1914), "Easter, 1916," and "In Memory of Major Robert Gregory" (1918). By drawing on all the sources of Yeats's poetry—Celtic myth, the heroic vision of Maud Gonne, the aesthetic discipline of *fin-de-siècle* Romanticism—"The Grey Rock" is of singular interest in proposing a complex myth justifying the direction of Yeats's entire poetic career.

The poem is easier to analyze if we chart out, as one recent critic has done, five distinct time periods, each set behind the other:

    1)   Yeats's narrative present;
    2)   the historic past of the Rhymer's Club poets and of Maud Gonne;
    3)   the mythological past in three periods—
        a)   the assembly of the gods at Slievenamon,
        b)   the earlier battle between the Irish and the Danes,
        c)   the still earlier promise of immortality from Aoife to her lover.[11]

Yeats had previously juxtaposed his own present with a mythological past in "No Second Troy" (1910) and the other Helen poems, but this is the first Yeats poem with the peculiarly modern complexity (despite its archaizing content) of asking the reader to unify the disparate levels rather than doing so in the central consciousness of the meditative persona.[12]

Each set of characters in the poem is to be compared with another and all are to be taken as foils for the poet. For instance, when Aoife poignantly calls out, "Why should the faithfullest heart most love/ The bitter sweetness of false faces?" (*VP*, 275), she masks the poet's own feeling of betrayal in love by Maud Gonne. The story of her unnamed lover, who chooses death in

battle to save the life of a king's son, rather than two hundred years of life
and love with her, has deep resonance in the poet's feeling of having lost
Maud to Irish politics. At the same time, Aoife is not only a mask for Yeats,
but also for his beloved Maud.

> *I knew a woman none could please,*
> *Because she dreamed when but a child*
> *Of men and women made like these.*

(*VP*, 272)

Maud and Aoife both dream of transforming the mortal into an immortal
image and both fail, because man and ghost cannot change places. Peter Ure
has argued accordingly that "The Grey Rock" betokens Yeats's "rejection of
the inhuman spiritual in favor of that in human life which is heroical and
passionate, and . . . only to be found in a human context" (*Towards a
Mythology*, 32).

If only human life is heroic, however, what of the dead poets of the
Rhymers' Club? Yeats ascribes a more passionate fulfillment to them than to
anyone else in the poem. They function essentially as Yeats's daimonic
guides, bringing him to understand the total, ecstatic commitment needed
for his chosen role as myth-maker. They show him the worldly pitfalls
everywhere facing the artist:

> *You had to face your ends when young—*
> *'Twas wine or women, or some curse—*
> *But never made a poorer song*
> *That you might have a heavier purse,*
> *Nor gave loud service to a cause*
> *That you might have a troop of friends.*

(*VP*, 273)

Men like Dowson and Johnson handed Yeats the mask of the isolated,
passionate, and self-sufficient artist (which they had inherited in turn from
Pater, Rossetti, and ultimately, from Shelley and Blake), but Yeats had
changed its lines significantly, taking on new commitments such as ten years
of "Theatre business, management of men" (*VP*, 260). Like his erstwhile
colleague Dowson pleading to ingratiate himself once more with his beloved
Cynara, Yeats writes that he too has been faithful, in his fashion.

The laughing company of gods are masks for both the Rhymers and for
Yeats in their mysterious ecstasy that lies beyond the passions of all living
men, except perhaps the visionary artist. Remembering that Yeats identifies
with Aoife as an heroic counterpart who shares his sorrow, we can see her
transformation into one of their laughing company as a valuable lesson for
the poet similarly preoccupied with private loss. By imagining "that room/
Those wine-drenched eyes" that are so much opposed to his own passionate

commitment to life, he becomes for the moment his daimonic opposite and shares in their divine exaltation. Theirs may seem "a cup that is filled from Lethe's wharf" (*Myth*, 331), but in their own timeless vision, they have awakened to an even higher order of reality. The multiple actions of "The Grey Rock" allow Yeats to define that timelessness as an opposite quality necessary for his own imaginative wholeness, and he adds the "laughing lip" (also in the contemporary heroic poem "Upon a Dying Lady") to the "proud steady gaze" of his heroic canon.

Yeats finds "the rights twigs for an eagle's nest" (*VP*, 288) in his self-created mythology of "The Fisherman" (1914), "A man who is but a dream":

> Maybe a twelvemonth since
> Suddenly I began,
> In scorn of this audience,
> Imagining a man,
> And his sun-freckled face,
> And grey Connemara cloth,
> Climbing up to a place
> Where stone is dark under froth,
> And the down-turn of his wrist
> When the flies drop in the stream;
> A man who does not exist,
> A man who is but a dream.
>
> (*VP*, 348)

Poetically, Yeats conveys a sense of the power that this supposedly non-existent image has over his imagination by describing it with an extremely vivid particularity, while "the reality" is portrayed at its lowest common denominator, "The witty man and his joke/ Aimed at the commonest ear." If we describe the poem in the language of "Anima Hominis," the first picture embodies the "heart's discovery of itself" through an image of its opposite, the second presents the "crude allegories" that drive the poet to isolate himself in reverie (*Myth*, 325). The poet retreats into his dream image at the end of the poem because he needs to keep this whole man alive until his audience is ready to accept the possibility of heroic action in modern Ireland.

Yeats soon found other heroes for his verse in the martyrs of the Easter Rising. In front of his amazed eyes, Irish men and women succeeded in realizing the total commitment that he had previously only found possible in imaginary and legendary beings, like "The Fisherman" or the gods of "The Grey Rock." People that he knew and had mocked for their cowardice in "September, 1913," had resigned their parts "In the casual comedy" by giving their lives to free Ireland from British tyranny. Yet Yeats could not simply celebrate their deaths. "Easter, 1916" and the four poems pendant to it in *Michael Robartes and the Dancer* express Yeats's deep ambivalence about the value of these sacrificial deaths and of all self-effacement in public causes. The individual facing death is often heroic in Yeats's work, but never when he denies his own individuality to become a passing figure in a crude allegory.

Truth flourishes in solitude for Yeats, and in "Easter, 1916" (written September 1916) the saving quality of the martyred heroes is their turning from the grimy public mirror of Dublin to seek out solitary heroic masks. Insofar as Yeats celebrates their deaths, he does so hoping to recreate them as heroic models who can teach the rest of Ireland to accept an antithetical destiny for itself. The first and third stanzas locate the heroes amidst the familiar settings of Irish town and country life, while the fourth makes them a part of the daily ritual of the family, a heroic litany to be intoned with the evening prayers of mother and child. The least rhetorical stanza (also the most biographical) is the second, where we feel Yeats most directly confronting his ambivalence. A sweet voice turns shrill, but a sensitive nature finds the power of bodily force, and a lout leaves pride and drunkenness behind to unite with his fellows in struggle. Balancing these positive and negative images, Yeats decides that the mask deserves his praise, but he can never again see heroism with the simple clarity of "The Fisherman." A man can unite with his mask in passion, but unless he brings wisdom with him, "A terrible beauty is born."

Yeats's later poems on the Easter Rising and its aftermath take as their point of departure the ambivalent query of "Easter, 1916," "Was it needless death after all?" (*VP*, 394). Yeats answers his question affirmatively with the grizzly, dehumanized images of bone and blood in "Sixteen Dead Men" (December 1916 or 1917) and "The Rose Tree" (April 1917), where light-hearted ballad rhythms further deflate the urgency of the heroes' sacrifice. In these public debates about the future of Ireland, the heroes have lost their personalities and become no more than abstract symbols to be weighed in the "give and take" (*VP*, 395) of politics. "On A Political Prisoner," written in 1919 after public eulogizing had subsided, weighs politics in the crucial Yeatsian balance of personality, and finds its effect on a once free and vital self utterly debasing: "Blind and leader of the blind/ Drinking the foul ditch where they lie" (*VP*, 397). The final poem of the series, "The Leaders of the Crowd" (1918–19), again emphasizes the sacrifice of personal integrity to the values of the mob: "So the crowd come they care not what may come" (*VP*, 398).

In the elegies written on the death of Major Robert Gregory, by contrast, Yeats is able to gauge the hero's life in terms of the poet's own spiritual and poetic values, assuring Gregory an immortality he could never have achieved on his own. In "Shepherd and Goatherd," written in February-March 1918 soon after the Irish airman's death in the European war, Yeats projects two speakers, versions of himself like Hic and Ille, who assess the hero's place in two opposing views of reality. The poem's pastoral convention is perhaps too recondite to express Yeats's personal sorrow, particularly when compared with the far more accessible "In Memory of Major Robert Gregory."[13] "Shepherd and Goatherd" succeeds admirably, however, in sketching the tragedy of the hero and the apotheosis of the soul in death, two of Yeats's primary concerns in *Per Amica*, almost as if the poem attempted to distill the wisdom espoused by the friendly light of the silent moon.

The song of death and the song of reincarnation are the still points in the poem's turning world or mortality, but before the dramatic dialogue reaches these climactic moments, Yeats concentrates on characterizing the speakers themselves as diametrically opposed types. The young shepherd writes his poem impulsively, as would Hic, in order to escape from his emotions in the face of Gregory's tragic death:

> I thought of rhyme alone,
> For rhyme can beat a measure out of trouble
> And make the daylight sweet once more.
>
> (*VP*, 339)

The imagery of speckled bird (the title of Yeats's autobiographical novel) and evening shadows expresses himself as much as it does the dead hero, for the shepherd can only see all around him as part of a sequence of transitory images in the natural world. The old poet "made like music" in his own youth, he tells us, but he can no longer expend energy in lamenting the ephemeral world. Instead, facing Gregory's untimely death and his own imminent demise, the goatherd transforms mortality into an image of its anti-self, the dead soul dreaming its way back to an imperishable bliss so unlike our life that all mortal knowledge must be lost before that bliss can be embraced.

The one finds self, the other, anti-self, and on that distinction rests everything that each singles out for praise in the dead man. For the shepherd, Gregory is the sum total of his achievements:

> He that was best in every country sport
> And every country craft, and of us all
> Most courteous to slow age and hasty youth,
> Is dead.
>
> (*VP*, 339)

The aged goatherd is indifferent to Gregory's achievements. If Gregory attained unity in life, the goatherd says, it is not because of his diverse merits, but "Because of what he had dreamed,/ Or the ambitions that he served." For the old man, as for Yeats, life is a struggle between opposites, and "outrageous war," as he sings, "Of all 'twas pain or joy to learn" (*VP*, 342).

Like both of the speakers of the poem, Gregory was an artist, a composer of pipe tunes. In the worldly eye of the young shepherd, these few tunes cannot compensate for the loss of a brilliant life and prospects, whereas the subjective goatherd finds solace in the music's expression of its creator's mind:

> He had often played his pipes among my hills,
> And when he played it was their loneliness,
> The exultation of their stone, that cried
> Under his fingers.

(*VP*, 339)

These lines contain a significant echo from a poem Yeats had written five years earlier to his great friend and patroness, Robert Gregory's mother, "To a Friend Whose Work Has Come to Nothing." Writing this poem of tribute as much for Lady Gregory as for himself (*L*, 647), Yeats hopes to reassure his bereaved friend that her dreams for an Irish cultural renaissance also sustained Robert during the all too brief period of his accomplishments. The life of the artist is lonely, but if lived sincerely in pursuit of the dream image that transfigures the self, then its rewards will endure.

If Yeats wrote the self-effacing "Shepherd and Goatherd" for his patroness, there is no question that he wrote "In Memory of Major Robert Gregory" for himself.[14] It gives us all of Yeats's characteristic modes in one burst—a love poem spoken to his wife; an emotional and probing analysis of four exemplary dead friends; a catalogue of values for Ireland to emulate in building a great unified civilization; a statement on the discipline of artistic vision; and finally, a virtuosic presentation of Yeats's assumption of opposite selves, forging within the poem a passionate, timeless moment apotheosizing the hero and the imagination of the poet who conceives him whole.

Yeats deliberately placed his elegy immediately after "The Wild Swans at Coole." Just as he refuses to let those swans die from his imagination, so too he makes use of the past of his dead friends, unwilling to allow the physical fact of mortality to isolate him as he ages. The narrator who opens the poem is preoccupied with death and losses just as he is beginning a new life. Because he cannot share with his wife all the friends who were dearest to him, and because he would forestall a foolish quarrel over an irretrievable past, he begins to recreate those friends' images as they were in life. He goes on to stage amicable quarrels of his own with those figures, construing them as opposite selves. The strategy is similar to that followed in *The Trembling of the Veil* (1922), the autobiographical volume that examines and criticizes the friends whose lives meshed so crucially with Yeats's own poetic and personal development.

The portraits in Yeats's various autobiographical volumes are almost always tinged with heroic qualities, but they are also ironic portrayals of men and women divided from their masks, unable to integrate self-images in life and art. Yeats's self-portrayal in the poem shows a similar division between the person he is and the one he would like to be. He places himself in the tower setting befitting a hero or mage, but he is a sorry figure compelled continually to rake the coals of his past: "All, all are in my thoughts to-night being dead." These dead men never escaped from their inner divisions to attain a full command of life; Yeats dwells on their lives precisely so that he can avoid their fates, but at the start of the poem it is by no means clear that the poet will succeed in creating a new exalted self-possession.[15]

Following the initial ironic portrait of the poet, the next three portrayals of dead friends all share in the characteristic Yeatsian division of personality into conflicting selves: Lionel Johnson, scholar and dreamer; John Synge, "enquiring" and "simple"; George Pollexfen, horseman and astrologer. Moreover, each of them represents something Yeats might have become. Many times in youth, he found himself on Johnson's ascetic path leading toward some "measureless consummation" and away from even imagining a life of action in the world. At other times, particularly in the decade of work for the Abbey Theatre (ca. 1900–10), Yeats like Synge, followed his audience's lead toward choosing "the living world for text." There were still other times in his career when, along with his uncle Pollexfen, Yeats was only too willing to see that living world in the light of a deterministic occult system. More than Yeats himself admits in the poem, these men were his alter egos, "A portion of my mind and life, as it were." Yeats leaves behind their self-divisions (and by analogy, his own) in the first half of the poem, and moves on toward a comprehensive unifying image, Robert Gregory envisioned as the ideal Renaissance courtier:

> Soldier, scholar, horseman, he,
> And all he did done perfectly
> As though he had but that one trade alone.
>
> (*VP*, 327)

In successive stanzas, we see Gregory as a lover of nature, as a daring athlete, as a visionary painter, and as a gifted artisan. While each adds a new facet to his personal achievement, the wider perspective is always that of the aristocratic coterie to which he belonged and which remains his loyal audience. The first person plural that predominates in the first two stanzas returns in stanza VI and IX–XI, allowing Yeats both to identify himself with Gregory and that community's standards and to ascribe to Gregory his own visionary achievements. In the stanza on Gregory as painter, we perceive the affinity between Gregory's visual talent and Yeats's verbal ability to render the grey rock of Irish mythology:

> We dreamed that a great painter had been born
> To cold Clare rock and Galway rock and thorn,
> To that stern colour and that delicate line
> That are our secret discipline
> Wherein the gazing heart doubles her might.
>
> (*VP*, 326)

Yeats's admiration for Gregory's paintings follows from his own recent pledge of faith to the "*rock-born, rock-wandering foot*" (*VP*, 276); in praising Gregory Yeats is in effect praising himself, Synge, and the other writers of the Irish Renaissance who found an artistic interest in the desolate landscape and lives of the Irish peasantry. By singling out the "secret discipline" of art, Yeats recasts Gregory's achievement in words normally reserved for his own quest for poetic or occult revelation.

In the poem Yeats makes Gregory an image of his own aspirations for unity, Hic and Ille, Shepherd and Goatherd, fused into one. In Gregory's diversity he finds qualities to lend wholeness to the life that he and his wife are beginning to lead in their tower. Like Gregory, they have a life grounded in the sights and sounds of nature (Stanza VII), in the companionship of a supportive community (Stanza VIII), and finally, in the discipline and execution of fine and domestic arts (Stanzas IX–X). Gregory would have been their "heartiest welcomer," gazing lovingly at "the old storm-broken trees," or counselling them "In all lovely intricacies of a house." He had the contemplative reach of Lionel Johnson, the physical energy of his fellow horseman, George Pollexfen, and the great delight in all passionate life of John Synge. Gregory remains all these things and more, because he assumes for the poet the proportions of an ideal anti-self, the unified man that Yeats would most like to be.

In the climactic stanza XI, Yeats assesses the total impact of Gregory's life and death as a war-hero, dramatizing both gains and losses through a magnificent reworking of the house imagery with which the poem began:

> Some burn damp faggots, others may consume
> The entire combustible world in one small room
> As though dried straw, and if we turn about
> The bare chimney is gone black out
> Because the work had finished in that flare.
>
> (*VP*, 327)

In contrast to the explosive image that follows, the fire of "damp faggots" symbolizes a self-contained life of slow maturation, and the all-consuming fire, the possibilities of heroic action, where one small room can take on the dimensions of "the entire combustible world," if the deeds conceived there are splendid enough. This heroic world contains great risks, and potentially, even greater losses; the vital spark of fire in the chimney can go "black out."

Yeats would have us remember that this tragic world is also one of significant achievement: "the work had finished in that flare." Yeats seems to identify himself in this context with the unheroic life of those who "burn damp faggots." For the first time in five stanzas, however, he has removed Gregory from the center of our attention with an indefinite focus. Is not the poet then also included in this vision of consummation, illuminating our world with his conception of imaginative unity?[16]

Elsewhere, Yeats felt that an appropriate image for his art was the slow-burning fire rather than the blaze of a Major Robert Gregory. When writing in *The Trembling of the Veil* about the tragic lives of the Paterian generation of the 1890s (Johnson, Dowson, Davidson, Symons et al.), Yeats returned to these two images as alternative paths for the artist: "They had taught me that violent energy, which is like a fire of straw, consumes in a few minutes the nervous vitality, and is useless in the arts. Our fire must burn slowly, and we must constantly turn away to think, constantly analyze what we have done. . . . Only then do we learn to conserve our vitality" (*Au*, 318). In the elegy, Yeats is very much concerned with conserving his vitality, analyzing what he has achieved by describing whom he has loved. By imagining and glorifying the antithetical, non-intellectual life that burns up its world, he shows evidence of an imagination that can embrace its opposite and thereby survive.

In the final stanza Yeats turns inward to conserve the energy he has expended in resurrecting Robert Gregory. The poet analyzes his own emotion in the face of the images he has called to mind. The elegy began amidst private quarrels, but it concludes in the universal tragic emotions of woe and wonder. The poet glances again at Synge, Pollexfen, and Johnson, and the affections he felt for them at each stage of life, "Until imagination brought/ A fitter welcome," an admiration worthy of his present maturity and self-possession. The final lines come to remind us that Yeats has given his heart to that whole and intense image of Robert Gregory, so different from himself, yet so essential to his psychic unity.

"Not a Poor Fool Understands" (*VP*, 381)

In his effort to strike a balance between the opposing claims of natural and imaginative life, between the "sensual music" of generation and the magnificent "monuments of unageing intellect" (*VP*, 407), Yeats needs one paramount symbol that is both natural and imagined to effect the resolution he seeks, whether it be a rooted tree, a dancer, or a singing golden bird. With much more modest visionary tools, Yeats's fools attain similar enduring visions of reality. Because they have a special kind of wisdom inaccessible to normal men and women, they put us directly in touch with an invisible kingdom without ever losing hold of the tangible reality before their eyes.

Obviously none of the fool poems is as great as "Sailing to Byzantium" or "Among School Children" where similar thematic reconciliations take place, but they are remarkable texts for illuminating the central thrust of Yeats's imagination in his middle period. Like the poems of lovers and heroes, they grow out of inner biographical quarrels, but they often succeed more fully in devising autonomous masks to which we can turn as sources of mysterious wisdom.

The poems in this middle period in which Yeats speaks as beggar, fool, or hermit come in two distinct groups, each circling around the concerns of a contemporary play, the revised *Hour Glass* (1913) and *The Cat and the Moon* (1917). The lyrics of 1913 extend the social critique of the opening poems of *Responsibilities*, as well as introduce the fool as a vehicle for spiritual authority. The lyrics of 1918 arrange themselves around Yeats's quest for personal wisdom, the central theme of *The Wild Swans at Coole*. Like the play to which they are related, the earlier lyrics are generally more didactic. Where *The Hour Glass* simply tries to prove to its protagonist that a spiritual world exists, *The Cat and the Moon* and the later fool lyrics all use that conviction to allow their characters to free themselves from the straitjacket of modern materialism. By eschewing discursive logic and material values, these later fools liberate both themselves and their creator.

One of the most pressing issues for Yeats in *Per Amica* is whether meaningful art grows best in the soil of fulfilled or unfulfilled desire. One of the earliest formulations of the question is that of King Guaire in Yeats's parable "The Three Beggars" (1913):

> "Do men who least desire get most,
> Or get the most who most desire?"

> (*VP*, 295)

The question of how to satisfy worldly expectations gives impetus to all of the beggar and fool poems in *Responsibilities*. Two of the poems, "Beggar to Beggar Cried" and "Running to Paradise" are posed back to back as an antiphonal pair, two speakers in middle age, one choosing a respectable middle-class life, the other a far-off paradisal dream. The other three poems all enact the debate internally, most clearly in "The Hour Before Dawn," which brings together two argumentative characters to make claims for this world and the next, the merry life of a good wind blowing, and the dreamy sleep of longing for the end of time. The other fables are not as schematic, but are equally concerned with the opposition between worldly existence and a possibly superior spiritual mode of being. In adopting masks of "the old crane of Gort" and of a giddy hermit, who in "his hundreth year,/ Sang unnoticed like a bird" (*VP*, 299), Yeats humorously attempts to assess the possibility of a simple harmony between self and world. Though some of the poems make choices of one mask over another, taken as a whole, the series reflects Yeats's preference to treat his various opposite selves ironically, since none of these self-images affords him complete escape from the pain of unfulfilled desire.

One way of channelling that pain is through teaching. Taking the form of fables, the poems thinly disguise Yeats's need to draw a moral from his bitter experience: excessive desire does hamper fulfillment. The beggars fight and lose the chance for King Guaire's promised treasures, while the crane, whom Yeats has kept aloof from the fray, has silently learned the lesson of the little parable played out before him. The old hermit also desires least and gets most; compare his unconscious mystic fulfillment to the pedantic sages' witty discussion of the fate of the soul after death. Those who remain obsessed by their own rhetoric, like the antagonists of "The Hour Before Dawn," can never grow emotionally. Yeats refuses to resolve their debate because the characters are not really open to choosing between this world and the next.

The two songs sung in the first person are the more satisfying of the group, because Yeats does not resort to such elaborate fables for dramatizing internal quarrels, but instead, lets the personae speak powerfully for themselves. "Running to Paradise" is clearly motivated, as are most of Yeats's compensating dreams, by disappointments in love: "never have I lit on a friend/ To take my fancy like the wind" (*VP*, 301). In "Beggar to Beggar Cried," motivated by the threat of a paternity suit,[17] Yeats projects his wish to be settled and done with the pains of love onto a lusty beggarman wishing to rid himself of the devil between his thighs. As lover, Yeats might agonize over his disappointed passion and misguided affairs, but as fool he can imagine a satisfying alternative life, respectability, security, and vicarious enjoyment of freedom in "The wind-blown clamour of the barnacle-geese" (*VP*, 300). The beggar who articulates this private wish is *"frenzy-struck."* This ambiguous epithet suggests that he is either mad, like those other beggars who fight under "the frenzy of the beggars' moon" (*VP*, 296), or that he is the recipient of a spiritual revelation, entering, like The Wise Man in *The Hour Glass*, into some "frenzy of the mind" (*VPl*, 587, 637). The folkloric use of the barnacle-goose as a symbol of immortality provides confirmation that the seemingly naive speaker has intuited some deeper truth about life.[18] His new unity is also Yeats's in confronting and partly transcending the dilemmas of middle age by cultivating such personae who translate his longing into song.

Yeats's fools in *The Wild Swans at Coole* sing in very different keys from the generally quarrelsome tones of 1913. They are iconoclastic visionaries and intuitive dreamers. Whether they speak with the arrogant certitude of conviction, as do Billy Byrne and Tom O'Roughley, or whether they hide behind their own reputed dull wits, as do the unnamed fools at the end of the volume, all are vehicles for expressing Yeats's imaginative pleasure in meeting with his own opposites, as they in turn meet with natural or dream images antithetical to them.

All four poems raise problems of interpretation connected with the inception of *A Vision* in 1917–18. The latter poems, "Two Songs of a Fool" and "Another Song of a Fool," following the exposition of the fool as a representative of the dissociation of thought in the last stage of "The Phases of the Moon," have hardly ever been interpreted except as illustrations of Yeats's contention in *A Vision* that the fool's "thoughts are an aimless reverie; his acts are aimless like his thoughts; and it is in this aimlessness that he finds his joy" (*AV*(B), 182).[19] Because each of Yeats's fools undergoes a learning process, it is hard to see the relevance of aimlessness to what in fact, are purposive meditations, however illogical they might seem. My effort in what follows is to restore the life of these poems as exercises in the free play of a mask with its opposites.

Of all the speakers, Billy Byrne in "Under the Round Tower," seems most willing to ignore the opposite image that his creator contrives for him, but even he ends by internalizing its lessons. In the first stanza, he deliberately spurns middle-class creature comforts, preferring, he says, to sleep on a cold tombstone. Billy is no stoic, as he soon betrays in a dream whose patterned symbols unfold the inner workings of his mind. His unsatisfied passion for rich living transforms the circuits of sun and moon into a beautiful ceremony, interpreted when he awakes as an omen that his luck has changed. It is beside the point to note, as Thomas Parkinson does, that this dance is a "symbol for the solved antimony of both sex and nature," since Billy Byrne is not concerned with metaphysical solutions.[20] Instead, he translates his vision of beatitude into the language of unsatisfied desire from which it sprang (like Yeats in "Anima Hominis" XII), and steals his way proudly to the creature comforts he spurned the night before. A vision of Billy's opposite leads him toward the fulfillment he most desired.

"Tom O'Roughley" defines a more spiritual fulfillment, along the lines of the main themes of *Per Amica*: first, assuming the mask of an opposite type, and second, viewing that world of masks from the perspective of an eternal soul. Yeats's persona in the poem is brashly iconoclastic, a Blakean philosopher of contraries. To the straight road of the "logic-choppers" he opposes the winding path of the butterfly, not going directly after its prey like eagle or hawk, but following, as Yeats explains in a note, "the crooked road of intuition" (*VP*, 827). We remember from *Per Amica* that Yeats's Daimon showed him an alternative to both winding path and straight line, the daimonic "zigzag" (*Myth*, 361), a word that recurs in Yeats's poetry only in the second stanza of "Tom O'Roughley." The stanza is a prelude to eternal life, where the intuitive butterfly can no longer serve as Tom's guide:

"If little planned is little sinned
But little need the grave distress.
What's dying but a second wind?
How but in zig-zag wantonness
Could trumpeter Michael be so brave?"
Or something of the sort he said,
"And if my dearest friend were dead
I'd dance a measure on his grave."

(VP, 338)

Impetuosity in life does not lead to punishment in death, but rather provokes an encounter with the archangel of the Last Judgment, Michael. His wantonness is not sexual license, but in Tom's archaic, countrified diction, unrestrained movement, and his bravery, not courage but glory. Tom sees the archangel Michael as the highest embodiment of his ideal of freedom. When Tom envisions himself dancing a measure on his friend's grave, he effectively internalizes the angel's daimonic lead toward wanton, brave, and untrammelled imaginative action. Where the butterfly's wings point out to Tom his crooked path through this life, Michael's zigzagging trumpet heralds his joyful way into the next in Yeats's most optimistic poem about the interpenetration of natural and spiritual realms.

A Yeatsian butterfly, emblem of the soul, points the way towards a series of natural, occult, and imaginative transformations in "Another Song of a Fool," a poem short enough to cite in full:

This great purple butterfly,
In the prison of my hands
Has a learning in his eye
Not a poor fool understands.

Once he lived a schoolmaster
With a stark, denying look;
A string of scholars went in fear
Of his great birch and his great book.

Like the clangour of a bell,
Sweet and harsh, harsh and sweet,
That is how he learnt so well
To take the roses for his meat.

(VP, 381–82)

To elucidate the poem's mystery, we can tell any number of parables about reincarnation, talk learnedly about the alchemical transformation of spirit into matter, or annotate source passages in *The Hour Glass* (*VP1*, 639) or *A Vision*.[21] But, in all such commentary, we must see that the witty process of the poem is sacrificed to an interest in its bare content. The poem is about what it claims to be about, the speaker's discovery of the true learning in a butterfly's eye. Any valid interpretation must come to terms with the fool's curious reasoning through antithetical images.

The central problem to be solved in the poem is how can man, knowing the limitations of his reason, talk sensibly about matters of instinct (as Yeats tries throughout *Per Amica*). The fool unwittingly raises the issue in the first stanza; he is intuitively aware of a superior learning reflected in the butterfly's eye, and that he, as a mere fool, is in no position to understand that animal wisdom. In the second stanza he drops his humility to speak with the authority of one who has the answer to the question he had earlier posed. In Yeats's antithetical manner, he has become his opposite, one very much like the schoolmaster whose image he summons before us.

But why propose that the butterfly had been a schoolmaster in a previous existence? Whatever that animal wisdom may be, we suppose that it is instinctive and not learned. Yeats's fool is about to show us how our assumptions are wrong. His proof lies in the following associative chain of reasoning: the initial thought of the butterfly's mysterious learning suggests to the fool the only learning that he has ever known at the hands of a schoolmaster and his frightful birch. In turn, this experience calls to mind the image of a schoolbell, sweet in sound, but harsh in its constant call to face the hated master. The fool then takes this conjunction of opposites as a paradigm for all learning experiences and for that of the butterfly in particular. "Sweet and harsh, harsh and sweet"—through trial and error experiments with many harsh flowers, the butterfly naturally learns what seems to us his instinctive wisdom, namely, to take the sweet "roses for his meat."

Where is the aimless fool of *A Vision*, "a straw blown by the wind, with no mind but the wind" (*AV*(B), 182)? Yeats's wise fool has moved deliberately through both intuition and its opposite, a peculiar attempt at reasoning through images. Once the fool submits to *Per Amica*'s poetic discipline of imagining himself as his opposite, then he can succeed with a problem that neither intuition nor reason alone could solve. The poet submits to the same discipline in creating the wandering, singing fool as *his* opposite. He becomes the Daimon who forces the fool to take up the mask of all that he "most lacks, and it may be dreads" (*Myth*, 335), the logic of the hated schoolmaster, to which the fool joins his native receptivity to the inflowing of images from the *Anima Mundi*. This interchange between sophisticated and simple allows Yeats's poem to revel in the freedom and joy of self-creation through the mask. It is a Yeatsian success story, overcoming inner division and pointing the way to psychic unity.

When Yeats finished *Per Amica*, he immediately perceived its efficacy as a structure for his poetry. He described it to his father as "a system which I hope will interest you as a form of poetry. I find the setting it all in order has helped my verse, has given me new framework and new patterns. One goes on year after year gradually getting the disorder of one's mind in order and this is the real impulse to create" (*L*, 626). *Per Amica* helped Yeats clean house in middle age, putting between two covers all his quarrels with himself and his world. "And yet, and yet," Yeats continued to ask, "Is this my dream or the truth?" (*VP*, 329). Had he articulated but a part of the creative opposition between man and the world soul? Did the theoretical outline of *Per Amica* need to be filled out with evidence of new quarrels drawn not merely from the self, but from reservoirs beyond the inflow of his own buried life? Marriage unleashed a flood of new subconscious material that became *A Vision*, and Yeats once again had to sweep the untidy room.

6

Epilogue: On Reading Yeats
Without *A Vision*

I take as my starting point Harold Bloom's eloquent critique of the book
that so many critics have considered the triumphant summing up of a
career: [1]

> It is possible to read *A Vision* many times over, becoming always more fascinated with it,
> and still to feel that Yeats went very wrong in it, that the book with all its inventiveness
> and eloquence, nevertheless is not adequate to Yeats's own imagination. This feeling
> need not be a reaction against the mere complications of the work. . . . More germane to
> a reader's uneasiness may be a sense that the book is nothing if it is not wisdom
> literature, yet it is sometimes very unwise (210).

Where *Per Amica* for the most part explains itself in terms familiar and
congenial to readers of Yeats's poetry, *A Vision* does not. Yeats himself
acknowledges *Per Amica* as the imaginative starting point for the later work
(*AV*(B), 8), but very soon in *A Vision* the imaginative structure of *Per
Amica*—the poet, his masks, and a supernatural Daimon mediating between
the two—gets lost in the transformation of this predominantly aesthetic relationship into a cosmological and religious one. In *Per Amica*, the Daimon is
a passionate anti-self, intimately involved in every creative act of the poet; in
A Vision, he becomes a figure for a distant godhead, vital to the poet's
system, in fact containing all other categories within his being, but ultimately, just another category, as passionless and undramatized as the rest.
By obscuring his focus on the antithetical Daimon, Yeats loses touch with
the poet's creative quarrels with himself. Though the work has much to teach
us as an imaginative reordering of history, as a poetic theory it finally fails. [2]

    Per Amica succeeds as a poetic theory precisely because its concerns are
so personal to Yeats. In "Anima Hominis," the poet is interested in the
psychology of those types most important for his own *oeuvre*—poet, hero,
and saint. Though his esoteric concerns in "Anima Mundi" often seem
extraneous to the poet when filtered through the archaic language of a
Henry More, there too Yeats deals with the central imaginative problem of

his own visionary poetry, the evocation and ordering of mental images. Given the autobiographical thrust of most of Yeats's previous work in prose and in verse, it is somewhat surprising that *A Vision* should have been conceived as a vast psychological panorama covering the whole of humanity. By comparing Yeats's successive presentations of the Daimon in *Per Amica* and in the two versions of *A Vision*, we can establish an excellent index of how the cosmological emphasis of the later works carried Yeats farther and farther away from his imaginative vision of himself and of his necessary poetic opposites.

The crucial characteristics of the Daimon in *Per Amica* are his individuality, his insatiable drive for power over man's life, and his ability to bestow aesthetic rewards upon the poet. Always the dramatist, Yeats shapes his daimonic speculations into a scenario: The Daimon, in all ways opposite to the individual he singles out, is bound to him with the intensity of a lover, and in fact conspires with the man's sweetheart against him. He will not loosen his controlling grip until he has led his chosen one to perform "the hardest work among those not impossible" (*Myth*, 336). Encountering "that other Will" in the "deep of the mind" (*Myth*, 337), the chosen man must internalize the power and wear the mask of his spirit guide, though these will bring him only disappointment and defeat in the world. He reacts stubbornly to the Daimon's mastery, wishing for the return of his individuality. Meanwhile, the Daimon bears his man's stubbornness as he would a lover's fickleness and forces him "again and again to the place of choice" (*Myth*, 361), where he must become hero, saint, or holy fool in his own poetic world, or else remain just another figure in the casual comedy. When Yeats is in that place of innocence where he makes a new aesthetic personality, he no longer knows "when I am the finger, when the clay" (*Myth*, 366), so completely has he identified with his daimonic opposite. The Daimon may be a figure out of a deterministic mythology, but his ultimate effect in *Per Amica* is the unselfconscious creation of art.

Though man may live in a fallen state, the aesthetic triumph at the end of *Per Amica* represents the poet's remarkable staying power in a confused and divided world. Yeats came to call this achievement of balance "Unity of Being" (*AV*(B), 258), a term that he associates with Dante's image of a "perfectly proportioned human body" (*AV*(B), 291).[3] In the lunar wheel of personality and in its alternating cycles of history, certain men and ages manifest unity of mind and body, thought and desire, but we lose sight of how that magnificent balance of Byzantium or of some figure of the Italian Renaissance is attained.

The 1925 *Vision* is the one place where Yeats attempts an extended elaboration of the concept, based on the idea of *Per Amica* that the Daimon "is in possession of the entire dark of the mind" (*AV*(A), 28). When man rejects that dark subconscious impulse and seeks to live only in the light (a characteristic of the *primary* phases), the Daimon plunges him into darkness, but when the *antithetical* man encourages the dark daimonic mind to express itself in the very events of his life, then light and dark coexist, and man achieves unity: "such men are able to bring all that happens, as well as all that they desire, into an emotional or intellectual synthesis and so to possess not the Vision of Good only but that of Evil" (*A V*(A), 28–29). The 1925 *Vision* preserves *Per Amica*'s interest in aesthetics, interpenetrating consciousnesses, sexual discord and union, and most importantly, the passionate bond between man and Daimon, now seen as being of the opposite sex. When man and woman unite in passion, they reproduce "the relation of man and *Daimon*," and become "an element where man and *Daimon* sport, pursue one another, and do one another good or evil" (*A V*(A), 27). Now located primarily in a metaphysical realm, Daimons contrive to use men as instruments for their own inhuman fulfillment. There is even a mythological creature born out of the union of men and the perfected spirits of Phase 15, "begotten in tragedy" but "brought forth in joy" (*A V*(A), 244).

These moments of mythological fancy shine forth in the midst of prose horribly burdened with the terminology of *Mask, Will, Creative Mind, Body of Fate,* and the even more abstruse *Husk, Passionate Body, Celestial Body* and *Spirit.* Yeats lived with his own invented symbolism for so many years that there is no section of the 1937 *Vision* that escapes this depersonalized rhetoric.

Daimon, the center of Yeats's vision in *Per Amica* and the chief mythological agent in the 1925 book, is reduced to a faded image of its former power and glory, a stage-manager, like Yeats himself, handing out roles and pulling the strings, as in the puppet-like *Commedia dell'Arte*:

> The stage-manager, or *Daimon*, offers his actor an inherited scenario, the *Body of Fate,* and a *Mask* or rôle as unlike as possible to his natural ego or *Will,* and leaves him to improvise through his *Creative Mind* the dialogue and details of the plot. . . . But this is *antithetical* man. For *primary* man I go to the *Commedia dell'Arte* in its decline. The *Will* is weak and cannot create a rôle, and so, if it transform itself, does so after an accepted pattern, some traditional clown or pantaloon. (8)

This is one of the more vivid passages in *A Vision* because it maintains a link to dramatic metaphor. More typically, Yeats describes the Daimon solely from a perspective of cosmic metaphysics. Rather than actively struggling with men and women for fulfillment, the Daimon's dramatic focus lies in interaction with other Daimons who may be able to grant him his ultimate goal, "deliverance from birth and death" (240). Human beings are reduced to reflections in the Daimon's "memory of the events of his past incarnations" (83). The Daimon remembers us into existence, and we go busily about our revolutions on the wheel.

Though his daimonic philosophy lost its imaginative force in the rigid categories of *A Vision*, Yeats's poetry never did, even in the poems based most directly on the system itself. However one evaluates "The Phases of the Moon" and "The Double Vision of Michael Robartes" within Yeats's poetic canon, they are far more compelling than any analogous prose passages in *A Vision*. Yeats claimed to have expressed in their phantasmagoria of images and masks his "convictions about the world" (*VP*, 852), the same phrase he uses to introduce the reveries of *Per Amica*.

"The Phases of the Moon" is certainly one of the most provocative of Yeats's poems, and has been interpreted variously as a doctrinal presentation of the apocalyptic aesthetic of *A Vision* and as either the culmination of the visionary quest initiated in "Ego Dominus Tuus," or as a parody of it.[4] I see the poem as antiphonal to that earlier debate, preserving its setting and its tension between magical and poetic images, but providing us with two new figures of the mage: Michael Robartes who sings the song of the lunar phases, and the poet in his tower assiduously copying down the song to provide a structure for new poems. The revelations themselves are couched in some of the most difficult language in Yeats's poetry, reminding us of the poet's claim in *Per Amica* that he has "delighted in all that displayed great problems through sensuous images or exciting phrases" (*Myth*, 343). The Robartes persona of the poem has so completely internalized his new doctrine that he is unaware of the obscurity of much of his wisdom. Our response to these difficulties is complicated by the fact that in the frame of the poem Yeats smirks at his personae, while in its doctrinal portions, he depends heavily on their occult expertise.

The song of the lunar phases intoned by Robartes and Aherne is the centerpiece around which the system of *A Vision* is built, but Yeats's interest in the phases of the moon antedates the revelations to his wife. Though Yeats was certainly a practicing astrologist, no source, occult or literary, provides as powerful a model as *Per Amica*'s wheel of reincarnations, including both moments of release and cyclic return, the Condition of Fire, and "the wheel where the world is butterfly" (*Myth*, 341). When we consider that the struggle to make permanent artistic form out of the impermanent but recurrent emotions of life has been a primary concern of the poet since his earliest lyrics, then the subject matter of "The Phases of the Moon" seems far less occult in its attempt to mediate between the changes of human life and the cycle that controls them.

To describe his cycle of impulsive, physical life progressively giving way to greater self-consciousness, and then turning, after the full of the moon, to self-absorption in the common dream of humanity, Yeats draws upon contrasts of personality types made in both "Ego Dominus Tuus" and *Per Amica*. The sentimentalists, rhetoricians, and practical men find their places at the end of the wheel serving the world; the saint is allowed a special form of escape, again following the lead of *Per Amica*'s "bowman who aims his arrow at the centre of the sun" (*Myths*, 340); the hero grows out of the phases of those who follow an adventurous dream. Almost every type of personality is characterized by some imagery of mental or physical struggle, reminding us of the role of "the Daimon who would ever set us to the hardest work among those not impossible" (*Myth*, 336), a phrase that Yeats echoes in describing both impulsive and obedient character types (lines 41–42, 91–92). Yeats's task in "Phases" is to articulate a harsh vision of the world, dominated at every point by the daimonic legacy of *Per Amica* that there is no meaningful change without frightful inner struggle.

In *Per Amica*, there is one moment of release into the Condition of Fire. Though there are two non-human incarnations in the poem, neither of them offers release. "The crumbling of the moon" (*VP*, 375) comes to remind the poet that all such hopes for apocalyptic or aesthetic completion are in vain. The perfect images at the full of the moon must avoid all contact with the incompleteness of human life; all they can do in their loneliness is contemplate other such "separate, perfect and immovable/ Images" (*VP*, 375). Their opposites in the dark last phase of the moon are just as helplessly "cast beyond the verge," according to Robartes/Yeats, "crying to one another like the bats" (*VP*, 376).

This final image calls to mind one that Yeats used to describe himself at the conclusion of "Anima Mundi": "I am baffled by those voices that still speak as to Odysseus but as the bats" (*Myth*, 366). Yeats returns to this image of the bafflement of all occult communication at the most esoteric point in his most esoteric poem with a certain degree of mocking, self-referential irony. In the penultimate image of the poem, a bat gyres above the poet's tower, a dark image of Yeats's need for communication with a realm that must inevitably remain impenetrable to all but the true mage.

Only one more image in "Phases of the Moon" need detain us, "the wagon-wheel/ Of beauty's cruelty and wisdom's chatter" (*VP*, 377), because it links the poem to the central concerns of *The Wild Swans at Coole* and *Michael Robartes and the Dancer*. The image has been pinned by a recent critic to the phases on either side of the full moon's perfection, one dominated by body, and the other by mind,[5] but whether or not Yeats intended us to identify specific phases, the emotional resonance of the descriptions of beauty and wisdom directs us to other contemporary poems: "beauty's cruelty" conjures "The Wild Swans at Coole," "Broken Dreams," and "The Living Beauty"; while "wisdom's chatter" suggests "The Dawn," "The Scholars," and "Michael Robartes and the Dancer." In every one of Yeats's important poems of the middle period, he attempts to bring beauty and wisdom to bear upon one another, for without the tempering of these opposites, beauty remains cruelly indifferent to man and wisdom divorces itself from sensuous life.

"The Phases of the Moon" will never be seen as a great poem precisely because its vision of life separates such necessary opposites into separate points on a wheel. The far more successful poem, "The Double Vision of Michael Robartes," goes on to forge out of images of wisdom and beauty a new phantasmagoric unity. Analyzing "The Double Vision" solely as a dramatization of two of the phases of the moon, we cannot help but find it a failure poetically.[6] For all the poem's sacral atmosphere and emphasis on the transcendent image, it is precisely the humanness of the dancer that captivates the Robartes/Yeats persona. We remember Yeats's acknowledgement in *Per Amica* that the poet is by no means a saint and must find a more vital fulfillment. Yeats finds his in "The Double Vision" by incorporating in the poetic revelation both sacred and profane, ideal beauty and sordid pain. The chief agent in this visionary drama is the autonomous image of the dancing girl that restores to the dessicated, abstract world of the inhuman moon a vision of human wholeness.

The poem begins and takes place entirely in "the mind's eye," Yeats's habitual term for locating his visionary poetry in the reader's consciousness. The opening vision is a peculiar achievement, the most vivid portrayal of a negation anywhere in Yeats's work:

> Under blank eyes and fingers never still
> The particular is pounded till it is man.
> When had I my own will?
> O not since life began.
>
> Constrained, arraigned, baffled, bent and unbent
> By these wire-jointed jaws and limbs of wood,
> Themselves obedient,
> Knowing not evil and good;
>
> Obedient to some hidden magical breath.
> They do not even feel, so abstract are they,
> So dead beyond our death,
> Triumph that we obey.

(VP, 382)

Yeats animates this phantasmagoria of inchoate matter by attributing to it an ego, and just as suddenly, he denatures it by switching to objective, third-person reportage. We watch matter struggling to be born only to see it lapse without any will back into the void and the inhuman control of the supernatural.

Robartes's second vision has all the formulaic qualities of traditional allegorical symbolism, but with none of its religiosity or subtlety of hidden meaning. A Sphinx, gazing "upon all things known, all things, unknown," is reduced to an emblem of the "triumph of intellect," while its counterpart, the similarly frozen Buddha, with eyeballs "fixed on all things loved, all things unloved" (*VP*, 383), represents an abstract conception of love. In *A Vision* (B), Yeats calls the one "introspective" and the other "outward-looking" (207), but in the poem, neither is more inward or outward than the other. Occultism seems to have triumphed over poetry.

Yeats chooses a third image to represent the fulfillment attained at the full moon, but the system itself is ironically deflated by the human image of the dancer, the perfect soul become the perfect body. The enraptured dancer is so completely involved in her dance that she compels even Michael Robartes to abandon his systematic manipulation of images and return to an appreciation of the sensuous reality that alone gives life to poetry.

> So she had outdanced thought.
> Body perfection brought,
>
> For what but eye and ear silence the mind
> With the minute particulars of mankind?
> Mind moved yet seemed to stop
> As 'twere a spinning-top.
>
> (*VP*, 383-84)

Like Keats's urn, the dancer has the power to exist in time, and yet to overthrow time. She is that "passing bell" whom "the ringers in the tower have appointed" as a permanent feature of Yeats's broadened poetic consciousness (*Myth*, 332).

The final movement of the poem confirms this diminution of the allegorical, for Sphinx, Buddha, and the dialectic of abstract ideas and images are completely forgotten. Robartes/Yeats has obviously been transported on the wings of his vision of the girl, thrilled to have escaped from the painful abstract unfeelingness of the first tableau. All that matters to him now is expressing the revitalizing "frenzy" (that word associated with both madness and revelation) into which the dancer's image has flung him:

> And yet in flying fling into my meat
> A crazy juice that makes the pulses beat
> As though I had been undone
> By Homer's paragon.
>
> (*VP*, 384)

The startling shift in diction (we feel that we are once again hearing a Yeats poem) reminds us that the poet has been liberated from the constraints of an excessively sacerdotal role. He had presumed to be able to explain the images that came to him from beyond, but the ideal human image of the dancer, breaking out of the systematic context in which he himself had placed her, has excited him in a way that hieratic revelation and exegesis could never do. Now he remembers that he is only a visitor in "the sacred house" of Cormac; his true home is "amid the whirlwinds that beset its threshold" (*Myth*, 333). In his ritualistic conclusion, he humbly expresses his gratitude for the birth of the image and applauds the creative energy it has afforded his song.

Accepting this visionary mantle forces Yeats to confront whatever images appear in the mind's eye, no matter how unsettling. If by chance the imagined images provide a seemingly secure structure for the poet's dreams, as the spreading laurel tree does in "A Prayer for My Daughter," so much the better. But if they threaten the poet with destruction of his own artifice and all the values he holds dear, as does the slouching beast of "The Second Coming," the poet knows that he is nevertheless responsible to the "vast image out of *Spiritus Mundi*" that troubles his sight (*VP*, 402). Juxtaposing these poems in *Michael Robartes and the Dancer* as alternate visions of birth, and repeating in each the key phrases "ceremony" and "innocence," Yeats obviously paired them in his imagination. In both, the private apocalypse of "The Double Vision" is reimagined in new ways; having sought and found suitable mysterious images to satisfy the demands of a personal mythology, the poet turns his contemplative gaze to traditional images which can speak to his whole society. The central lesson of *Per Amica* and its dominating Daimon is that the poetic image does not belong to "Anima Hominis" but to "Anima Mundi." It is therefore the poet's responsibility to shake off the merely personal as he creates and to subordinate self-expression to the claims that the world soul makes upon him: "Surely some revelation is at hand" (*VP*, 402).

As first conceived, each poem was embedded in political and biographical matrices from which it needed to be extricated. It is well-known that "The Second Coming" was begun as a poem about the political situation of Europe in the aftermath of World War I, in particular, the menacing Russian Revolution. The manuscript drafts for "A Prayer for My Daughter" printed by Stallworthy also show that poem's equally private inception. In several finished stanzas that Yeats intended as a conclusion, Yeats asks a grown-up Anne to revisit the scene of his private agony at Coole and allay the old ghost of his heartache:

> Daughter if you be happy and yet grown—
> Say when you are five and twenty—walk alone
> Through Coole Domain and visit for my sake
> The stony edges of the lake,
> Where every year I have counted swans, and cry
> That all is well till all that's there
> Spring sounding on the still air
> And all is sound between the lake and sky.

(41)

Anne is not only his link with an uncertain future, envisioned apocalyptically, but also with the painful childless past, when poems of longing were the only births he could conceive. Yeats writes the poem to exorcise private ghosts, but in the process of that exorcism something new emerges, and the public poetic myth triumphs over the need for self-vindication.

In "A Prayer for My Daughter" Yeats offers us a bifurcating vision of possible paths through life. Following immediately upon "The Second Coming," the poem begins with a vision of "the murderous innocence" in nature, an imaginative extreme that Yeats quickly leaves behind in his search for a truly "radical innocence," a life of the soul that can begin to redeem fallen humanity. The language of the poem is secular, but its intent is fully religious: an offering of the best that humanity has to offer the future. For Yeats, that offering is twofold: an external life of custom and ceremony, of innocence and beauty, and an internal life capable of supreme moments of beatitude and love.

The philosophy that supports the rhetorical and symbolic structure of "A Prayer" is not the cosmic warfare of *A Vision* but rather the internal struggle of the soul to overcome its own petty hatreds and find some imperishable internal bliss. The spiritual climax of the poem is directly dependent on statements in *Per Amica*:

> Considering that, all hatred driven hence,
> The soul recovers radical innocence
> And learns that it is self-delighting,
> Self-appeasing, self-affrighting,
> And that its own sweet will is Heaven's will;
> She can, though every face should scowl
> And every windy quarter howl
> Or every bellows burst, be happy still.

(VP, 405)

The movement of the stanza is typical of Yeats, who at his best always grounds philosophical generalization in biography. When his daughter learns to shut out the world's windy hatred and rely instead on internal powers of receptivity, then she can know and live through Heaven's will, without renouncing (as does the saint) personal happiness. We recall Yeats's climactic reverie in "Anima Mundi" on the "innocence" of the aesthetic partnership between man and Daimon, entered into, Yeats writes, "the moment I cease to hate" (*Myth*, 365). R.P. Blackmur has written that Yeats's "magical philosophy, all the struggle and warfare of the intellect, is precisely what Yeats in this poem *puts out of mind*, in order to imagine his daughter living in innocence and beauty."[7] But it is not put out of mind at all, for Yeats has internalized its lessons and finally found public symbols to teach that wisdom to the widest possible audience.

"A Prayer for My Daughter" is about the recovery of innocence, though even while it is propounding that religious ideal, the poem recognizes the almost insuperable barriers to attaining it. The future belongs only to the sleeping babe who may some day experience the innocence and beauty we are denied. Or does it belong to a rough beast far more powerful than the levelling wind by Yeats's tower, powerful enough to tear our whole world apart? Seen through the oracular aid of the Daimon, the visionary sphinx is itself the image of the Daimon, the supernatural opposite that forces the poet to take up the most difficult possible task: imagining, describing, and predicting the course of his destructive civilization.

The beast is not only the poet's Daimon, but our own. In *Per Amica*, Yeats speaks of the Daimon who comes to an entire nation or culture, creating a new order out of its vaguest desires. Society and Daimon recognize each other as necessary opposites, and daimonic history becomes a part of human history. In "The Second Coming," Yeats dramatizes this mutual recognition in two ways. In the opening stanza he presents a generalized vision in which the modern world sees its own chaotic tendencies embodied. Immediately upon finding ourselves in the visionary trajectory of "the widening gyre," Yeats enacts his private moment of daimonic recognition for us, so that as he sees the all-powerful image of the beast for the first time, it is also born for us. This doubling was singled out in manuscript with the phrase "The Second Birth" (Stallworthy, 20, 22), a metaphor far closer than the religious one to the process of Yeats's imagination in the poem. He is both the mother of the vision and its midwife, allowing the seed from the *Anima Mundi* to be set growing and then delivering it as a completed image with prophetic significance for our world.

A world whose moral center has collapsed needs a powerful counter-force to infuse its history with new purpose. The sphinx bears the secret of a future that we ourselves must unriddle. Yeats intimates that the beast will initiate a new societal, and perhaps, cosmic unity by drawing the analogy with the birth of Christ and what it initiated. The opening stanza presents a disintegrating vision of A.D. 1919 without any interpretive historical comment, but by the end of the poem there can be no doubt that the dissolution is the direct consequence of twenty nightmarish centuries of Christian history. Although in his vision of the new Messiah, Yeats avoids stating the consequences of this new birth, he does give us one remarkably evocative detail that is far more than merely scenic. The ominous desert birds, understandably indignant at having their massive perch so suddenly disrupted, represent but a small fragment of all that is to be overturned as the unknown creature makes its way to our impotent civilization.

The future course of that civilization was described by Yeats in a burdensome three-page note to the poem, dropped in subsequent printings. Apparently, Yeats came to perceive that a full technical understanding of the

interlocking gyres, constantly spinning in relation to each other's movements, strangled the poem. The predictive historical model of *A Vision*
claims the ability to dissect that circumscribed future. Yeats is far more
honest about his limitations in the poem. The final words of the vision, "The
darkness drops again" (*VP*, 402), make clear its inadequacy as prophetic
history. But as poetry, that darkness is essential to its power. What would
"The Second Coming" have been with a third stanza illuminating that
uncertain darkness? Just one more paragraph in the historical mythology of
"Dove or Swan."

Yeatsian history is not truly dialectical, since there is no progress: only
reversals, ebb and flow. "The widening gyre" that symbolizes this pattern is
itself a recapitulation of an earlier Yeatsian reversal, the image of the wild
swans "wheeling in great broken rings" away from the poet who would keep
them still for himself. That poem eventually gave way to an opposite gesture
of liberation, as does "The Second Coming." The rough beast slouching
toward Bethlehem is replaced in our consciousness by a similarly unknown
opposite, the future of Yeats's sleeping babe. As the child's soul grows
toward a "radical innocence" of its own, it too becomes a daimonic image
mediating between our world and an unseen, unknowable ideal. At the
beginning of the next phase of his career, Yeats sums up the knowledge he
has gained in a half a lifetime's exploration and partnership with that unseen
opposite:

> The abstract joy,
> The half-read wisdom of daemonic images
> Suffice the ageing man as once the growing boy.
>
> (*VP*, 427)

Yeats is responsible for interpreting "the half-read wisdom" of the daimonic
images he has envisioned, but only that half accessible to human understanding. Though he may have envisioned the impending destruction of his
civilization, the poet remains radically innocent. The vision comes to him as
Heaven's will, sent by its messenger, the immemorial Daimon. As the
shadow of Yeats's times darkened his life, the Daimon drew Yeats deeper
into "the desolation of reality" (*VP*, 563). In assessing his contribution to our
culture, we must also remember the "radical innocence" of Yeats's first years
courting his daimonic Muse, when the dark grew luminous and the void
fruitful.

Appendix

Poems Added for *The Wild Swans at Coole*, Macmillan, 1919.

In Memory of Major Robert Gregory
An Irish Airman Foresees His Death
Under the Round Tower
Solomon to Sheba
The Living Beauty
A Song
To a Young Beauty
To a Young Girl
Tom O'Roughley
Shepherd and Goatherd
A Prayer on Going into My House
The Phases of the Moon
The Cat and the Moon
The Saint and the Hunchback
Two Songs of a Fool
Another Song of a Fool
The Double Vision of Michael Robartes

WSC II—published March 11, 1919.

Notes

Introduction

1. T.S. Eliot, "The Poetry of W.B. Yeats," in *The Permanence of Yeats*, eds. James Hall and Martin Steinmann, 300.

2. Richard Ellmann, *Yeats: The Man and the Masks*, 220; hereafter *Man and Masks*.

3. Harold Bloom, *Yeats*, 198.

4. See Morton Irving Seiden, *William Butler Yeats: The Poet as Mythmaker*, 68–72; Peter Ure, *Yeats, The Playwright: A Commentary on Character and Design in the Major Plays*, 86–89; for more directed summaries, see B.L. Reid, *William Butler Yeats: The Lyric of Tragedy*, 78–88; Leonard E. Nathan, *The Tragic Drama of W. B. Yeats: Figures in a Dance*, 161–64.

5. Robert Langbaum, *The Mysteries of Identity: A Theme in Modern Literature*, 162; Langbaum summarizes his thesis in his chapter title, "Exteriority of Self."

6. Lawrence Lipking, *The Life of the Poet: Beginning and Ending Poetic Careers*, 15–20.

7. I date the middle period from the publication of Yeats's *Collected Works* in 1908 to *Michael Robartes and the Dancer* and *Four Plays for Dancers* (both 1921), when Yeats entered a new phase in beginning to annotate his poetry with material from the drafts of *A Vision*. For the dates of composition I have relied primarily on Richard Ellmann, *The Identity of Yeats*, 2nd ed. (hereafter *Identity*); A.N. Jeffares, *A Commentary on the Collected Poems of W.B. Yeats* (hereafter *Commentary*); and A.N. Jeffares and A.S. Knowland, *A Commentary on the Collected Plays of W.B. Yeats*.

Chapter 1

1. For a discussion of the reintroduction of the Robartes mythology from 1915 to 1925, see Michael Sidnell, "Mr. Yeats, Michael Robartes and Their Circle," in *Yeats and the Occult*, ed. George Mills Harper, 225–54.

2. Langbaum, 163, characterizes the poem's speakers as "Hic, the poet Yeats started out as, and Ille, the poet he was in the process of becoming."

3. Yeats had received an otherworldly revelation several months before writing "Ego Dominus Tuus," but he was ambivalent about its authenticity; see my discussion of the Leo Africanus episode below. The original placement of the poem in *The Wild Swans at Coole* (1917), was just before *At the Hawk's Well*, a much bleaker statement about visionary revelation.

4. Bloom, 197, 204, has best emphasized the poem's striking doctrinal qualities.

5. A.N. Jeffares, *The Circus Animals: Essays on W.B. Yeats*, 4, cites these lines as the earliest poetic formulation of the mask.

6. Virginia Moore, *The Unicorn: William Butler Yeats's Search for Reality*, 146.

7. Warwick Gould, "'Lionel Johnson Comes the First to Mind': Sources for Owen Aherne," in *Yeats and the Occult*, 284, points out the correspondence between the occult stories of the nineties and *Per Amica*'s discussion of the mask.

8. The quoted phrases are from a lecture by Paul Verlaine, reported by Yeats earlier in "Discoveries," where he describes the French poet as one who delighted in "singing his own life" (*E&I*, 270–71).

9. Yeats notes this change in several prefaces around 1904–05. He writes of "a change that may bring a less dream-burdened will into my verses," and of "the search for more of manful energy" in his plays (*VP*, 814, 849).

10. Some months earlier (in February 1908), Yeats's friend, the designer Gordon Craig, began publishing *The Mask*, a theatrical journal. The first issue included "The Actor and the Übermarionette," a theoretical essay by Craig that stressed the need for actors to wear masks so as not to be affected by personal emotions. On Craig's influence on Yeats's dramatic practice, see James W. Flannery, "W.B. Yeats, Gordon Craig and the Visual Arts of the Theatre," in *Yeats and the Theatre*, ed. Robert O'Driscoll and Lorna Reynolds, 82–108; and Karen Dorn, "Dialogue into Movement: W.B. Yeats's Theatre Collaboration with Gordon Craig," 109–36.

11. Robert O'Driscoll, "Yeats on Personality: Three Unpublished Lectures," in *Yeats and the Theatre*, 32. O'Driscoll (5) lists some of the distinguished members of Yeats's audience, representatives of two generations of revolt against Victorianism: George Bernard Shaw and Edmund Gosse from the nineties, and Ezra Pound and W.C. Williams from the emerging modernist camp.

12. *Uncollected Prose* by W.B. Yeats, ed. J.P. Frayne and Colton Johnson, II, 413.

13. See "The Later Yeats," *The Literary Essays of Ezra Pound*, ed. T.S. Eliot, 378–81; hereafter *Literary Essays*.

14. "Extracts from an MS Book given Yeats by Maud Gonne, Christmas, 1912," TS, 10, 13–14; hereafter "Extracts." All references to Yeats typescript material, by permission of Michael and Anne Yeats, are to the Curtis Bradford transcriptions, catalogued in James Lovic Allen and M.M. Liberman, "Transcriptions of Yeats's Unpublished Papers in the Bradford Papers at Grinnell College," *Serif*, 10, (Spring 1973), 13–27. The full text of Yeats's later essay on this medium is in George Mills Harper and John S. Kelly, "Preliminary Examination of the Script of E[lizabeth] R[adcliffe]," in *Yeats and the Occult*, 130–71. The editors comment (165n.) that Pound seems to have read and corrected Yeats's manuscript. Yeats's use of the Homeric blood sacrifice here is closely echoed several years later in Pound's Canto I.

15. G.M. Harper, "'A Subject of Investigation': Miracle at Mirabeau," in *Yeats and the Occult*, 187. Harper has connected this prose paragraph with "The Fisherman," completed in June 1914 (187, n. 8). Though the poem also celebrates a double, its setting is at odds with Yeats's summary of this prose subject: "I too had my conception of the Divine Man, and a few days before had schemed out a poem, praying that somewhere upon some seashore or upon some mountain I should meet face to face with that divine image of

myself" (187). A year and a half later, Yeats makes this same prayer on "the wet sands" in the final stanza of "Ego Dominus Tuus."

16. For a summary of the episode, see Arnold Goldman, "Yeats, Spiritualism, and Psychical Research," in *Yeats and the Occult*, 115–21. On the question of religious faith and supernatural experience, see James L. Allen, "Belief Versus Faith in the Credo of Yeats," *Journal of Modern Literature*, 4 (1975), 692–716, and my own discussion of "Anima Hominis" V in Chapter 2. For Yeats's borrowings from himself, see *Ex*, 34–37 and "An Exchange of Letters with Leo Africanus," TS, 27–31 (hereafter "Leo Africanus"); *L*, 588 and "Leo Africanus," TS, 22.

17. "Leo Africanus," TS, 11, 25, as corrected by George Mills Harper, in correspondence with the author.

18. *Passages from the Letters of John Butler Yeats*, ed. Ezra Pound, 24; hereafter *Passages*.

19. J.B. Yeats, *Letters to His Son W.B. Yeats and Others, 1869–1922*, ed. Joseph Hone, 187; hereafter *Letters to His Son*.

20. Although Leo had appeared several times before (on May 9, 1912, for the first time), the exchange of letters did not take place until August 1915. See "Leo Africanus," TS, 8, 24.

21. "Extracts," TS, 51. This passage became part of "Lines Written in Dejection" (*VP*, 343). Pages 52–57 of this MS book contain the final working drafts of "Ego Dominus Tuus," dated December 5, 1915. An earlier untitled version exists, dated October 5, 1915, on note sheets, Nos. 1–12, MS. 13,587 in the National Library of Ireland, printed with some errors of transcription in Mary C. Flannery, *Yeats and Magic: The Earlier Works*, 129–36. Flannery dates this draft 1912, but presents no valid corroborating evidence; Richard Ellmann, *Identity*, 290, dates the poem October 5, 1915.

22. Richard Ellmann, *Eminent Domain: Yeats among Wilde, Joyce, Pound, Eliot, and Auden*, 71 and 139n., gives Mrs. Yeats as a source for Pound's witticism; for Pound's attitude to Yeats at this time, see 61–71.

23. *Shelley's Prose, Or The Trumpet of a Prophecy*, ed. David Lee Clark, 170.

24. For an excellent discussion of Yeats's attitude toward Wordsworth at this period, see Hugh Kenner, "The Sacred Book of the Arts," *Irish Writing*, No. 31 (Summer 1955), 33–34.

25. For a useful summary of Yeats's relationship to Dante, see George Bornstein, "Yeats's Romantic Dante," *Colby Library Quarterly* 15 (1979), 93–113.

26. Brian John, "'To Hunger Fiercely After Truth': Daimonic Man and Yeats's Insatiable Appetite," *Eire*, 9 (1974), 98.

27. "The Hero as Poet," *The Works of Thomas Carlyle*, ed. H.D. Traill, Centenary ed., V, 86. Though Yeats disliked Carlyle (*L*, 608), we should not be surprised at the borrowing since Yeats himself acknowledged the pervasive effect that Carlyle had on self-educated men in the 1880's, when Yeats first encountered Dante's poetry (*AU*, 214).

28. Giorgio Melchiori, "Yeats and Dante," *English Miscellany*, quotes *Paradiso*, xvii. 58–60.

29. Keats to Benjamin Bailey, November 22, 1817, No. 43, in *The Letters of John Keats, 1814–1821*, ed. Hyder E. Rollins, I, 185. Cf. *Paradise Lost*, 8.460–90, and Yeats's similar phrase in his "J.M. Synge and the Ireland of His Time": "The imaginative writer shows us the world . . . as we were Adam and this the first morning" (*E &I*, 339).

30. Brian John, "Yeats and Carlyle," *N&Q*, n.s. 17 (1970), 455.

31. The first published mention of the term to become so central in the later Yeats is in a letter to JBY, October 17, 1918 (*L*, 653). It probably derives from Mrs. Yeats's automatic script, where it occurs frequently in the material that was to become *A Vision*. In *Au* (190), Yeats attributes the term to his father. For the role of "unity of being" in *AV*, see Chapter 6.

Chapter 2

1. G.C. Spivak, "Finding Feminist Readings: Dante-Yeats," *Social Text: Theory, Culture, and Ideology*, 3 (1980), 84.

2. A.E. Waite, *The Pictorial Key to the Tarot*, 140; G.V. Downes, "W.B. Yeats and the Tarot," in *The World of W.B. Yeats*, ed. Robin Skelton and Ann Saddlemeyer, 52, identifies Waite as a member of Yeats's Order of the Golden Dawn.

3. T.R. Whitaker, *Swan and Shadow: Yeats's Dialogue with History*, 302, n.22, points to a recorded conversation of Yeats's in 1916, in which he discussed "Freud and Jung and the Subconscious Self, applying the doctrine to art." For more on Yeats's relation to Freud, see below my discussion of "*Anima Hominis*" XII.

4. J.H. Miller, *Poets of Reality: Six Twentieth Century Writers*, 73, uses this as an example of Yeats's successful embodiment of abstract ideas in concrete images.

5. Quotations from the sections of *Per Amica* under discussion will not be paginated.

6. See letters written by Yeats to Lady Gregory during the summer of 1917, *L*, 628–32: "Iseult has always been something like a daughter to me and so I am less upset than I might have been" (63), hardly the rationalization of a passionate lover.

7. M.A. Lofaro, "The Mask with No Eyes: Yeats's Vision in *Per Amica Silentia Lunae*," *Style*, 10 (1976), 60–61, n.4, sees the final paragraph as a digression from the main thrust of Yeats's reverie, failing to take into account the formative role of allusion and quotation in Yeats's discourse.

8. Walter Pater, *Marius, The Epicurean, His Sensations and Ideas*, 2 vols, I, 148; hereafter *Marius*.

9. In 1922, Yeats ascribes both praise and blame to Pater's *Marius* (*Au*, 302–33).

10. Louis MacNeice, *The Poetry of W.B. Yeats*, 115.

11. "The Dark Interpreter," *The Posthumous Writings of Thomas DeQuincey*, ed. A.H. Japp, 2 vols., I, 12. The essay was originally intended for *Suspiria de Profundis*. See below my discussion of "Anima Hominis" VIII.

12. *Blake: Complete Writings*, ed. Geoffrey Keynes, 184.

13. Simeon Solomon, *A Vision of Love Revealed in Sleep*, 8.

14. George Moore, *Vale*, 166.

15. "The Poet and the Actress" TS, 7. Yeats was here developing a phrase from his 1909 Journal (*Mem*, 157).

16. David S. Thatcher, *Nietzsche in England: The Growth of a Reputation*, 161–63.

17. Walter Pater, *The Renaissance: Studies in Art and Poetry*, 190.

18. "Houses of Commons & Houses of Lords . . . seem to me to be something else besides Human Life," *Complete Writings*, 600.

19. The chief secondary sources for the summary that follows are Angus Fletcher, *Allegory: The Theory of a Symbolic Mode*; E.R. Dodds, *The Greeks and the Irrational;* Rudolph Otto, *The Idea of the Holy*, trans. J.W. Harvey.

    Yeats gives a bibliography of his own primary sources in "Swedenborg, Mediums, and the Desolate Places" (*Ex*, 61), but he makes clear that he knew the ancients primarily through the seventeenth century Platonists. Henry More, *The Immortality of the Soul*, treats the souls of departed men as daemons, Books II and III; Ralph Cudworth, *The True Intellectual System of the Universe*, 4 vols., ed. Thomas Birch, is a compendium of ancient traditions. On the daemon or demon, see I, 465; II, 228, 271, 306-8, 496, 526, 539; III, 360; IV, 35.

    Other principal ancient sources that might have been known to Yeats are as follows: the pre-Socratics, particularly Heraclitus and Empedocles in John Burnet, *Early Greek Philosophy*, a book that Yeats certainly knew in the 1930s, since he refers to it in *A V*(B), 67; Plato, *Phaedo, Timaeus, Symposium*, and *Republic* (relevant passages noted below); Plotinus, *Ennead*, III, iv, though he did not come to know this work in detail until after 1917 when Stephen MacKenna's translation began appearing; Plutarch, as a summarizer of Platonic and neo-Platonic traditions, in "On the Cessation of Oracles," and "A Discourse Concerning the Daemon of Socrates." The latter is definitely described in the Swedenborg essay (*Ex*, 56), in "Anima Hominis" VII, and in "Extracts," TS, I. In an entry dated July 21 [1913], he notes the similarity between Plutarch's description of the daimon and "spiritist guides," and marks down page references to a seventeenth-century translation, Plutarch's *Morals* (Philemon [Holland], 1657), 995, though Bradford, in a marginal annotation, notes that he found the quotation on 1221-22.

    On the daimon in Romantic poetry, see J.B. Beer, *Coleridge, The Visionary*, Ch. 4; Neville Rogers, *Shelley at Work: A Critical Inquiry*, Ch. 5; Charles Patterson, *The Daemonic in the Poetry of Keats*, Ch. I.

    On Yeats's daimonic tradition, see Bloom, 232; Langbaum, 161-65; James Olney, "Sex and the Dead: Daimones of Yeats and Jung", *Studies in the Literary Imagination*, 14 (1981), 43-60; F.A.C. Wilson, *W.B. Yeats and Tradition* (London: Gollancz, 1958), 244-45. Langbaum and Wilson concentrate on Plutarch and Blake as analogues, Olney on the pre-Socratics and Plato, and Bloom on the Shelleyan epipsyche and various muse figures in Keats.

20. *Agamemnon*, I, 1475ff; *Aeschylus*, Loeb Classical Library, II, 131-33.

21. *Plato*, Loeb Classical Library, V, 179.

22. The fascinating theory of Julian Jaynes, *The Origin of Consciousness in the Breakdown of the Bicameral Mind*, suggests that the Daimon may have become an especially useful concept in the sixth and fifth centuries B.C., when the majority of men were no longer hearing god-voices from the right hemisphere of the brain, but remained receptive to that earlier form of internalized external control.

23. The Romantic poets got much of their daimonic lore from Thomas Taylor who followed the neo-Platonists in stressing the allegorical uses of the daimon; for his influential reading of the *Odyssey*, see *Thomas Taylor, The Platonist: Selected Writings*, ed. Kathleen Raine and G.M. Harper, 321-42.

24. In August 1913, Yeats describes a similar "breath" or "shiver" in response to his call during a seance to a private daimon, Petre the Malachite, "Extracts," TS, 18.

25. *The Oxford Book of Modern Verse*, Chosen by W.B. Yeats, xxx. Frank Kermode,

Romantic Image, 61-63, sees Pater's image of the Mona Lisa owing much to Rossetti and the tradition of the *femme fatale*, to which Yeats links his Daimon in Section VIII.

26. "On the Cessation of Oracles," *Complete Works*, I, 441; F.A.C. Wilson, p. 245, overlooks this passage in describing Yeats's borrowings from Plutarch, though he is generally correct in noting the way in which Yeats separates himself from the idealized daimon in Plutarch and Platonism.

27. Helen Vendler, *Yeats's VISION and the Later Plays*, 10-11, has made a cogent case for seeing the daimon as the Muse (Maud Gonne) joined "with the *femme fatale* of the 1890's"; for useful exegeses of Section VIII in spiritual and psycho-sexual terms, see Bernard Levine, *The Dissolving Image: The Spiritual-Esthetic Development of W.B. Yeats*, 70; and Seiden (See Introduction, n.4), 69.

28. *Confessions of an English Opium Eater*, with introductory note by William Sharp, 108; Yeats acquired this edition in 1887, and it remains in the possession of Anne Yeats. For evidence that Yeats read and echoed DeQuincey, see Stuart Peterfreund, "'The Second Coming' and *Suspiria de Profundis*: Some Affinities," *AN&Q*, 15 (1976) 40-43.

29. For a discussion of Yeats's intention here, see James Olney, *The Rhizome and the Flower: The Perennial Philosophy—Yeats and Jung*, 118; hereafter *Rhizome*.

30. On the background of "phantasmagoria" as an imaginative confrontation with reality, especially in crisis situations, see Ian Bell, "The Phantasmagoria of Ezra Pound," *Paideuma*, 5 (1976), 361-86.

31. Joseph Ronsley, "Yeats's Lecture Notes for 'Friends of My Youth,'" in *Yeats and the Theatre*, 69.

32. Edwin Ellis, "Himself," *Fate in Arcadia*, 158-63; Arthur Symons, "The Obscure Night of the Soul," *Poems*, 2 vols., I, 188-89.

33. *Egoist*, 5 (June-July 1918), 87.

34. Ezra Pound, *Translations*, 287; in 1917 Yeats based his own ghost play, *The Dreaming of the Bones*, on the tragic story of the lovers, for which see my Chapter 4.

35. G.M. Harper, *Yeats's Golden Dawn*; Appendix K, "Is the Order of R.R. & A.C. to Remain a Magical Order?," 261.

36. Honoré de Balzac, *Edition Définitive of the Comédie Humaine*, trans. George Burnham Ives et al., XLII, 292.

37. William H. O'Donnell, "Yeats as Adept and Artist: *The Speckled Bird, The Secret Rose*, and *The Wind Among the Reeds*," in *Yeats and the Occult*, 60.

38. Yeats connects this passage to the later work (*AV*(B) 9), and echoes it in the description of the Great Wheel as "every completed movement of thought or life," (*AV*(B) 81).

39. Whitaker, 28-33, connects Yeats's cyclical model with Blake, Balzac, Heine, Emerson, Carlyle, Hallam, Pater, Ibsen, and the historians J.W. Draper and J.S. Stuart-Glennie; Donald Pearce, "Philosophy and Phantasy: Notes on the Growth of Yeats's 'System,'" *University of Kansas City Review*, 18 (1952), 169-80, traces the development of the historical myth through Yeatsian images of Rose and stone.

40. See below my discussion of "Anima Mundi" XI.

41. Langbaum, 158, has taken this image to mean "the pattern where the world is soul, suggesting that our identity is not single but many-layered, that we have lived many lives,"

basing his interpretation of Yeats's "stream of souls" (*Ex*, 397) in "Introduction to *The Resurrection*" (1934).

42.   *The Gay Science*, trans. Walter Kaufmann, 133.

43.   Ernest Dowson and Oscar Wilde died in 1900, Lionel Johnson in 1902, John Davidson and John Synge in 1909; only Arthur Symons survived with Yeats well into the twentieth century.

Chapter 3

1.   See John Vickery, *The Literary Impact of the Golden Bough*, Ch. 6.

2.   "Ezra Pound: Letters to William Butler Yeats," ed. C.F. Terrell, *Antaeus*, No. 21/22 (1976), 34. Pound also comments on this book of the *Odyssey* in "The Constant Preaching to the Mob" (1916), in *Literary Essays*, 65, from which Yeats quotes a phrase on "The Seafarer" in "*Anima Hominis*" VIII.

3.   G.R.S. Mead, *Quests Old and New*, 229.

4.   Yeats associated Mathers with Goethe's ageless Faust (*Au*, 187). On Yeats's influential reading of Goethe, see Marjorie Perloff, "Yeats and Goethe," *Comparative Literature*, 23 (1971), 125-40.

5.   By implying a succeeding great influence, Yeats probably meant his reading of Nietzsche in 1902.

6.   For a characterization of Jung's hesitancy versus Yeats's ardency in belief, see Olney, *Rhizome*, 229-33.

7.   George Bornstein, *Transformations of Romanticism in Yeats, Eliot, and Stevens*, 44.

8.   Cleanth Brooks, "Yeats: The Poet as Myth-Maker," in *The Permanence of Yeats*, 75, compares this bird to the golden bird of "Sailing to Byzantium." A personification of the phoenix in human terms can be found in "The Tree of Life" (1906), *E&I*, 272.

9.   Yeats quotes similar versions of this sentence at least three other times: "Swedenborg . . . ," *Ex*, 37; "Leo Africanus," TS, 40; and *On The Boiler* (1939), *Ex*, 449. In two of these instances, he mentions Villiers de l'Isle-Adam as the source.

10.   Yeats was ambivalent about this duality, as can be seen in the Leo Africanus episode, where he initially wanted to reject Leo's braggadocio manner for having obscured his childhood memory of the "faint voice" of a supernatural being near him (TS, 14). The spirit's characteristic "faint voice" recurs in Section IV.

11.   Yeats narrates the same incident of a voice speaking of God's love at least four other times: *The Celtic Twilight, Myth*, 68; *The Speckled Bird*, ed. William H. O'Donnell, I, 48; *Mem*, 126; and *Au*, 378-79.

12.   Basil Willey, *The Seventeenth Century Background: Studies in the Thought of the Age in Relation to Poetry and Religion*, 163-64.

13.   Samuel Taylor Coleridge, *Biographia Literaria*, ed. John T. Shawcross, I, 202.

14.   Yeats draws upon the Swedenborg essay for many of his assumptions and examples, as well as upon an exposition of Henry More's positions in even greater detail in "Leo Africanus," TS, 32-34; see especially More, 172-73, 190.

15. "A Treatise on Morals," *Shelley's Prose*, 183, 193. In earlier editions, these passages were printed under the heading, "Speculations on Metaphysics."

16. Langbaum, 173, argues that this represents a new conception of identity in the Western world, but Yeats could have found very similar sentiments in Pater's *Marius*:

    And might not the intellectual frame also, still more intimately himself as in truth it was, after the analogy of the bodily life, be a moment only, an impulse or series of impulses, a single process, in an intellectual or spiritual system external to it, diffused through all time and place—that great stream of spiritual energy, of which his own imperfect thoughts, yesterday or to-day, would be but the remote, and therefore imperfect pulsations? (II, 68-69).

17. F.A.C. Wilson, *Yeats's Iconography*, 97; hereafter *Iconography*.

18. Yeats referred to Sturge Moore's poetry in 1910 as "some beautiful water plant sowing and resowing itself in the stillness of his mind. . . . One feels that his mind is moved by thoughts and instincts and metaphors that think in him and not he in them." (Ronsley, in *Yeats and the Theatre*, 78-79). The connection with the transmigrating thought of "Anima Mundi" is clear.

19. Jacob Boehme, *Six Theosophic Points and Other Writings*, 148.

20. Jon Stallworthy, *Between The Lines: Yeats's Poetry in the Making*, 127, 130.

21. Harper and Kelly, in *Yeats and the Occult*, 159.

22. The original version was more explicit about their permanence: "But, kindly old rout/ Of the fire-born moods,/ You pass not away" (*VP*, 142).

23. The same events are recorded in "Extracts," TS, 22, after Sept. 16, 1913, where the woman is identified as Maud Gonne; on prevision, see "Leo Africanus," TS, 26.

24. The theory also exists in embryo in *The Speckled Bird*, II, 36.

25. Yeats indulges here in speculative ancient history. Pericles, the illegitimate son of Aspasia and the famed orator Pericles, was not "brief-lived," but lived to hold the generalship of Athens in 406 B.C., when he was executed for his part in the loss of the fleet in the battle of Arginusae.

26. In the first edition of *Per Amica* (1918), Yeats substituted "live" for "move" in the second line of the quotation from Shelley: "live there/ And move like winds of light on dark and stormy air." Bloom (188-89) has argued that Yeats purposely distorts the quotation to make Shelley assert Yeats's own claim for the soul's survival after death, rather than the Shelleyan interest in the dead man's survival in the poet's heart. Yeats, however, had summarized Shelley's intention in "The Pathway" (1900-08) in *Collected Works in Prose and Verse of William Butler Yeats*, VIII, 187: "those who die move through the minds of living men, as Shelley believed." The textual error was silently corrected in the second edition of *Per Amica* in *Essays*, 528.

27. Yeats used Ben Jonson's phrase again in a draft of "The Gift of Haroun Al-Rashid" (1923); see Stallworthy, 76.

28. Vendler, 152, notes the source. The phrase also appears in the first draft of "A Meditation in Time of War," circa. November 1914, in "Extracts," TS, 45.

29. Thatcher, 148; the annotated passage is from *Nietzsche as Critic, Philosopher, Poet, and Prophet*, ed. Thomas Common, 126. Nietzsche extends the argument to include Christ as subverter of classical values in *The Genealogy of Morals*, "First Essay," Sec. 7-8, a book that Yeats owned (Thatcher, 143).

30. See *L*, 581–84, July 22 & August 5, 1913.

31. For prose antecedents of Section XVIII, see *Ex*, 40–41, 51–56, and "Leo Africanus," TS, 31, 36–38.

32. Yeats describes Blake's view of Reason and Will in his interpretive chapter, "The Necessity of Symbolism," in *The Works of William Blake, Poetic, Symbolic, and Critical*, eds., Edwin J. Ellis and W.B. Yeats, I, 240.

33. For a potential source for this image, see Boehme, 149.

34. Vendler, 28, suggests that it results from the free, aesthetic experience of reading poetry.

35. For a fuller view of Yeats's attitude to Carlyle and Swinburne in this period, see *L*, 608; "the rhetoric of Swinburne" is a phrase repeated from "Art and Ideas" (1913; *E&I*, 351), an opinion Yeats claims to have gotten from William Morris (*Au*, 145).

36. Yeats used the same account in at least four other places: *The Speckled Bird*, I, 44; "Leo Africanus," TS, 26; *Au*, 379; and *AV*(B), 233. Compare the more humble divine communication in "Anima Mundi" V, *Myth*, 347–48.

37. "Epilogue," TS, 2, catalogued in Allen and Liberman (see Chapter 1, n. 14), 16. The parable is reminiscent of Plate V in Blake's *The Marriage of Heaven and Hell* which, viewed right side up, shows Satan falling from the top of the picture into the fires of hell, but when reversed in Blake's antithetical way, shows him in glory, standing with a fiery halo around his head; *The Illuminated Blake*, ed. D.V. Erdman, 102.

38. "Crisis in Poetry" (1886–95) in Stéphane Mallarmé, *Selected Prose Poems, Essays, and Letters*, trans. Bradford Cook, 34–43.

39. Cf. *The Speckled Bird*, II, 5, and *Au*, 347, where Yeats retells some of these same stories.

40. Arthur Rimbaud, "Une Saison en Enfer" (1872), *Oeuvres*, ed. Paterne Berrichon, 268.

41. *Axel*, trans. M.G. Rose, 126, 170. Yeats quotes the line from *Axel* (written 1872, publ. 1890, trans. 1925 with preface by W.B. Yeats) in at least four other places, twice in connection with Lionel Johnson. Compare the prefatory lines to *The Secret Rose* (1897), *Myth*, 144; "The Holy Places" (1906), *E&I*, 296; "Lionel Johnson" (1900–08), *Collected Works* (1908), VIII, 187; and "The Tragic Generation" (1922), *Au* 305.

42. After *Per Amica*, Yeats's concerns turned increasingly toward the political ideal of unity of culture. In "If I Were Four-and-Twenty" (1919), where he considers these same French poets to whom Iseult had introduced him, he highly appreciates them as "men in whom an intellectual patriotism is not distinct from religion" (*Ex*, 264–65), a conjunction of values he recommends to Ireland. For a fuller discussion, see Daphne Fullwood, "The Influence on W.B. Yeats of Some French Poets (Mallarmé, Verlaine, Claudel)," *Southern Review*, 6, N.S. (1970), 356–79.

Chapter 4

1. Curtis B. Bradford, *Yeats at Work* (Carbondale: Southern Illinois Univ. Press, 1965), 171.

2. See Bradford, 181, for the sentence quoted above from Yeats's *Autobiographies*; Vendler, 178. The reference to Coole Lake can also be found in the drafts of "A Prayer for My Daughter," in Stallworthy, 38–42.

3. Nathan (See Introduction, n.4), 161–65, laid the groundwork for reading these plays in terms of the ideology, if not the psychology of *Per Amica*.

4. "Decorative Plays," rev. of *Four Plays for Dancers, Literary Review*, 2 (1922), 465.

5. Bloom, 296; for autobiographical readings of the play, see also Ellmann, *Man and Masks*, 215-16; Wilson, *Iconography*, 69-70.

6. Barton R. Friedman, "*On Baile's Strand* to *At the Hawk's Well*: Staging the Deeps of the Mind," *JML*, 4 (1975), 634.

7. *Masks of Love and Death*: *Yeats as Dramatist*, 207, 204.

8. Between September 1909 and March 1910. See *Mem*, 230, 233, 243.

9. Joesph Hone, *W.B. Yeats 1865-1939*, 2nd ed., 304.

10. Wilson, *Iconography*, 212; Vendler, 188; and Bloom, 308 all ask us to dismiss or minimize the political concerns of the play. David R. Clark, "Yeats, Theatre, and Nationalism," in *Theatre and Nationalism in Twentieth-Century Ireland*, ed. Robert O'Driscoll, 149-55, provides the best political view of the play.

11. Akhtar Qamber, *Yeats and the Noh*, 63, mentions forgiveness as the norm in Noh drama.

12. Nathan, 235, associates this passage with the confrontation of Emer and Bricriu.

13. Wilson, *Iconography*, 122; Vendler, 218; Bloom, 301.

14. Richard Taylor, *W.B. Yeats*: *Irish Myth and Japanese Nō*, 147.

15. The final lyric from *At the Hawk's Well* was initially printed as "The Well and the Tree" in *Responsibilities and Other Poems* (1916); all the lyrics from *The Dreaming of the Bones* and *The Only Jealousy of Emer* were included in *Selected Poems* (1929); see *VP*, 780-86.

Chapter 5

1. William H. Pritchard, "The Uses of Yeats's Poetry," in *Twentieth Century Literature in Retrospect*, ed. Reuben A. Brower, 119.

2. Denis Donoghue, "The Human Image in Yeats," in *William Butler Yeats*: *A Collection of Criticism*, ed. Patrick J. Keane, 109, sees the volume as being "at the very heart of the human predicament, groping for values through which man may define himself without frenzy or servility."

3. Arnold Goldman, "The Oeuvre Takes Shape: Yeats's Early Poetry," in *Victorian Poetry*, ed. Malcolm Bradbury and David Palmer, 197-221, has traced such a pattern of dialectical response in the volumes through *In the Seven Woods* (1904).

4. See the author's "Freeing the Swans: Yeats's Exorcism of Maud Gonne," *ELH*, 48 (1981), 411-26, especially the discussion of "Baile and Ailinn" (1901).

5. Robert W. Caswell, "Yeats's Odd Swan at Coole," *Eire*, 4 (1969), 81-86.

6. Cf. *Passages*, 39-43 for JBY's invidious distinction between "companionable" and "solitary" poets discussed above in chapter 1.

7. For a useful comparison, see Graham Martin in *An Honoured Guest: New Essays on W.B. Yeats*, ed. Denis Donoghue and J.R. Mulryne, 54-72.

8. On the Yeatsian genre of tragic love poems in this period, see B.L. Reid (See Introduction, n. 4), 107-8.

9. See *L*, 633-34 for a sense of the severe emotional strain related to composition of the poem.

10. Brooks, in *The Permanence of Yeats*, p. 79; Peter Ure, *Towards a Mythology: Studies in the Poetry of W.B. Yeats*, 65; hereafter *Towards a Mythology*.

11. Frank Hughes Murphy, *Yeats's Early Poetry: The Quest for Reconciliation*, 121–24.

12. It is interesting to note in this connection that Yeats won *Poetry* magazine's annual award for this poem, and gave the bulk of the prize money to his modernist mentor, Ezra Pound.

13. See Daniel Harris, *Yeats: Coole Park & Ballylee*, 118–26, for the best discussion of the literary sources and conventions of the poem.

14. This is borne out by the fact that Yeats was particularly asked by Margaret Gregory, the dead man's wife, to include a stanza on Gregory as horseman, a side of his nature that did not interest Yeats nearly as much as his artistic talent. See Marion Witt, "The Making of an Elegy: Yeats's 'In Memory of Major Robert Gregory,'" *Modern Philology*, 48 (1950), 117.

15. George T. Wright, *The Poet in the Poem: The Personae of Eliot, Yeats, and Pound*, 108, comments on Yeats's ironic self-portrayals which "make through the deliberate placing of emphasis on the shortcomings of the hero, the transcending of those weaknesses more heroic."

16. Pritchard, in *Twentieth Century Literature in Retrospect*, 122, shares my conviction that the stanza expresses a "self-consummation—for reader and poet."

17. Jeffares, *Commentary*, 138.

18. Daniel Hoffman, *Barbarous Knowledge: Myth in the Poetry of Yeats, Graves, and Muir*, 44. The bird is also used mysteriously in Yeats's late poem "High Talk."

19. See, for instance, John Unterecker, *A Reader's Guide to William Butler Yeats*, 153–54; Sidnell, in *Yeats and the Occult*, is a heartening exception in a recent discussion of the self-conscious persona in "Two Songs of a Fool."

20. *W.B. Yeats: The Later Poetry*, 161–62.

21. On the man who dreams that he is a butterfly dreaming that he is a man, see *The Complete Works of Chaung Tzu*, trans. Burton Watson, 49. *The Hour Glass's* butterfly hovering above the corpse and signifying the rebirth of the soul may derive from Blake's illustrations of Young's "Night Thoughts" (IV.687). See S. Foster Damon, *A Blake Dictionary: The Ideas and Symbols of William Blake*, 140.

Chapter 6

1. For an eloquent defense, see A.G. Stock, *W.B. Yeats: His Poetry and Thought*, 146–64.

2. If *A Vision* is to be salvaged I agree with Bloom that Whitaker's historiographical reading makes more sense than Vendler's predominantly aestheticist view; Northrop Frye, "The Rising of the Moon: A Study of *A Vision*," in *An Honoured Guest*, 8–33, presents a generally adequate critique of the work's importance and inadequacy as a structure of symbolism.

3. See Chapter 1, n. 31.

4. Vendler, 22; Sidnell, in *Yeats and the Occult*, 234–35; Harris, 104.

5. Stuart Hirschberg, "Yeats's 'The Phases of the Moon,'" *Explicator*, 32 (1974), item 75.

6. For a reading that assesses the poem's success on these same grounds, see Stuart Hirschberg, "The Shaping Role of *A Vision* on W.B. Yeats's 'The Double Vision of Michael Robartes,'" *Studies* (Dublin), 68 (1979), 109–13.

7. "The Later Poetry of W.B. Yeats," in *The Permanence of Yeats*, p. 57.

Bibliography

Aeschylus. *Agamemnon*. Ed. Herbert Weir Smyth. Loeb Classical Library. 1926; rpt. London: Heinemann, 1946.

Allen, James Lovic. "Belief Versus Faith in the Credo of Yeats." *Journal of Modern Literature*. Special Yeats Number, 4 (1975), 692–716.

Allen, James L., and M.M. Liberman. "Transcriptions of Yeats's Unpublished Papers in the Bradford Papers at Grinnell College," *Serif*, 10, No. 1 (1973), 13–27.

Balzac, Honoré de. *Séraphita. Edition Définitive of the Comédie Humaine*. 53 vols. Trans. George Burnham Ives et al. Philadelphia: George Barrie, 1899. XLII.

Beer, J.B. *Coleridge, the Visionary*. New York: Collier, 1962.

Bell, Ian. "The Phantasmagoria of Ezra Pound." *Paideuma*, 5 (1976), 361–86.

Bishop, John Peale. "Decorative Plays." Rev. of *Four Plays for Dancers*, by W.B. Yeats. *Literary Review*, 2 (1922), 465.

Blackmur, R.P. "The Later Poetry of W.B. Yeats." *The Permanence of Yeats*. Eds. James Hall and Martin Steinmann. 1950; rpt. New York: Macmillan, 1961, 38–59.

Blake, William. *Complete Writings*. Ed. Geoffrey Keynes. London: Oxford Univ. Press, 1972.

———. *The Illuminated Blake*. Ed. David. V. Erdman. Garden City, N.Y.: Anchor-Doubleday, 1974.

———. *The Works of William Blake, Poetic, Symbolic, and Critical*. 3 vols. Eds. Edwin J. Ellis and W.B. Yeats. London: Quaritch, 1893 I.

Bloom, Harold. *Yeats*. New York: Oxford Univ. Press, 1970.

Boehme, Jacob. *Six Theosophic Points and Other Writings*. 1620; rpt. Ann Arbor: Univ. of Michigan Press, 1970.

Bornstein, George. *Transformations of Romanticism in Yeats, Eliot and Stevens*. Chicago: Univ. of Chicago Press, 1976.

———. "Yeats's Romantic Dante," *Colby Library Quarterly*, 15 (1979), 93–113.

Bradford, Curtis B. *Yeats at Work*. Carbondale: Southern Illinois Univ. Press, 1965.

Brooks, Cleanth. "Yeats: The Poet as Myth-Maker." *The Permanence of Yeats*. Eds. James Hall and Martin Steinmann. 1950; rpt. New York: Macmillan, 1961, 60–84.

Burnet, John. *Early Greek Philosophy*. 1892; rpt. London: Adam & Charles Black, 1908.

Carlyle, Thomas. *Heroes and Hero-Worship. The Works of Thomas Carlyle*. Centenary ed. 30 vols. London: Chapman and Hall, 1897; rpt. New York: AMS Press, 1969. V.

Caswell, Robert W. "Yeats's Odd Swan at Coole." *Eire* 4 (1969), 81–86.

Chuang Tzu. *The Complete Works of Chuang Tzu*. Trans. Burton Watson. New York: Columbia Univ. Press, 1968.

Clark, David R. "Yeats, Theatre, and Nationalism." *Theatre and Nationalism in Twentieth-Century Ireland*. Ed. Robert O'Driscoll. Toronto: Univ. of Toronto Press, 1971, 149–55.

Coleridge, Samuel Taylor. *Biographia Literaria*. Ed. John T. Shawcross. London: Oxford Univ. Press, 1907.

Cudworth, Ralph. *The True Intellectual System of the Universe*. 4 vols. Ed. Thomas Birch. 1678; rpt. London: J.F. Dove, 1820.

Damon, S. Foster. *A Blake Dictionary: The Ideas and Symbols of William Blake*. Providence: Brown Univ. Press, 1965.

DeQuincey, Thomas. *Confessions of an English Opium Eater*. Ed. William Sharp. London: Walter Scott, 1886.

————. *The Posthumous Writings of Thomas DeQuincey*. 2 vols. 1891; rpt. Hildesheim: Georg Olms Verlag, 1975. I.

Dodds, E.R. *The Greeks and the Irrational*. Berkeley and Los Angeles: Univ. of California Press, 1951.

Donoghue, Denis. "The Human Image in Yeats." *William Butler Yeats: A Collection of Criticism*. Contemporary Studies in Literature. Ed. Patrick J. Keane. New York: McGraw-Hill, 1973. 100–118.

Dorn, Karen. "Dialogue Into Movement: W.B. Yeats's Theatre Collaboration with Gordon Craig." *Yeats and the Theatre*. Ed. Robert O'Driscoll and Lorna Reynolds. Yeats Studies Series. Niagara Falls, N.Y.: Maclean-Hunter, 1975, 109–36.

Downes, Gwladys V. "W.B. Yeats and the Tarot." *The World of W.B. Yeats*. Ed. Robin Skelton and Ann Saddlemeyer. Seattle: Univ. of Washington Press, 1965, 51–53.

Eliot, Thomas Stearns. Rev. of *Per Amica Silentia Lunae*, by W.B. Yeats. *Egoist*, 5 (1918), 87.

Ellis, Edwin. *Fate in Arcadia*. London: Ward & Downing, 1892, pp. 158–63.

Ellmann, Richard. *Eminent Domain: Yeats Among Wilde, Joyce, Pound, Eliot, and Auden*. London: Oxford Univ. Press, 1970.

————. *The Identity of Yeats*. 2nd ed. 1964; rpt. New York: Oxford Univ. Press, 1968.

————. *Yeats: The Man and the Masks*. 1948; rpt. New York: Dutton, 1958.

Flannery, James W. "W.B. Yeats, Gordon Craig, and The Visual Arts of the Theatre." *Yeats and the Theatre*. Ed. Robert O'Driscoll and Lorna Reynolds. Yeats Studies Series. Niagara Falls, N.Y.: Maclean-Hunter, 1975, 82–108.

Flannery, Mary C. *Yeats and Magic: The Earlier Works*. New York: Harper & Row, 1978.

Fletcher, Angus. *Allegory: The Theory of a Symbolic Mode*. Ithaca: Cornell Univ. Press, 1964.

Friedman, Barton. "*On Baile's Strand* to *At the Hawk's Well*: Staging the Deeps of the Mind." *Journal of Modern Literature*. Special Yeats Number, 4 (1975), 625–50.

Frye, Northrop. "The Rising of the Moon: A Study of *A Vision*." *An Honoured Guest: New Essays on W.B. Yeats*. Eds. Denis Donoghue and J.R. Mulryne. New York: St. Martin's Press, 1966, 8–33.

Fullwood, Daphne. "The Influence on W.B. Yeats of Some French Poets (Mallarmé, Verlaine, Claudel)." *Southern Review*, 6 New Series (1970), 356–79.

Goldman, Arnold. "The Oeuvre Takes Shape: Yeats's Early Poetry." *Victorian Poetry*. Stratford-Upon-Avon Studies, No. 15. Eds. Malcolm Bradbury and David Palmer. London: Edward Arnold, 1972, 197–221.

————. "Yeats, Spiritualism, and Psychical Research." *Yeats and the Occult*. Ed. George Mills Harper. Yeats Studies Series. Toronto: Macmillan, 1976, 108–29.

Gould, Warwick. "'Lionel Johnson Comes the First to Mind': Some Sources for Owen Aherne." *Yeats and the Occult*. Ed. George Mills Harper. Yeats Studies Series. Toronto: Macmillan, 1976, 255–84.

Gregory, Lady Augusta. *Visions and Beliefs in the West of Ireland*. 2 vols. New York: Putnam, 1920.

Harris, Daniel. *Yeats: Coole Park & Ballylee*. Baltimore: Johns Hopkins Univ. Press, 1974.

Harper, George Mills, ed. *Yeats and the Occult*. Yeats Studies Series. Toronto: Macmillan, 1976.

————. *Yeats's Golden Dawn*. London: Macmillan, 1974.

Hirschberg, Stuart. "The Shaping Role of *A Vision* on W.B. Yeats's "The Double Vision of Michael Robartes." *Studies*, 68 (1979), 109–13.

_____"Yeats's 'The Phases of the Moon.'" *Explicator*, 32 (1974). Item 75.

Hone, Joseph. *W.B. Yeats, 1865-1939.* 2nd ed. 1943; rpt. London: Macmillan, 1962.

Hoffman, Daniel. *Barbarous Knowledge: Myth in the Poetry of Yeats, Graves and Muir.* London: Oxford Univ. Press, 1967.

Jaynes, Julian. *The Origin of Consciousness in the Breakdown of The Bicameral Mind.* Boston: Houghton Mifflin, 1976.

Jeffares, A. Norman. *The Circus Animals: Essays on W.B. Yeats.* Stanford: Stanford Univ. Press, 1970.

_____. *A Commentary on the Collected Poems of W.B. Yeats.* Stanford: Stanford Univ. Press, 1968.

Jeffares, A. Norman, and A.S. Knowland. *A Commentary on the Collected Plays of W.B. Yeats.* Stanford: Stanford Univ. Press, 1975.

John, Brian. "'To Hunger Fiercely after Truth': Daimonic Man and Yeats's Insatiable Appetite." *Eire*, 9, (1974), 90–103.

_____. "Yeats and Carlyle." *Notes and Queries.* New Ser., 17 (1970), 455.

Keats, John. *The Letters of John Keats, 1814-1821.* Ed. Hyder E. Rollins. 2 vols. Cambridge: Harvard Univ. Press, 1958. I.

Kenner, Hugh. "The Sacred Book of the Arts." *Irish Writing.* W.B. Yeats: A Special Number. No. 31 (Summer 1955), 24–35.

Kermode, Frank. *Romantic Image.* New York: Macmillan, 1957.

Langbaum, Robert. *The Mysteries of Identity: A Theme in Modern Literature.* New York: Oxford Univ. Press, 1977.

Levine, Bernard. *The Dissolving Image: The Spiritual-Esthetic Development of W.B. Yeats.* Detroit: Wayne State Univ. Press, 1970.

Levine, Herbert. "Freeing the Swans: Yeats's Exorcism of Maud Gonne." *ELH*, 48 (1981), 411–26.

Lipking, Lawrence. *The Life of the Poet: Beginning and Ending Poetic Careers.* Chicago: Univ. of Chicago Press, 1982.

Lofaro, Michael A. "The Mask with No Eyes: Yeats's Vision in *Per Amica Silentia Lunae*." *Style*, 10 (1976), 51–66.

MacNeice, Louis. *The Poetry of W.B. Yeats.* 1941; rpt. New York: Oxford Univ. Press, 1969.

Mallarmé, Stéphane. *Selected Prose Poems, Essays, and Letters.* Trans. Bradford Cook. Baltimore: Johns Hopkins Univ. Press, 1956, 34-43.

Martin, Graham. "The Wild Swans at Coole." *An Honoured Guest: New Essays on W.B. Yeats.* Eds. Denis Donoghue and J.R. Mulryne. New York: St. Martin's Press, 1966, 54–72.

Mead, G.R.S. *Quests Old and New.* London: G. Bell, 1913.

Melchiori, Giorgio. "Yeats and Dante." *English Miscellany*, 19 (1968), 153–79.

Miller, J. Hillis. *Poets of Reality: Six Twentieth Century Writers.* 1965; rpt. New York: Anthanaeum, 1974.

Moore, George. *Vale.* London: Heinemann, 1914.

Moore, John Rees. *Masks of Love and Death: Yeats as Dramatist.* Ithaca: Cornell Univ. Press, 1970.

Moore, Virginia. *The Unicorn: William Butler Yeats's Search for Reality.* New York: Macmillan, 1954.

More, Henry. *The Immortality of the Soul. A Collection of Several Philosophical Writings.* London: James Flesher, 1662.

Murphy, Frank Hughes. *Yeats's Early Poetry: The Quest for Reconciliation.* Baton Rouge: Louisiana State Univ. Press, 1975.

Nathan, Leonard E. *The Tragic Drama of William Butler Yeats: Figures in a Dance.* New York: Columbia Univ. Press, 1965.

Nietzsche, Friedrich. *The Gay Science.* Trans. Walter Kaufmann. 1882; rpt. New York: Vintage, 1974.

———. *Nietzsche as Critic, Philosopher, Poet, and Prophet*. Ed. Thomas Common. London: Grant Richards, 1901.

O'Donnell, William H. "Yeats as Adept and Artist: *The Speckled Bird, The Secret Rose*, and *The Wind Among the Reeds*." *Yeats and the Occult*. Ed. George Mills Harper. Yeats Studies Series. Toronto: Macmillan, 1976.

O'Driscoll, Robert, and Lorna Reynolds, eds. *Yeats and the Theatre*. Yeats Studies Series. Niagara Falls, N.Y.: Maclean-Hunter, 1975.

Olney, James. *The Rhizome and the Flower: The Perennial Philosophy—Yeats and Jung*. Berkeley and Los Angeles: Univ. of California Press, 1980.

———. "Sex and the Dead: Daemones of Yeats and Jung." *Studies in the Literary Imagination*. Special Issue. W.B. Yeats: The Occult and Philosophical Background. 14 (1981), 43–60.

Otto, Rudolph. *The Idea of the Holy: An Inquiry into the non-rational factor in the idea of the divine and its relation to the rational*. 2nd ed. Trans. John W. Harvey. 1926; rpt. London: Oxford Univ. Press, 1950.

Parkinson, Thomas. *W.B. Yeats: The Later Poetry*. 1964; rpt. Berkeley and Los Angeles: Univ. of California Press, 1971.

Pater, Walter. *Marius, The Epicurean: His Sensations and Ideas*. 2 vols. 1885; rpt. London: Macmillan, 1910.

———. *The Renaissance: Studies in Art and Poetry*. The 1893 Text. Ed. Donald L. Hill. Berkeley and Los Angeles: Univ. of California Press, 1980.

Patterson, Charles. *The Daemonic in the Poetry of Keats*. Urbana: Univ. of Illinois Press, 1970.

Pearce, Donald. "Philosophy and Phantasy: Notes on the Growth of Yeats's 'System.'" *University of Kansas City Review*, 18 (1952), 169–80.

Perloff, Marjorie. "Yeats and Goethe." *Comparative Literature* 23 (1971), 125–40.

Peterfreund, Stuart. "'The Second Coming' and *Suspiria de Profundis*: Some Affinities." *American Notes and Queries*, 15 (1976), 40–43.

Plato. *Apology, Phaedo, Symposium, Timaeus et al.* Loeb Classical Library. 8 vols. 1914–29; rpt. London: Heinemann, 1952–53. I.V.VII.

Plotinus. *Enneads*. 5 vols. Trans. Stephen Mackenna. Library of Philosophical Translations. London: Warner, 1917–30.

Plutarch. *Essays and Miscellanies. Complete Works*. 6 vols. New York: Crowell, 1909.

Pound, Ezra. "Ezra Pound: Letters to William Butler Yeats." Ed. C.F. Terrell. *Antaeus*, Nos. 21/22 (1976), 34–49.

———. *The Literary Essays of Ezra Pound*. Ed. T.S. Eliot. 1935; rpt. New York: New Directions, 1968.

———. *Translations*. New York: New Directions, 1963.

Pritchard, William H. "The Uses of Yeats's Poetry." *Twentieth Century Literature in Retrospect*. Ed. Reuben A. Brower. Cambridge, Mass.: Harvard Univ. Press, 1971, 111–32.

Qamber, Akhtar. *Yeats and the Noh*. New York: Weatherhill, 1974.

Reid, B.L. *William Butler Yeats: The Lyric of Tragedy*. Norman: Univ. of Oklahoma Press, 1961.

Rogers, Neville. *Shelley at Work: A Critical Inquiry*. Oxford: Clarendon, 1956.

Rimbaud, Arthur. *Oeuvres*. Ed. Paterne Berrichon. Paris: Mercure de France, 1912.

Ronsley, Joseph. "Yeats's Lecture Notes for 'Friends of My Youth.'" *Yeats and the Theatre*. Eds., Robert O'Driscoll and Lorna Reynolds. Yeats Studies Series. Niagara Falls, N.Y.: Maclean-Hunter, 1975, 60–81.

Seiden, Morton. *William Butler Yeats: The Poet as Mythmaker*. E. Lansing: Michigan State Univ. Press, 1962.

Shelley, Percy Byshhe. *Shelley's Prose, Or the Trumpet of a Prophecy*. Ed. David Lee Clark. Albuquerque: Univ. of New Mexico Press, 1954.

Sidnell, Michael. "Mr. Yeats, Michael Robartes, and Their Circle." *Yeats and the Occult*. Ed. George Mills Harper. Yeats Studies Series. Toronto: Macmillan, 1976, 225–54.

Solomon, Simeon. *A Vision of Love Revealed in Sleep*. London: Printed for the Author, 1871.
Spivak, Gayatri Chakravorty. "Finding Feminist Readings: Dante—Yeats." *Social Text: Theory, Culture, and Ideology*, 3 (1980), 73–87.
Stallworthy, Jon. *Between the Lines: Yeats's Poetry in the Making*. Oxford: Clarendon, 1963.
Stock, A.G. *W.B. Yeats: His Poetry and Thought*. Cambridge: University Press, 1964.
Symons, Arthur. *Poems*. 2 vols. London: Heinemann, 1921, I, 188–89.
Taylor, Richard. *W.B. Yeats: Irish Myth and Japanese Nō*. New Haven: Yale Univ. Press, 1976.
Taylor, Thomas. *Thomas Taylor, The Platonist: Selected Writings*. Eds. Kathleen Raine and George Mills Harper. Bollingen Series 88. Princeton: Princeton Univ. Press, 1969.
Thatcher, David S. *Nietzsche in England: The Growth of a Reputation*. Toronto: Univ. of Toronto Press, 1970.
Unterecker, John. *A Reader's Guide to William Butler Yeats*. New York: Farrar, Straus & Cudahy, 1959.
Ure, Peter. *Towards a Mythology: Studies in the Poetry of W.B. Yeats*. London: Hodder & Stoughton, 1946.
———. *Yeats the Playwright: A Commentary on Character and Design in the Major Plays*. London: Routledge & Keagan Paul, 1963.
Vendler, Helen. *Yeats's VISION and the Later Plays*. Cambridge: Harvard Univ. Press, 1963.
Vickery, John. *The Literary Impact of The Golden Bough*. Princeton: Princeton Univ. Press, 1973.
Villiers de L'Isle Adam. *Axel*. Trans. Marilyn Gaddis Rose. Dublin: Dolmen, 1970.
Waite, Arthur Edward. *The Pictorial Key to the Tarot*. New York: University Books, 1959.
Whitaker, Thomas R. *Swan and Shadow: Yeats's Dialogue with History*. Chapel Hill: Univ. of North Carolina Press, 1964.
Willey, Basil. *The Seventeenth Century Background: Studies in the Thought of the Age in Relation to Poetry and Religion*. 1934; rpt. Garden City, N.Y.: Doubleday, 1953.
Wilson, F.A.C. *W.B. Yeats and Tradition*. London: Victor Gollancz, 1958.
———. *Yeats's Iconography*. London: Victor Gollancz, 1960.
Witt, Marion. "The Making of an Elegy: Yeats's 'In Memory of Major Robert Gregory.'" *Modern Philology*, 48 (1950), 112–21.
Wright, George, T. *The Poet in the Poem: The Personae of Eliot, Yeats, and Pound*. Perspectives in Criticism No. 4. Berkeley and Los Angeles: Univ. of California Press, 1960.
Yeats, John Butler. *J.B. Yeats: Letters to His Son W.B. Yeats and Others 1869–1922*. Ed. Joseph P. Hone. New York: Dutton, 1946.
———. *Passages from the Letters of John Butler Yeats*. Ed. Ezra Pound. Dundrum: Cuala, 1917.
Yeats, William Butler. *Autobiographies*. London: Macmillan, 1955.
———. *The Cat and the Moon and Certain Poems*. Dublin: Cuala, 1924.
———. *Collected Works in Prose and Verse of William Butler Yeats*. Stratford-on-Avon: Shakespeare Head, 1908. VIII.
———. *A Critical Edition of Yeats's* A Vision *(1925)*. Eds., George Mills Harper and Walter Kelly Hood. London: Macmillan, 1978.
———. Drafts, revisions etc. of poems published in *The Wild Swans at Coole*. MS. 13,587. The National Library of Ireland, Dublin, Ireland.
———. "Epilogue" filed with drafts of *Per Amica Silentia Lunae*. TS. Curtis Bradford Papers. Grinnell College, Grinnell, Iowa.
———. *Essays*. London: Macmillan, 1924.
———. *Essays and Introductions*. London and New York: Macmillan, 1961.
———. "An Exchange of Letters with Leo Africanus." TS. Curtis Bradford Papers. Grinnell College, Grinnell, Iowa.
———. *Explorations*. New York: Macmillan, 1963.
———. "Extracts from an MS Book Given Yeats by Maud Gonne, Christmas, 1912." TS.

Curtis Bradford Papers. Grinnell College, Grinnell, Iowa.

———. *Four Plays for Dancers.* New York: Macmillan, 1921.

———. *Letters of W.B. Yeats.* Ed. Alan Wade. London: Rupert Hart-Davis, 1954.

———. *Memoirs.* Ed. Denis Donoghue. New York: Macmillan, 1973.

———. *Mythologies.* London and New York: Macmillan, 1959.

———. ed. *The Oxford Book of Modern Verse.* Oxford: Clarendon, 1936.

———. *Per Amica Silentia Lunae.* London: Macmillan, 1918.

———. "The Poet and the Actress." TS. Curtis Bradford Papers. Grinnell College, Grinnell, Iowa.

———. *Responsibilities and Other Poems.* New York: Macmillan, 1916.

———. *Selected Poems.* London: Macmillan, 1929.

———. *The Speckled Bird.* Ed. William H. O'Donnell. 2 vols. Dublin: Cuala, 1973.

———. *Uncollected Prose of W.B. Yeats* Eds. John P. Frayne and Colton Johnson. 2 vols. New York: Columbia Univ. Press, 1975, II.

———. *The Variorum Edition of the Plays of W.B. Yeats.* Ed. Russell K. Alspach. London and New York: Macmillan, 1966.

———. *The Variorum Edition of the Poems of W.B. Yeats.* Eds. Peter Allt and Russell K. Alspach. New York: Macmillan, 1957.

———. *A Vision.* 1938; rpt. London: Macmillan, 1962.

———. *The Wild Swans at Coole.* Dundrum: Cuala, 1917.

Index